Peach

Ty Cobb
in His Time
and Ours

Richard Bak

SPORTS
MEDIA
GROUP

All inquiries should be addressed to:
Sports Media Group
An imprint of Ann Arbor Media Group LLC
2500 S. State Street
Ann Arbor, MI 48104

Printed and bound in Canada.

09   08   07   06   05   1   2   3   4   5

ISBN 13: 978-158726-257-9
ISBN 10: 1-58726-257-6

Library of Congress Cataloging-in-Publication Data

Bak, Richard, 1954-
Peach : Ty Cobb in his time and ours / Richard Bak.
p. cm.
Includes bibliographical references and index.
1. Cobb, Ty, 1886-1961. 2. Baseball players--United States--Biography. I. Title.
GV865.C6B34 2005
796.357'092--dc22

2005001462

Book and jacket design by Somberg Design
www.sombergdesign.com

TO THE MEMORY OF

JERRY MALNAR

Contents

A fan's snapshot of the Peach at Navin Field, circa 1917.

Foreword

BY ERNIE HARWELL

Anyone familiar with the movie *Field of Dreams* remembers the scene where an Iowa farmer named Ray Kinsella (played by Kevin Costner) introduces novelist Terence Mann (James Earl Jones) to "Shoeless Joe" Jackson (Ray Liotta) and several ethereal teammates on a diamond carved out of a cornfield.

"You wouldn't believe how many guys wanted to come play here," says Shoeless Joe. "I had to beat them off with a stick."

"Hey, that's 'Smokey Joe' Wood!" says Ray, surveying the field in astonishment. "And Mel Ott ... and Gil Hodges...."

"And Ty Cobb wanted to play," interrupts Shoeless Joe. "None of us could stand the son of a bitch when we were alive, so we told him to stick it!"

While pure fantasy, the dialogue in this Capraesque baseball film is instructive. More than 40 years after he passed away in his native Georgia, Tyrus Raymond Cobb is still sorely in need of a press agent.

As history would have us believe, the "Georgia Peach" was baseball's last angry man, a wholly irredeemable crank who, when he wasn't busy intentionally spiking infielders, probably pulled the wings off flies for amusement. Sporting razor-sharp spikes, he'd slice a player from chin to shin just to swipe a base or score a run. His rotten disposition didn't change off the field, either. He was rude, abusive, selfish, obnoxious, vindictive, and utterly lacking in any virtues. In the end he finally died as he had lived—bitter and friendless.

At least that is what we've all heard and read for years. But is this a complete and fair portrait?

No, argues author Richard Bak, whose *Peach: Ty Cobb in His Time and Ours* gives us a welcomed, balanced look at the life of the man who has fascinated so many of us through the years. *Peach*, an expanded and revised version of an earlier title on Cobb, combines page after page of compelling photographs with an engaging narrative. The author helps us all with his sharp insight into Cobb, his times, and the forces that helped shape his character inside and outside the ball yard.

The Peach produced numbers with which we've all become familiar: 4,191 base hits, a dozen batting titles, 892 stolen bases, a .367 batting average over 24 big-league seasons. His "vying nature," as he once described it, wasn't the kind that could be turned on and off like a spigot. It won games, but it also alienated many around him. However, Cobb never could have been the player he was without this temperament, observed sportswriter Harry Salsinger, a cultured man who came to know Cobb extremely well during their 51-year friendship. "The trouble with most ballplayers is that they are too phlegmatic, taking matters as they come," Salsinger contended. "Cobb never did. He created his own situations. Cobb had his faults as all mortals have, but he had virtues as well. Physical courage was one of them. His enemies were many and bitter, but nobody ever called him a coward."

The author, like Salsinger before him, makes a case for empathy and discernment when dealing with such a polarizing figure as Cobb. Although everybody can claim to have at least some of Ty's imperfections, fewer of us can also boast his tremendous gifts of drive, intelligence, dedication, and courage. For all of his bad points—and as the author amply illustrates, there were many—there still is much to admire about Cobb, whose good points are routinely buried beneath the weight of his soiled reputation and unflattering apocrypha. How many people, for instance, know of the nonprofit health care system he founded in north Georgia, still going strong after more than a half century? Or of the educational foundation he established, which to date has helped put several hundred Georgians—black and white—through college? The writer is no apologist for Cobb; indeed, this new edition has even more examples of the man's frequently noxious behavior than the original. But if this biography seems at other times to be unusually sympathetic to its subject, it's because it was written with the thought that no person passing through this world even approaches perfection, so those of us in glass houses had better be careful where we pitch our baseballs.

All of us have our impressions of Cobb—from reading about him, watching feature films, documentaries, and plays about him, or even perhaps from actually having met him. I crossed paths with Ty several times, and I have to admit that I still have difficulty trying to sort out the many contradictions in this very complex man.

My first meeting with the Great One came in 1941. I had just started my job as sports director for radio station WSB in Atlanta. Word came that Ty was visiting his hometown of Royston, Georgia, so I suggested that the station send me there to interview him.

"He's a mean old man and he won't even talk to you," was the response. "But go anyway and do the best you can."

I made the journey. Ty met me at the door with a hearty welcome. I had no trouble at all with the interview. He talked for the entire 15-minute show and was both gracious and entertaining. The visit proved to me that every man has to judge for himself.

Looking back, I can see where Ty had varying degrees of influence on several other memorable occasions in my life. In fact, I hold him responsible for the first severe spanking of my life. Let me explain.

When I was growing up in Washington, Georgia, swatting at sawdust baseballs and doing tongue-tied imitations of my favorite announcers, the name Ty Cobb was burned deep into my psyche. Not only did we schoolboys and our fathers consider the Georgia Peach the greatest ballplayer of all—greater than even Babe Ruth—he was one of our state's most famous native sons. Doc Green, the local druggist, had once played semipro ball with Cobb and would not let me or anyone else forget it.

It was after our family moved to Atlanta that I first got the chance to see

this living, breathing legend in action. Cobb was scheduled to play in an exhibition game against the Georgia Tech team, and my buddies persuaded me to go with them and to sneak into the game without paying.

Now, my dad didn't object to me going to the game. He loved baseball. But he didn't approve of me sneaking into the game—Ty Cobb or no Ty Cobb. When I came home that night he gave me the whipping of my life.

Ty also had an influence on my so-called literary career. One year I covered the Masters golf tournament for WSB. Cobb, a good friend of fabled golfer Bobby Jones, was a Masters regular. One day I sat around and listened as he and some golfers exchanged stories.

Grantland Rice, the granddaddy of all sportswriters, was in the group. Cobb turned to Rice and said, "Granny, you won't remember this. But when you were sports editor of the *Atlanta Journal* in 1904, you got a lot of letters and telegrams from around Anniston, Alabama, telling you how great I was while I was playing there.

"You finally came down to Anniston, saw me in action, and wrote a glowing story which helped me on my way. I never admitted it until now, Granny, but I was the guy who sent all those."

I wrote down this surprising story and submitted it to the *Saturday Evening Post*, which snapped it up. That marked my first sale to a major national publication.

I had occasion to meet Ty several more times in the last few years of his life. He was always a gentleman. As sick old men are wont to do, he slowed down considerably toward the end, suffering the effects of a long, losing bout with cancer and other ailments. When he died on July 17, 1961, I was in my second year of broadcasting in Detroit. The club asked me to write a tribute to be read over the public address system that night, which I gladly did. Here is what I wrote:

> Baseball's greatest player—Tyrus Raymond Cobb—died today in his native Georgia.
>
> Cobb was a genius in spikes. His mind was the keenest ever to solve the strategy of the diamond. He was fiery and dazzling on the base paths. For 24 years of high-tensioned baseball action, his name led all the rest. He was the best—in hitting, base-stealing, run-making—in everything.
>
> Cobb's rise to fame in the early 1900s kept step with the progress of baseball as a national spectacle. His dynamic spirit was a symbol for the ever-growing industrial community he represented: Detroit, Michigan.
>
> And now, here in a baseball stadium where the cheers were the loudest and longest for this greatest of all Tigers, let us stand and pay final tribute to him in a moment of respectful silence.

On that long-ago summer night, I pronounced Cobb the greatest of them all. No one has come along since to make me change my mind, though several of his important records have been broken since his death. The very next year, 1962, former Tigers farmhand Maury Wills stole 104 bases for the Los Angeles Dodgers, breaking Ty's single-season mark of 96. Another of his stolen-base records was eclipsed in 1977, when Lou Brock of the St. Louis Cardinals registered career steal number 893.

Eight years later, amid great hoopla, another mark was shattered. At precisely 8:01 p.m. on September 11, 1985, Pete Rose of the Cincinnati Reds slapped a 2–1 pitch from San Diego's Eric Show into left field for career hit 4,192. The confetti-filled storm of applause from the sellout crowd at Cincinnati's Riverfront Stadium delayed play for seven minutes. It was 57 years to the day since Cobb had played his last major-league game.

Despite his distaste for the modern game, I think Ty would have approved of Rose, a throwback to baseball's earlier days who had earned his nickname "Charlie Hustle" through an aggressive, unrelenting style of play. (Although Ty, remembering "the teach" Kid Elberfeld applied on him as a rookie, would have frowned on Rose's trademark headfirst slides.)

Rose was an astute student of the game's history and its immortals. To his credit, the new base-hit king acknowledged that the crown as baseball's greatest hitter still belonged to the ghost that he had chased since entering the major leagues in 1963. "At no time did I say I'm a better hitter than Cobb," said Rose, who would retire in 1986 with 4,256 base hits, but with a career batting average far below Cobb's. "He was the greatest hitter in history. Nobody will ever hit .367 again."

Over the last few decades the study of sports in American society has taken on a greater importance. The result has been a steady stream of books and films that have broken out of the Frank Merriweather mode I knew as a boy. Their

unvarnished studies portray athletes as human beings with faults, instead of as infallible, milk-drinking gods. They come across as more sympathetic and genuine, and thus more heroic.

In discussing this country's pantheon of sports heroes, it's problematic whether Tyrus Raymond Cobb is spending eternity inside a skybox or inside the furnace room. What seems certain is that we will never see his like again—to which those old ballplayers stepping out of Ray Kinsella's cornfield would surely add, "Thank God!"

A wide-eyed Tyrus Raymond Cobb photographed in 1887, not long after his birth in the small Georgia farming community known as The Narrows.

CHAPTER ONE

Somewhere in Georgia

*Somehow the idea of staring at the rump of
a balky mule while I steered a plow behind him
didn't strike me as fitting work.*

TY COBB

One temptation facing biographers is to write that so-and-so put such-and-such a place "on the map." In the case of Tyrus Raymond Cobb, born December 18, 1886, in The Narrows in Banks County, Georgia, such a cliché would be more than a literary misdemeanor. It would be geographically incorrect.

The Narrows, then and now, is more a state of mind than an actual dot on the Rand McNally. The name refers to a community of scattered farms in the Appalachian foothills of northeast Georgia. Like the two historical markers that today line Georgia Highway 105, it honors a Confederate victory at the Battle of the Narrows, which was fought in a gap in the nearby mountains in the fall of 1864.

No markers honor Cobb's birthplace. The house where he was born—a 13-room white frame dwelling that belonged to his maternal grandfather, Caleb Chitwood—burned down years ago. A small frame house has since been built on the site; at last report, a Southern Baptist minister and his wife were living there. Sprinkled about the property are a few outbuildings from the original homestead: a well shelter, a corn crib, and the old cotton house. Not that these traces of Cobbiana engender much excitement among the locals.

In fact, a couple of decades ago, when Pete Rose was on the verge of overtaking Cobb as baseball's all-time base-hit champion, an out-of-town writer visited The Narrows to ask about the community's most famous native. Those who knew Ty Cobb generally were of the opinion that records were made to be broken. The lack of passion about the subject disappointed the writer, though the indifference was perhaps understandable in the light of a recent event. Area

The house in which Ty was born on December 18, 1886.

residents were still buzzing about the poultry farmer who had buried a large number of dead chickens in a shallow grave. The built-up gases had exploded, showering feathers and chicken parts all over the old Chitwood place.

Presumably no ghosts complained. Explosions, after all, were old hat to Caleb Chitwood, who had survived the six-week siege and fall of Vicksburg as an infantry officer in the Army of Tennessee. Paroled on July 8, 1863, along with twenty thousand other Confederates, Chitwood broke his vow not to take up arms again against the Union and was captured a second time in Raleigh, North Carolina, near the close of the war. Such tenacity served Captain Chitwood well when he returned to Banks County after the fighting ended. He was able to scratch out a decent living growing cotton, eventually employing several tenants on his two hundred or so acres of land. In the summer of 1883 the mildly prosperous farmer reluctantly allowed his 12-year-old daughter, Amanda, to be married at the Chitwood "plantation." The groom was a 20-year-old schoolteacher named William Herschel Cobb.

William, born and raised across the state line in North Carolina, had recently graduated with first honors from North Georgia Military College in Dahlonega. Eager to raise their social standing, the North Carolina Cobbs insisted they were related to the more distinguished Georgia Cobbs, a family that included several prominent men of the Old South. Despite the tenuous lineage, the tall, dignified William was always careful to emphasize the family's bloodlines to his and Amanda's three children.

The first of these was Tyrus Raymond, born when Amanda was only 15. William, who read widely, had always admired the story of the ancient Phoenician city of Tyre, which in 332 B.C. had put up a gallant but doomed resistance to the legions of Alexander the Great. Hence his first-born's unique name. By the time Ty was six, he was sharing his parents' attention with a brother and a sister. John Paul was born in 1888, followed by Florence Leslie in 1892.

As a rural schoolteacher, William was always captive to the whims of the community he served. One-room schoolhouses survived only in areas where families could afford a schoolmaster's pay and spare their children's participation in the crushing load of everyday chores. Consequently, for the first few years of his marriage William moved his family throughout northeast Georgia. One of Ty's earliest memories was "of a buggy, bumping along a clay road" as his father traveled to yet another village and another teaching position. "I seem to recall that I was barefooted and wore a hickory shirt under a pair of bib overalls," Ty said in his autobiography. "With my legs dangling over the tailgate, I was busy winding yarn around a small core ball. It was slow work."

So was setting down roots. There were stops in farm communities like Commerce, Lavonia, Carnesville, and Hickory Grove. Finally, sometime in the early 1890s, when Ty was five or six, the peripatetic teacher was offered a position in Royston, Georgia. The town of about five hundred people was located in Franklin County, about 75 miles northeast of Atlanta.

At the time America was still a constellation of small towns. In many ways, turn-of-the-century Royston resembled those drowsy "little white towns in the hills" Thornton Wilder paid homage to in his play *Our Town*. There was a commercial area, its wide, dusty streets flanked by sleeping dogs and pimpled with horse apples. Awnings shaded the plank sidewalks in front of the post office, bank, pool hall, saloon, blacksmith, barbershop, feed store, and other businesses common to Main Streets everywhere. The surrounding countryside was a quilt of cleared fields and rolling hills, intersected by narrow packed-dirt roads and topped by the occasional farmhouse. The soil was rich here, enabling cotton, corn, and wheat farmers to prosper and local commerce to thrive. The citizens of Royston had the money to support a good school and to pay the new schoolmaster a living wage. William Cobb was able to buy a comfortable two-story house in town and, a few years later, a hundred-acre farm on which he raised cotton and other crops to supplement his teaching salary.

In his old age, Ty would often reminisce about the small-town sensations of his youth. The sound of croaking frogs near a favorite swimming hole. The sight of rockers and flower boxes on a wide veranda. The smell of red clay as it baked and shimmered in the sun. "I felt secure and, like all small boys, I harbored big dreams," he later said of this idyllic period.

Some of Ty's fondest memories centered around his regular trips to his paternal grandparents' house. They lived in the Smoky Mountains near Murphy, North Carolina, about a hundred miles from Royston. As a boy Ty often spent most of each summer there in an attempt to escape the heat and humidity of Georgia. William's father, "Granddad Johnny," was an avid outdoorsman and colorful raconteur who could get his grandson's heart pumping with a vigorous day-long tramp through the woods, or stop it completely with stories of tracking bears with only his musket and his wits.

"There he was, glaring at me red-eyed," the lean, bearded old man would say, packing his pipe with tobacco as he settled into another tall tale. "A slavering monster, twelve feet tall, with fangs as long as a corncob and claws on him the size of a scythe. Looked like a fieldpiece couldn't bring him down . . . and me with just a long-rifle."

"What happened?" Ty would gasp.

Granddad Johnny would take his time lighting his pipe.

"Tyrus," he'd finally say with a solemn expression, "if I'd missed, you wouldn't be here today."

Granddad Johnny "couldn't talk without being dramatic," Ty would later admit. But he dearly loved his father's parents. Simple, dignified, and wise in the ways of the natural world, they instilled in him a lifelong passion for the outdoors.

As was the case with most rural youths of his generation, Ty grew up around firearms, knives, and fishing rods. He took his dogs, including a favorite hound named Old Bob, into the fields, hills, and streams to hunt deer, raccoon, opossums, and fowl. (He once sneaked Old Bob onto the train to Granddad Johnny's place.) As a hunter, Ty displayed the same lightning reflexes and superb hand-eye coordination that would make him such a great hitter; hunting partners would always remember Ty as a crack shot. This easy familiarity with weapons, taken for granted in his time and place, would later get him in trouble in the urbanized North.

Even a shooting accident when he was about 14 didn't diminish his enthusiasm for firearms. On one occasion, while slaughtering hogs, he propped a loaded .22 rifle against a fence. The rifle discharged, hitting him in the left shoulder. Doctors, unable to find the bullet, sewed up the wound and pronounced him fit. Ty wasn't as sure, but he didn't complain. For the rest of his life he walked around with the slug imbedded near his left clavicle.

It has been observed that those who speak most longingly of small towns never had to live in one. Certainly, for all the bucolic charms of growing up in Royston, there were disadvantages as well: gossip, bigotry, narrowmindedness, limited opportunities, and a suffocating sameness to life. These factors, coupled with others viewed as uniquely Southern, all had a part in shaping Ty's character.

When Ty was young, keepers of the Confederate faith still numbered in the millions. Although the Confederacy had been defeated three decades earlier, misty-eyed memories of the Old South were kept alive through countless monuments, memoirs, pamphlets, regimental histories, sermons, memorial addresses, and various veterans' organizations. According to historian Charles Reagan Wilson, the movement was in effect "a functioning civil religion," its expressions of faith ranging from the lithograph of General Robert E. Lee hanging on the parlor wall to the ubiquitous rebel yell piercing the air at communal gatherings.

Ty's grandfathers, both of whom had fought for the Confederacy, undoubtedly told him stories of the war and its "sacred causes." (But Granddad Johnny, true to his iconoclastic nature, had been an anti-slavery Republican with a spotty service record.) Certainly Ty's father, mindful as he was of the family's famous name, mentioned the wartime exploits of a pair of Cobbs. Howell Cobb, born in 1815 in Franklin County, had been speaker of the U.S. House of Representatives, governor of Georgia, and secretary of the treasury in the years before secession. He presided over the convention that organized the Confederacy, then raised and commanded a regiment of volunteers. He was promoted to major general and commanded the District of Georgia for most of the war. His younger brother, Thomas Reade Rootes Cobb, was widely known for his published defenses of slavery, including the famous *Cobb On Slavery*. A brigadier general in command of Cobb's Legion during the Civil War, he bled to death during the Battle of

Fredericksburg after his femoral artery was severed by an explosion.

Also around were plenty of survivors of General William T. Sherman's infamous campaign to "make Georgia howl" in the closing months of the war. One diarist bitterly referred to Sherman as "the Nero of the 19th century." Stories of atrocities later dramatized in *Gone With The Wind*—the burning of Atlanta, the wanton destruction of the surrounding countryside, the plundering and the rape—were destined to be handed down from generation to generation. Memories die hard. Not too many years ago, an independent filmmaker named Ross McElwee came across an elderly lady who kept her grandmother's moldy old couch in the attic, its fabric punctured with holes where Union soldiers had plunged their swords more than a century earlier looking for valuables. In fact, it's quite possible that the bitter legacy of Sherman's march played a part in William Cobb's unusual naming of Tyrus. After the war Atlanta was referred to in some intellectual circles as "the Tyre of the South," calling to mind the fate of that other unlucky, sacked city. Some mused that when Ty broke into the major leagues as one of the game's few Southern players, he in a sense brought the flames of the Confederacy's funeral pyre with him—an overdrawn but convenient explanation for his complex, combustible personality. "He came up from the South, you know, and he was still fighting the Civil War," was teammate Sam Crawford's analysis. "As far as he was concerned, we were all damn Yankees before he even met us." A century after his birth, Cobb's home state was among several that still displayed the stars and bars on their state flags, proof of the former Confederacy's enduring fascination with "the Lost Cause."

As a boy, Ty was slim as a reed and had a temperament as flaming as his red

William Herschel Cobb, Ty's demanding and distant father. He represented the 31st District in the Georgia state senate from 1900 until his tragic death five years later.

hair. Intelligent and sensitive, he wore his combative, competitive nature like a sandwich board, for all to see. "You saw it the moment you set eyes on him," recalled Joe Cunningham, a classmate and next-door neighbor whose father ran a furniture store in Royston. "He just seemed to think quicker and run faster. He was always driving and pushing, even in grade school."

"I was a boy with a vying nature," is how Ty once described himself. "I saw no point in losing, if I could win." In fifth grade he once pummeled a schoolmate for misspelling a word that allowed the girls' team to win a spelling bee.

Ty won Cunningham's respect early, standing up to the larger boy in a schoolyard fight. They quickly became best friends. Whether he was accepting a dare to cross a tightrope strung across a downtown street or playing ball against the older boys, Ty felt compelled to measure himself, again and again, against those bigger and older than he was. In Cobb's South, these regular displays of primal honor were part of an entire cultural pattern. Throughout his life Ty demonstrated that he would rather be cut to pieces than surrender an inch, an attitude that traditionally drew admiration in the South but played to mixed reviews in the North. When Ty was beaten to a pulp by a bigger and stronger Charlie Schmidt shortly after joining the Tigers, for example, his teammates viewed his refusal to quit as foolishness, not courage, just one more lost cause engaged in by the hot-headed Georgian.

Honor preoccupied Ty and was at the root of many of his seemingly endless altercations as an adult. On one infamous occasion, he took umbrage at the way a Detroit fish merchant spoke to his wife on the telephone. Leaving his dinner guests behind, Ty rushed to redress the perceived insult. He stormed into the fish store and, at gunpoint, extracted an apology. Ty's heritage would often be taken into account when assigning blame for his irrational actions. In 1907, when he got into a fight with a black groundskeeper and his wife during spring training, the *Augusta Herald* ran a headline: "Georgia Peach Defends the Honor of the Southland." Five years later, Ty climbed into the stands in New York to beat senseless a foul-mouthed fan. "The fan yelled an epithet," sportswriter Fred Lieb recalled, "one that any Southerner would well resent. . . ." That particular fan had called Cobb a "half-nigger." In his world, those were more than just fighting words—they were grounds for justifiable homicide.

Throughout his life Ty was an unrepentant bigot, casually sprinkling his conversation with such pejoratives as "coon," "Sambo," and "shine" and "nigger." Such an attitude in the post-bellum South was hardly remarkable. In fact, due to a tangle of Jim Crow laws and customs, racism was firmly woven into the fabric of everyday life throughout America. As with all social prejudices, Ty's racial attitudes were the result of conditioning, not genetics. As a child he often worked or played alongside blacks, who composed about one-quarter of the population of Franklin County. In later years he would recall how he had learned to swim by repeatedly clinging to the neck of a young black man. The man would swim to the middle of a stream and then release Ty, forcing the youngster to reach shore on his own. Despite his occasional warm memory of contact with blacks, Ty as an adult was guilty of outrageous conduct toward black waiters, maids, grounds-

"There's nothing as useless on earth as knocking a string ball around a pasture with ruffians."

—WILLIAM H. COBB

keepers, and any other person of color who didn't exhibit the automatic deference white Southerners were raised to expect.

There's no excusing Ty's bigotry; the best one can do is to try to understand it. Like many farmers, William Cobb regularly employed black freedmen in his fields—as freed, that is, as uneducated former slaves and their offspring could be in a climate of suspicion, hostility, and almost insurmountable social barriers. Despite emancipation, most black Americans could not vote, hold office, or attend school with whites. Such restrictions not only reinforced the superiority whites on both sides of the Mason-Dixon line felt in the decades following the Civil War, but also manifested their fear that the country's growing number of blacks might somehow shed their traditional role of subservience. Although based on pseudoscience and anecdote, the conventional wisdom in turn-of-the-century America was that the Negro race was genetically inferior.

Negrophobia was especially pronounced in Georgia, which during Cobb's lifetime recorded more lynchings than any state except Mississippi. Royston and the rest of northern Georgia exercised a semblance of tolerance, but God help the black man who "forgot his place" in mixed society. Hoke Smith's influential *Atlanta Journal* daily "played up and headlined current stories of Negro crime, charges of rape and attempted rape, and alleged instances of arrogance, impertinence, surly manners, or lack of prompt and proper servility in conduct," wrote C. Vann Woodward in his landmark study of American race relations, *The Strange Career of Jim Crow*. Ty and his father both read the *Journal* religiously during its race-baiting heyday. It would be surprising if their racial attitudes were not partially shaped, or at least reinforced, by the paper's sensationalistic and inflammatory rhetoric.

At the century's turn, North and South were bound together by more than institutional racism. From Texas sandlots to Wisconsin playgrounds, from Kansas pastures to New York alleys, the favorite pastime by far was baseball. Sundays in particular were filled with adults and older boys who, freed for an afternoon from the chains of factory, field, or office, taxed their muscles socking and chasing a lopsided ball around some communal piece of ground. Idle youths, assuming they had completed (or ignored) their chores or schoolwork, had it even better, playing throughout the week. It's hard to overestimate the grip baseball had on the country's affections at the time. In absence of the professional sports and entertainment options future generations of Americans would take for granted, baseball usually was the only game in town. Actually, it was more than a game. It was a national obsession.

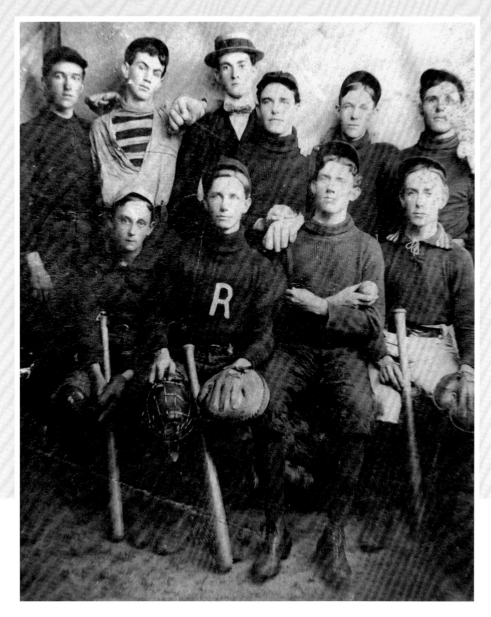

A skinny but determined Ty (front row, left) with his older, bigger Royston teammates sometime around 1900.

"Every town had its own town team in those days," said Sam Crawford, who recalled the glorious summer of 1898 when he and several other teenaged boys representing Wahoo, Nebraska, struck out for the open road in a horse-drawn grain wagon. "One of the boys was a cornet player, and when we'd come to a town he'd whip out that cornet and sound off. People would all come out to see what was going on, and we'd announce that we were the Wahoo team and were ready for a ball game. Every little town out there on the prairie had its own ball team and ball grounds, and we challenged them all. We didn't have any uniforms or anything, just baseball shoes maybe, but we had a manager. . . .

"We were gone three or four weeks. Lived on bread and beefsteak the whole time. We'd take up a collection at the games—pass the hat, you know—and that paid our expenses. Or some of them anyway. One of the boys was the cook, but all he could cook was round steak. We'd get 12 pounds for a dollar and have a feast. We'd drive along the country roads, and if we came to a stream, we'd go swimming; if we came to an apple orchard, we'd fill up on apples. We'd sleep anywhere. Sometimes in a tent, lots of times on the ground, out in the open. If we were near some fairgrounds, we'd slip in there. If we were near a barn, well . . ."

While "Wahoo Sam" was touring Nebraska in a wagon (and then quickly moving into the professional ranks with the Cincinnati Reds), his future team-mate was testing himself in town ball competition as a member of the Royston Rompers, a team comprised of 12-to-14-year-old boys. During vacations at Granddad Johnny's, Ty would hunt down a game in the mountain villages of Murphy and Andrews. No matter where the pasture or sandlot, opponents saw an earnest competitor awkwardly growing into a young man's body. In the outfield, he galloped like a puppy among the cow pies and wildflowers; in the infield, he choked back the instinct to turn his face at wickedly hit ground balls. Out of necessity he held his heavy homemade bats with hands wide apart on the handle. That grip, the only way the youngster could get around on the ball with his swing, would become his trademark through his professional career.

"It wasn't that I gave baseball a second thought as a career—skinny 90-pounder that I was," Ty once reflected. "My overwhelming need was to prove myself a real man. In the classroom, I was merely adequate—except for a flair for oratory, which brought me a few prizes. I couldn't hope to match my celebrated father for brains. In town ball—pitted against older boys and men at the age of 14— was the chance to become more than another schoolboy and the son of Professor Cobb."

Ty's feelings for his father were a deep blend of love, awe, and respect. "Professor" Cobb's lofty title had more to do with his exalted standing in the community than actual university credentials, but the townspeople's admiration was no less deserved for that reason. In addition to being a schoolmaster, landowner, and successful farmer, William by his late thirties had created a weekly newspaper, the *Royston Record* (which he wrote and edited), and been elected a state senator. He represented the 31st District in the Georgia state senate from 1900 until 1905, at which point he also was serving as Royston's mayor. As a legislator he was instrumental in reforming Georgia's public school system. He once delivered an address peppered with citations from history that showed education to be the foundation of democracy. Naturally, the voters of Franklin County elected him their first school commissioner. What spare time remained in William Cobb's busy life was spent reading mathematics, science, and classical literature.

Fifteen-year-old Ty was spending his winter school break at his grandparents' house in North Carolina when he received the following letter from his father. Like many educated men of the Victorian age, Professor Cobb's overblown prose stood in sharp contrast to his stiff and formal manner. But the correspondence reveals an affection that he had difficulty expressing to his son in person. That may be the reason, years later, Ty kept the letter tucked into his wallet and eventually had copies printed.

Royston, Ga., January 5th, 1902

Tyrus, Dear Boy—The first snow of the year of account is down today. It is two inches I reckon. It is all of a round fine hail not a single feathery flake, some lodge on the limbs of the trees. Our wheat and oats have stood the winter all right, wheat is up nicely. We are all snowed in today principally on account of the cold weather. Hardly a sound has been heard today. It is nearly six o'clock. I knew the past cold weather would furnish you with some fine scenery up there and I am glad you have been receptive of its austere beauty and solemn grandeur, as to color, sound, and picturesque contour or outline. That is a picturesque and romantic country with solitude enough to give nature a chance to be heard in the soul. The presence of man and the jargon of artificiality and show do not crowd out the grand aspects of God's handiwork among those everlasting hills covered with its primevil forest, nor hush the grand oratorios of the winds, nor check the rush of her living leaping waters.

To be educated is not only to be master of the printed page but be able to catch the messages of star, rock, flower, bird, painting and symphony. To have eyes that really see, ears that really hear and imagination that can construct the perfect from a fragment. It is truly great to have a mind that will respond to and open the door of the soul to all the legions of thoughts and symbols of knowledge and emotions that the whole universe around brings to us.

Be good and dutiful, conquer your anger and wild passions that would degrade your dignity and belittle your manhood. Cherish all the good that springs up in you. Be under the perpetual guidance of the better angel of your nature. Starve out and drive out the demon that lurks in all human blood and ready and anxious and restless to arise and reign.

Be good.

Yours affectionately,
W. H. COBB

Grandad Johnny had managed to provide his six children with at least partial college educations, and William expected to achieve no less for his own offspring, starting with the oldest. But Ty had the same jumbled feelings regarding the future that all youths have. William thought Ty might enjoy a career in law or medicine, once going so far as to have Ty apprenticed to the local doctor. The sight of blood didn't affect Ty at all. One memorable evening he assisted with the operation on a youngster who been shot in the stomach. At other times William thought his son might be right for a career in the military and spoke openly of securing for him an appointment to West Point or Annapolis.

If Ty wasn't sure what he wanted to be when he grew up, he knew what he didn't want to be: a farmer. Ty considered himself a "townie." He was so embarrassed at being seen working his father's crops in dirty overalls that he would hide in the lower end of the field rather than let a girl he was sweet on

> **"Going against my father came hard. But I had a burning zeal in me to find out what I could do on my own."** —TY COBB

catch him plowing like an ordinary clodhopper. He also showed little inclination to study harder than needed to pass a grade. To William's horror, it soon became obvious that what Ty really enjoyed more than anything else was playing ball. By 1901, when he was 14 years old, Ty had earned a spot as the starting shortstop (and occasional outfielder) on the local men's team, the Royston Reds.

"Ty was still a little, skinny, spare-built fellow," recalled Reds manager Bob McCreary, who clerked in the local bank. "But I thought at the time that he was about the best natural ballplayer I had ever seen."

William Cobb, who appears to have had little need or time for recreation, hardly knew a baseball from a boll weevil. Rather than force his intentions on Ty, he decided that the best strategy was to surrender to his son's fancy, with the expectation that he would eventually come around to more serious pursuits. Once before, when Ty had tried to swap some of his father's law books for a new fielder's glove, William had punished him so severely that Ty refused to discuss the particulars 60 years later in his autobiography. But now there was a subtle softening in William's objections. Assured by Bob McCreary that he would guarantee Ty's well-being, William allowed his son to accompany the team on a trip to the neighboring town of Elberton. Batting left-handed, Ty stroked three hits, including the game-winner in the eighth inning.

The heroics continued later that season against Harmony Grove. This time playing center field, Ty made a circus catch of a fly ball to save the game. The hometown crowd showered the young star with cheers, applause, and several dollars in change. Moments like this, Cobb later admitted, were his epiphany. "Once an athlete feels the peculiar thrill that goes with victory, he's bewitched. He can never get away from it." The catch was the talk of the town for days. With his son elevated into the unaccustomed role of local hero, a chagrined William proudly devoted space in the *Royston Record*, which normally shunned sports, to an account of the game.

The two major leagues, the established National and the upstart American, were concentrated in the Northeast and thus little more than a rumor to most of the rest of the country. Nonetheless, one spring day in 1902, 15-year-old Ty talked his father into letting him take a train to Atlanta, where the Cleveland Naps (named after their great slugger, Napoleon Lajoie) were training. Sneaking into Piedmont Park with his dollar Kodak, Ty saw his first big leaguers. His biggest thrill was striking up a conversation with veteran third baseman Bill Bradley, who posed for some snapshots. "After that," he said, "Bill Bradley was a hero of mine. I kept those pictures until they turned to dust."

At the same time as he was humoring Ty, William continued his campaign to find more practical applications for his baseball-loving son's energy. In the

spring of 1903, when Ty was in his junior year of high school, William assigned him a section of the family farm to put in the season's cotton crop. Wrestling with a hoe or a mule, sweating alongside black field hands like "Uncle Ezra," normally held no appeal for Ty. But this time proved different. William made him in effect the sole proprietor of this patch of land, trusting him to make all the decisions regarding purchasing and equipment. The responsibility of keeping the books, supervising the crop, and ensuring a decent return on investment produced a remarkable change in Ty. Watching his long hours of seeding and plowing slowly blossom into ten acres of whitish-gray cash crop, he felt the first stirrings of the visceral rewards of farming. He enjoyed speculating on what his labor would yield at harvest time and in the marketplace. In the process he felt closer to his father, whose own estimation of Ty began to swell.

"It was the sweetest thing in the world to be fully accepted by my father," said Ty. "All at once, he was willing to hear my ideas, discuss them, and even exchange opinions. We'd talk about crop production, English import of cotton which competed with our Georgia output, and I never felt closer to him than when he said, 'Do you think we should sell now, or hold on for a better price?'" Demonstrating a new enthusiasm for agribusiness, Ty took a job with a local cotton concern and learned all about ginning, baling, grading, and moving the crop to market.

More than cotton had been planted. The seeds of Ty's fabled business acumen (as well as his equally storied stinginess) also were sown that spring. "That was the most valuable lesson I ever received," he said 20 years later, by which time he had become independently wealthy through shrewd stock investments. "I learned to produce. I learned that money had to be earned. I learned the value of a dollar, the joy of earning it. I could not have learned it in any better way."

But always there was baseball to dash William's hopes. That year Ty pocketed a few dollars playing ball for a country nine in Anderson, South Carolina. Those first two play-for-pay games technically made him a "professional" and thus could have destroyed his amateur eligibility when he went on to college—which, of course, his father fully expected. In the spring of 1904, however, as the weeks to high school graduation were winding down, Ty secretly wrote letters to the six clubs then forming the brand new South Atlantic (Sally) League. The only reply came from the Augusta team. Manager and part-owner Con Strouthers invited Ty to a tryout at his expense. If he made the team, he would be paid $50 a month. Ty eagerly signed the enclosed contract and sent it back.

"If that one team hadn't answered," Ty later reflected, "I wonder if I'd ever have made baseball a career, for my ambition hung by a tenuous thread...suspended between my duty to my father, and my own desire."

Ty confided in his mother, who reluctantly gave her blessing. But he waited until the night before he was to leave to approach his father for his permission—and, just as important, for expense money. Instead of blowing up, the senior Cobb patiently tried to explain why it was imperative that Ty develop his mind, not his muscles. He also had considerable influence, he explained, which could help smooth a career path into law, medicine, or the military. "You are seventeen and this is the decisive moment for you," he lectured, pacing back and forth, hands clasped behind his back. "In baseball, you can't help but fall into the company of a riffraffish type of men who drink and carouse and lead a pointless life."

"I just have to go," Ty protested over and over.

The discussion went on through the night and into the small hours of the morning, when William finally capitulated.

"Well, son, you've chosen," he said wearily. "So be it. Go get it out of your system, and let us hear from you once in a while." With that he sat down and wrote six $15 checks to cover Ty's expenses. Although he wouldn't be around to fully appreciate it, in terms of return on investment it was the soundest business decision William Cobb ever made.

The following morning Ty traveled the 80 miles by train to Augusta. The charming city's reputation as a resort town, established in the years before highways and air conditioning made Florida more accessible to vacationers, had inspired the nickname of its Class C ball club, the Tourists. The team played at Warren Park.

Ty, practicing in his flaming red Royston uniform, was anything but an immediate hit. Eager to impress, he instead angered the older players by cutting in front of them on fly balls and grounders. He alternately dismayed and amused Con Strouthers by running the bases like an empty-headed fool. Strouthers, counting pennies, also was upset that the newcomer had broken two new bats in batting practice—at a cost of seventy-five cents apiece. As a result, Ty sat on the bench throughout the spring training schedule.

He did have a chance, however, to meet Sam Crawford when the Detroit Tigers checked into Warren Park during an exhibition swing in April. After the

Amanda Chitwood Cobb, Ty's mother. Amanda married in 1883 and was just 15 when she gave birth to Ty.

Tigers had beaten the Tourists, Ty hesitatingly approached Crawford, introduced himself, then began peppering the rangy center fielder with questions. Talkative and helpful at first, Wahoo Sam finally said, "Hell, I can't gab all day," then ended their session with a last piece of advice: "Don't drink on game days." Nobody in the entire state of Georgia could have predicted that in little more than a year, the brusque veteran and the skinny, stammering 17-year-old would be traversing the same outfield grass in distant Detroit.

In fact, few would have bet on Ty making the Tourists. However, on April 21, 1904, opening day against the Columbia (South Carolina) team, Strouthers unexpectedly penciled Cobb's name into the lineup. Augusta's first baseman was holding out in a contract dispute, so the starting center fielder was moved to first and Ty took over in center. In his first professional game, Ty batted seventh against Columbia's George Engel, a fastball pitcher. He grounded out in his first at-bat, but on his second attempt he drove an Engel pitch over third base and up against the left-field fence. As the ball bounced around the outfield, Ty circled the bases for an inside-the-park home run, narrowly beating the throw home with a head-first slide. He added a double his next time up. Although Columbia won, 8–7, his performance had impressed many in the crowd of fifteen hundred. A married couple from Cornelia invited him out to dinner that night, and a reporter for the *Augusta Chronicle* described the professional debut of "Outfielder T. Cobb" as "auspicious," his pair of extra-base hits "a better act than anyone could expect from a beginner."

Had William Cobb been sitting in Warren Park that afternoon, the classics scholar might have reminded his son of the Latin cautionary phrase *Sic transit gloria mundi:* "Fame is fleeting." For the following day Ty went hitless and was cut from the roster. Strouthers explained that his first baseman had signed and that Ty's services would thus no longer be needed. The youngster was convinced Strouthers just didn't like him.

Dazed, Ty fell in at his hotel with Thad Hayes, a pitcher who also had been cut. Hayes knew of a team organizing in Anniston, Alabama, that they might be able to catch on with.

Ty dreaded calling his father to explain his release and to ask his permission to head for Anniston, a sooty mill town halfway between Atlanta and Birmingham. However, instead of saying "I told you so" and demanding his return home, William Cobb gave his son the greatest surprise of his young life. "Go after it," said William. "And I want to tell you one other thing: Don't come home a failure."

Anniston was one of eight charter members of the Tennessee-Alabama League. The "outlaw" league (which meant that it operated outside of the jurisdiction of organized baseball) had just been created with five teams in Alabama and three in Tennessee. The caliber of play was somewhere between that of a good semipro league and a Class D circuit, the lowest of the organized leagues. By the time the Anniston Noblemen disbanded in July, Cobb had settled into a starring role for the sixth-place club. Typically playing left field and batting fifth, he hit .313 with a league-best eight triples, according to surviving scoresheets.

Ty's stint with "Annie-town" is the least reported part of his professional career, but it may have been the most valuable. It gave a teenager with only two games of professional experience under his belt a chance to sharpen his raw talent and boost his self-confidence against inferior competition. It also gave him his first prolonged taste of the baseball life, which he discovered he enjoyed. Ty admitted he "managed to look like the berries" in this group, although little mention of his exploits made the *Atlanta Journal* and other major dailies. When a brief blurb did appear, he often was referred to as "Cyrus" Cobb.

Before long, however, the *Journal's* up-and-coming sports editor, Grantland Rice, started receiving a stream of letters and postcards from fans named Jackson, Smith, and Kelly. One signed by a "Mr. Jones" informed Rice that "Tyrus Raymond Cobb, the dashing young star with Anniston, Ala., is going great guns. He is as fast as a deer and undoubtedly a phenom." It wasn't until years later that Cobb confessed to Rice that, eager to get back into organized ball, he had written the letters himself.

The ruse worked, to the extent that Rice wrote in his column that "rumors had reached Atlanta from numerous sources that over in Alabama there's a young fellow named Cobb who seems to be showing an unusual lot of talent." Rice even traveled to Anniston to see for himself. Faced with this kind of evidence from "interested fans" and a popular sportswriter, the Augusta Tourists had a change of heart. For at the same time that the Anniston Noblemen were disbanding, Con Strouthers was saying good-bye to Augusta. The Tourists' new management welcomed the "dashing young star" back into the fold, with Ty rejoining the lineup on August 9 in a game against Columbia. It didn't take long before Ty's propensity for ad-lib base running put him at odds with catcher-manager Andy Roth. "Be careful, junior," the tough veteran warned Cobb after he was twice thrown out while ignoring signs, "or you'll be catching another train out of town!"

Although he batted only an aggregate .237 during his two stints with Augusta, Ty returned to Royston in the fall of 1904 as a minor celebrity. Far from succumbing to the evils of dissipation, he had even managed to save $200 during his summer away from home. While William Cobb continued to be sparing in his praise, he had carried around a clipping of Grantland Rice's column during the season to show his legislative friends. Tragically for Ty, who over the winter signed a new contract with Augusta for $90 a month for the 1905 season, he wouldn't discover this small but meaningful item about his father until after he had been snatched away from him.

Like many preoccupied men, William Cobb could be blind to events unfolding in front of his eyes. A staple of gossip around Royston during the summer of 1905—by which time Ty was playing left field and batting leadoff for Augusta—was that Amanda Cobb had taken a lover. The rumors were not that easy to dismiss. At 34, Ty's mother was still young and attractive, and William often was out of town for days at a time. Amanda's paramour was said to be a family acquaintance, a local planter who was young, prosperous, and—unlike her frustratingly remote husband—attentive to her needs, emotionally and sexually.

One day William stood around downtown arguing with several men about closing a local brothel. The alleged house of ill repute, which happened to be one house over from the Cobbs' residence, was operated by the pair of sisters who lived there.

"Why don't you take care of your own house first?" one irritated citizen finally suggested.

The implication that he was a cuckolded husband should have brought a forceful, even physical, response from William. That he evidently did not challenge the man suggests that he either was already aware of Amanda's infidelity, or else thought the rumors too ridiculous to address.

Early in the evening of August 8, 1905, William left the house for the family farm. He probably would be there a couple of days, he told Amanda. Later that night, with Ty in Augusta and the other two children staying with friends, Amanda locked the windows and went to bed.

Meanwhile, after night fell, William doubled back to town. With a pistol in his coat pocket, he quietly climbed a ladder to the second-story landing outside his and Amanda's bedroom. As Amanda later testified, she was awakened about midnight by a shadowy figure trying to lift one of the bedroom windows. Scrambling for the loaded double-barreled shotgun that was always on hand when William was away, she pointed it at the intruder and pulled one of the triggers. A short while later, she pulled the other trigger.

The screams and explosions rocked the muggy night air. First on the scene was Ty's friend and next-door neighbor, Joe Cunningham, who was sickened by what he later described as "the worst thing I ever saw." William Herschel Cobb lay, barely breathing, in a pool of blood, brains, and viscera. The blasts had ripped out his stomach and blown off part of his head. Cunningham ran to find H. F. McCreary, a doctor and the father of Ty's old manager on the Royston Reds. The doctor pronounced William dead at 1:30 a.m.

Amanda Cobb was subsequently arrested on a charge of involuntary manslaughter, posted a stiff $7,000 bond, and was tried the following spring. She hired five defense attorneys. The prosecution, unwilling to ask the hard, indelicate questions about her alleged infidelity, failed to make its case. The all-male jury needed just one hour to return a verdict of not guilty.

The yellow frame house where Ty Cobb's father died no longer stands. The site is now the parking lot of a funeral home. All of the principals in the case are long gone. The shooting case will probably never be fully resolved. Yet, after all these years, it is still a topic of conversation around Royston, fueled by key unanswered questions that have been handed down from generation to generation like a grandmother's treasured quilts. Why were the windows closed on such a hot, stuffy summer night? Was it to guard against intruders or to provide privacy for a clandestine coupling? And why the significant delay between shots? Joe Cunningham, whose father built the coffin that William was buried in two days later, always maintained that Amanda didn't pull the trigger. Whispers swirled around town that her lover fired the fatal shots. "My father said he knew who the man was," Eugene Phillips, a retired general and lifelong Royston resident, told a reporter in 1994. "I knew who he was, but there's no sense in talking about it. He's long since dead." But others to this day insist that it truly was a case of mistaken identity; as proof of Amanda's fidelity, they point out that she never remarried. One modern researcher, Royston native Wesley Fricks, has conjectured that William was not even spying on his wife that night. Instead, Royston's mayor was

Ty (top row, third from right) and the 1905 Augusta Tourists. Within a ten-day span that summer the 18-year-old outfielder received two pieces of news that rocked his world: his father had been killed, and he was being called up to the big leagues.

lying in wait to see if some local men, upset over hizzoner's successful campaign to close the bawdy house next door, would carry through on their threat to torch his house in reprisal. It's a novel theory, supported circumstantially by the fact that the Cobbs' home was lost to a fire a couple of years later.

One of the few certainties about William Cobb's death is that it devastated Ty, who learned of the tragedy by telegram the following morning. He described it as "the blackest of days," but for the rest of his life he rarely spoke of it, and even in his autobiography he dismissed the episode in one sentence as "a gun accident." Although he was never close to his mother, he remained convinced outwardly of her virtue. "This isn't the kind of people Cobbs are," he insisted after hurrying home from Augusta.

The extent of the damage to Ty's psyche can only be guessed at. Today emotionally traumatized youths are routinely surrounded by a phalanx of social workers, child psychologists, and assorted other "grief counselors." None of these was available in the summer of 1905. The best recourse for the sorrowful 18-year-old was to wrap up as many loose ends as possible and return to the profession William Cobb had opposed. Only now the full and unequivocal approval Ty had so desperately sought from his father would be withheld forever.

CHAPTER TWO

An Infant Prodigy

He wasn't like this when he came up, you know. He was
only 18, and as scared as they all are. But he had all that talent,
and so the veterans went after him more mercilessly than I had ever
seen in all my years in the game. They ridiculed him, and splintered
his bats, even intercepted his mail from home. And I don't think
Mister Cobb has ever really trusted anyone but himself since then.

HARRY STEIN, *HOOPLA*

Ty rejoined the Augusta Tourists on August 16, 1905, just a week after his father's fatal shooting. Three days later, club president Charles D. Carr sold him to the Detroit Tigers.

It had already been a strange and tragic summer for Ty, one in which events were moving almost too fast. Just four months earlier he had startled the same Tiger ball club with his wild base-running and fielding antics during spring training exhibitions between Augusta and Detroit. "He's the craziest ballplayer I ever saw," remarked the Tigers' resident loon, Herman "Germany" Schaefer. At the time of his sale to Detroit, Augusta—a team that boasted several future major leaguers including infielder Clyde Engle and pitchers Eddie Cicotte and Nap Rucker—had fallen into a funk that left the team floundering near the bottom of the standings and its talented but immature left fielder counting the days until the end of the season. Away from the park, Ty had fallen in with a fast crowd. He was introduced to hard liquor, women, and the horsetrack, and found them all to his liking. At the park he became so nonchalant that during one game he missed a fly ball because he was munching on a bag of popcorn in the outfield. That particular episode cost the Tourists a run and caused Cicotte to punch Cobb in the dugout. The fight, just the latest of several confrontations involving Ty and his teammates, was judged a draw, but it prompted manager Andy Roth to sell him to Charleston for the insulting sum of $25. Team owners, however, recognized Cobb as a brilliant if mercurial asset. They killed the deal and dumped Roth

Opposite: A familiar sight around the American League for a quarter century: Ty Cobb, hands held wide apart, ready to smack the ball to any part of the field. This photograph shows Ty at bat at Chicago's West Side Park in 1906.

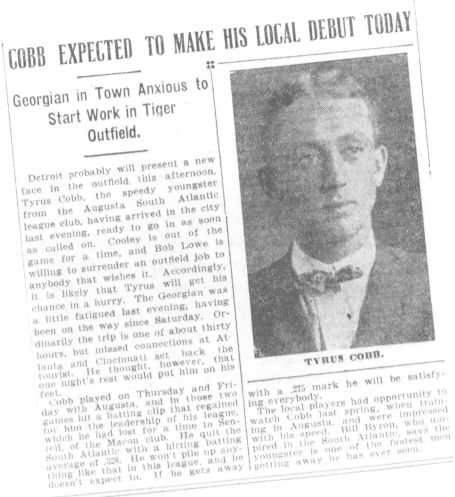

The *Detroit Free Press* announced Cobb's arrival in town in its August 30, 1905, edition.

instead, causing the rest of the team to shun the disruptive youngster from Royston. "He was a strange bird, the whole ball club knew it," Rucker said years later. "Say something to him and he was likely to give you a dirty look."

This was when one other major influence in Ty's life stepped forward. George Leidy, a career minor leaguer whose diamond smarts outweighed his skills, had been the Tourists' sore-armed outfielder and team captain when he was tapped to replace Roth. Leidy, whom Cobb described as "the type who tore into every play with all he had—a team man to the bone," had spent the best years of his life trying to make it to the majors. That Ty seemed intent on throwing away his own chance upset him deeply.

"The reason I made good in the majors was Leidy," Cobb acknowledged years later. The paternalistic Leidy, nicknamed "Dad," took Ty aside and through lecture and instruction turned his baseball career around. In the mornings before games Leidy taught him the mechanics of the hit-and-run, the drag bunt, the double steal, and the squeeze play. They worked on drawing the third baseman in on a fake bunt, then slapping the ball past him. Leidy had Ty bunt into a sweater placed strategically on the diamond, in spots where an infielder had little or no chance to make a play. "I bunted until I was worn out," recalled Ty.

But the grueling hours of self-improvement paid off in the afternoon, as Ty tore loose at bat and on the bases, using what he had just learned to upset and outthink opponents. And over evening meals and during postgame strolls through muggy Southern towns, Leidy counseled his young pupil on the rewards and recognition that came with being a big leaguer. "Stop breaking training," he lectured. "Stay sober. Apply yourself every minute. You're not playing ball, you're playing *at* it."

Then came the painful events of early August—his father's shooting, his mother's indictment for murder, and the rumors about her infidelity. Ty's sudden promotion to the major leagues evoked only one melancholy thought, he later admitted: "Father won't know it."

Cobb's final game for Augusta was on August 25, 1905. Play was stopped so fans could present him with a floral bouquet and a gold watch. Ty said thanks, shook hands, waved to the Warren Park crowd—and then struck out. "Let Detroit have him!" someone in the stands bellowed. Two subsequent singles produced Ty's final batting mark of .326, which would prove good enough to lead the Sally League.

As Ty would quickly learn, the American League was far removed from the Sally League in skill level and culture as well as in distance. That he was making the 725-mile train trip to Detroit at all was not entirely due to his talent but owed more to economics—and possibly a social disease.

That April the cash-strapped Tigers had left behind a promising pitching prospect, Eddie Cicotte, in lieu of the $500 the club owed Augusta for spring training expenses. However, Augusta agreed that the Tigers could later claim any player off its roster for the same amount. The Tigers, looking for a cheap replacement player for its injury-depleted outfield, decided against buying an experienced but more expensive player from the higher levels of organized baseball. Reviewing the Augusta roster, club officials seriously considered Clyde Engle. But largely on the advice of Detroit scout Heinie Youngman and pitcher Bill Donovan, as well as Sally League umpire Bill Byron (a native Detroiter), Tigers manager Bill Armour and club secretary Frank Navin settled on Cobb. Years later, Ty suggested that Engle wasn't selected because he was suffering from a venereal disease (an occupational hazard of professional ballplayers), which had affected his play. Whatever the reason, Ty headed north to finish out the year with the Tigers. Because he was joining Detroit before the end of the Tourists' season, Augusta received an additional $250 for his contract. Total purchase price: $750.

ᏬᏬ

On Wednesday, August 30, 1905, the *Detroit Free Press* ran a brief story about the newcomer's arrival, accompanied by a photograph. Under the headline "Cobb Expected to Make His Local Debut Today," readers got a brief summation of the unknown teenager that some competing dailies were identifying as "Cyrus" Cobb:

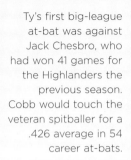

Ty's first big-league at-bat was against Jack Chesbro, who had won 41 games for the Highlanders the previous season. Cobb would touch the veteran spitballer for a .426 average in 54 career at-bats.

Detroit probably will present a new face in the outfield this afternoon. Tyrus Cobb, the speedy youngster from the Augusta South Atlantic league club, having arrived in the city last evening, ready to go in as soon as called on. Cooley is out of the game for a time, and Bob Lowe is willing to surrender an outfield job to anybody that wishes it. Accordingly, it is likely that Tyrus will get his chance in a hurry. The Georgian was a little fatigued last evening, having been on the way since Saturday. Ordinarily the trip is one of about thirty hours, but missed connections at Atlanta and Cincinnati set back the tourist. He thought, however, that one night's rest would put him on his feet.

Cobb played on Thursday and Friday with Augusta, and in those two games hit a batting clip that regained for him the leadership of the league, which he had lost for a time to Sentell, of the Macon club. He quit the South Atlantic with a hitting batting average of .328 [sic]. He won't pile up anything like that in this league, and he doesn't expect to. If he gets away with a .275 mark he will be satisfying everybody.

The local players had opportunity to watch Cobb last spring, when training in Augusta, and were impressed with his speed. Bill Byron, who umpired in the South Atlantic, says the youngster is one of the fastest men getting away he has ever seen.

As expected, Ty broke into the Detroit lineup that afternoon in a game against the New York Highlanders. In the top of the first inning, an estimated 1,200 "bugs" (as fans were then known) at wooden Bennett Park watched with mild curiosity as Cobb nervously trotted out to his position in center field, flanked by Matty McIntyre in left and Sam Crawford in right. In the bottom of the inning, Ty drew several stares and comments as he swung three bats in the on-deck area. No one could ever remember seeing a player do that before. Spectators and teammates may have thought the new fellow was showing off, but Ty had been following the ritual for some time. Throwing down the other two bats before entering the batter's box made his heavy, thick-handed club feel two-thirds lighter.

Ty, batting fifth, came up with a runner on third and two out. Facing him was Jack Chesbro, a grizzled spitballer who had won 41 games—still the modern record—a year earlier. Ty swung and missed Chesbro's first offering, took a called strike on the second, and then slapped the third pitch into the gap in left-center field for a run-scoring double. It was an auspicious beginning, although Ty went hitless the rest of the game and was thrown out attempting to steal second after reaching base on a walk. Observed the *Free Press*: "Cobb, the rookie, may consider a double and a walk a much better career-opener than usually comes a young ballplayer's way."

The following afternoon Ty contributed a pair of singles as the Tigers beat the Highlanders for the second straight game. The rookie's most memorable moment came on a stolen base attempt after his first hit. Waiting for him at second base was Norman "Kid" Eberfeld, a scrappy, sawed-off shortstop who had played several years for Detroit. As Cobb dove head first into the bag—a bush-

"You don't know what you've got .... in a year or two, no more, you can be up there making ten times the money you're getting now."

—AUGUSTA MANAGER GEORGE LEIDY TO COBB, 1905

league slide in 1905—Eberfeld put the "teach" on him, sticking his knee into Ty's neck and rubbing his nose into the dirt. Cobb got up sputtering and red-faced, as the crowd and veterans on both teams hooted and laughed. From that point on Ty rarely slid head first into a base.

With regular Jimmy Barrett sidelined with a bad leg, Ty started each of the Tigers' final 41 games. On September 23 he hit his first home run, an inside-the-park blow off Cy Falkenberg at Washington. "He went so fast that he almost ran over the two Tigers scoring ahead of him," reported one Detroit daily. "This kid can outleg the No. 1 horse hitch at the Central Fire Department." He wound up batting .240 for the season, with a couple of stolen bases, as the Tigers roared home a surprising third. Ty, whose play was occasionally brilliant but often unpredictable, deserved little of the credit, but everyone around the circuit recognized him as a raw talent—"an infant prodigy," as *Sporting Life* called him.

The Tigers thought enough of him to raise his annual salary from $1,200 to $1,500 for 1906—an important consideration, as he was now expected to provide for his widowed mother and sister. However, no amount of money could compensate Cobb for what happened in the spring of 1906, a period he later called "the most miserable and humiliating experience I've ever been through."

Specifically, Ty became the target of a relentless hazing campaign aimed, he thought, at driving him off the team. Starting in spring training and continuing throughout the season, a core group of veterans made life practically unbearable for him. They shoved him aside at the batting cage and turned away when he spoke to them. In the clubhouse they tied his clothes in knots. Back in the hotel after practice, they kept the grime-streaked youngster waiting in the hallway for hours as they took their time soaking in the communal bathtub. Perhaps the lowest moment was when Ty discovered his homemade bats had been destroyed.

His teammates' unexpected behavior shocked, angered, and ultimately inspired Ty. He had made it through his abbreviated 1905 stay in time-honored rookie fashion, keeping to himself while the veterans ignored him. But in the spring of 1906, last year's late-season substitute suddenly was a threat to someone else's full-time employment. With Sam Crawford a fixture in right field and newly acquired veteran Davy Jones conceded the center-field spot, Ty figured to compete with Matty McIntyre for the final outfield position. This left him wide open to abuse from the popular McIntyre and his circle of friends.

To his teammates, Ty was as much a foreigner as the millions of immigrants then flooding America's shores. At the century's turn, the overwhelming majority of big leaguers were Irish or German Catholics who hailed from the

Northeastern quadrant of the country. When Ty spoke, his thick drawl—which transformed the name of his home state into something approximating "Jo-ja"— immediately marked him an outsider, as did his youth, inexperience, and Baptist upbringing. Unlike most veteran ballplayers, the young Cobb neither smoked, chewed, cussed, nor frequented brothels (though this would soon change). He also had the appearance of a Southern rube. Although he would later fill out to an imposing 6-foot-1 and 190 pounds, at the time he was about three inches and 25 pounds smaller. His wispy, reddish-blond hair and wide blue eyes added to his vulnerable look. In Ty's mind, the treatment he received helped account for his legendary ferocity. "Those old-timers made a snarling wildcat out of me," is how he often put it.

From university dorms and infantry barracks to baseball clubhouses, hazing was a staple of American life, although it often crossed the line from innocent high jinks to mean-spiritedness and maliciousness. The following spring, for instance, Detroit veterans drove an unfortunate rube who had committed the gaffe of labeling his luggage "Jameson Harper, Ballplayer" out of camp and nearly out of his mind with a series of heckles, pranks, and cold shoulders. And in 1908, Philadelphia rookie "Shoeless Joe" Jackson, an ignorant mill hand from South Carolina, was so thoroughly humiliated by his teammates that he quit the club several times, forcing an exasperated Connie Mack to finally sell him to Cleveland.

In Ty's case, veterans encountered a high-strung, serious-minded, and stub-bornly proud teenager who simply refused to retreat an inch. Cobb made no

The Detroit Tigers gather inside Warren Park in Augusta for a team photo during spring training in 1906. *Top row, from left:* pitchers Bill Donovan and George Disch, first baseman Pinky Lindsay, catcher Tom Doran, outfielder Matty McIntyre, and pitchers John Eubank and George Mullin. *Middle row:* outfielder Bobby Lowe, catcher Lew Drill, pitcher Ed Killian, outfielder Sam Crawford, manager Bill Armour, pitcher Jimmy Wiggs, Cobb, outfielder Jimmy Barrett, shortstop Charlie O'Leary. *Bottom row:* pitcher Frank Kitson, catcher Jack Warner, third baseman Bill Coughlin, second baseman Germany Schaefer.

apologies for his defiance. "If I'd been meek and submissive and hadn't fought back," he later explained, "the world never would have heard of Ty Cobb."

Ty's principal antagonists were McIntyre and his roommate, pitcher Ed Killian. Cobb's future Hall-of-Fame outfield mate, Sam Crawford, didn't like the newcomer either but he apparently did little more than agitate in the background. Six years older than Cobb, Wahoo Sam was already a star with the Cincinnati Reds when Ty was still fielding grounders with the Royston Reds. The left-handed hitting Crawford was probably the top slugger of the deadball era. His 312 lifetime triples and 56 inside-the-park home runs, both major-league records, are as much a testimony to his power and surprising speed as they are to the cavernous ballparks of the period.

Crawford, the acknowledged star of the team since joining the Tigers in 1903, was a proud man with a high opinion of himself. Like Cobb, Crawford could be petulant, calculating, and vindictive. The thought of someone stealing his thunder accounted for Crawford's attitude toward Ty. Although the two would wind up playing 13 seasons together, they only barely tolerated each other. So tense was their relationship that Ty was convinced Crawford would occasionally foul off a pitch on purpose if it looked like Ty had a base stolen.

"The great American game should be an unrelenting war of nerves." —TY COBB

Late in life, Crawford gave his side of the story: "We weren't cannibals or heathens," he explained. "We were all ballplayers together, trying to get along. Every rookie gets a little hazing, but most of them just take it and laugh. Cobb took it the wrong way. He came up with an antagonistic attitude, which in his mind turned any little razzing into a life-or-death struggle. He always figured everybody was ganging up against him."

Ty never had much of a sense of humor, added Davy Jones, who did his best to befriend him. "Especially, he could never laugh at himself. Consequently, he took a lot of things the wrong way. What would usually be an innocent-enough wisecrack would become cause for a fist fight if Ty was involved." It's impossible today to apportion blame for what happened in Cobb's early years. But if it's true that Ty suffered from a persecution complex, then it's equally true that wiser or more charitable teammates should have recognized it and eased off.

That spring, Joe S. Jackson of the *Detroit Free Press* coined Ty's soon-to-be-famous nickname, "the Georgia Peach." Of course, nobody called him that in everyday conversation. To others Ty was simply "Cobb" or "Tyrus" or "T. C.," though Cobb, who delighted in his new moniker, was now wont to refer to himself in the third person as "the Peach." Predictably, photographers began posing him biting into his namesake fruit. As time went by "Peach" became the nickname of choice for many sportswriters and ballplayers.

At that, the name proved wonderfully descriptive. Tyrus Raymond Cobb *was* a peach of a player, as he proved when given the chance. When the 1906 season opened, the Tigers' outfield consisted of Crawford in right, Jones in center, and McIntyre in left. However, after Crawford injured his leg in a late April game against Chicago, Ty entered the starting lineup and, despite uneven play, stayed there. When Crawford was ready to come back, Armour benched Jones and installed Cobb in center.

Ty was determined to remain a major leaguer no matter what the price. He was still recovering from the butchery he had endured to cure an agonizing case of tonsillitis he had developed as the team worked its way north from spring training. Fearful of losing his spot on the roster, he had kept the condition to himself, until a high fever and swollen glands finally forced him to visit the physician of the Toledo hotel where the team was staying. Over three bloody sessions, each of which left Ty dazed from hemorrhaging and pain, the doctor went at his tonsils with more enthusiasm than surgical skill.

"He sat me in a chair, tipped it back and went to work, without anesthetic," remembered Cobb. "My tonsils were in such a condition that they had to be removed in sections. Each time a piece of them came out, blood surged into my mouth, choking me, and I had to demand a rest period. Putting a stranglehold on my neck, the doc would probe and cut for 10 or 15 minutes before letting me collapse on a sofa." Germany Schaefer, who had come along for moral support,

wound up half-carrying his teammate back to his room after each gory episode. Ty later would discover that the man who had happily hacked away at his tonsils had been committed to an insane asylum.

Not long afterward the Peach was "invalided" for several days at a Detroit hospital to drain and heal his raw and infected left hip, which had been rubbed into hamburger by repeated slides on Bennett Park's concrete-like base paths. The Tigers' home field had been built in 1896 on the site of an old hay market, and a decade later cobblestones still regularly emerged through the thin layer of topsoil. Pitcher Bill Donovan, whose own base-running style had earned him the sobriquet "Wild Bill," said of Cobb during this period: "Every time he slides he loses a pint of blood."

Despite his starting status, Ty remained shut off from most of the team. The scrappy teenager known to his hazers as "the Reb" ate alone, roomed alone, and continued to endure random acts of mayhem. On train trips he would be smacked in the back of the head by soggy wads of newspaper. Grabbing his hat after a meal, he would find that its crown had been crushed. He was never able to identify his attackers, though. "Who did this?" he would yell, his hands balled into fists. No one ever stepped forward. Veterans elbowed him aside at batting practice, stuffed horse turds in his shoes, and kicked over the water bucket when he reached for a drink. The ostracism became so bad that Ty took to spending his pregame warm-ups inside the groundskeeper's shack, looking for a temporary respite to settle his nerves. Although a few players, such as Donovan, Schaefer, and Jones, were friendly with him, Ty had no truly close companions. During his

"Edgar, they are not driving me off this team."

—COBB TO TEAMMATE EDGAR WILLETT, 1906

free time he would wander alone to a vaudeville show or take in a classical performance at the Detroit Opera House. Or he would stroll down to lush Belle Isle Park on the Detroit River. Edgar Willett, a rookie pitcher from Virginia, moved into Ty's cramped downtown hotel room for a time. More important than sharing expenses was the opportunity for companionship with a fellow Southerner. But a short while later the anti-Cobb faction convinced Willet that it was in his best interest to move out. After that, Ty's closest companion was the pistol he started carrying.

Beyond the physical isolation, it was his agile mind that truly set Ty apart from everyone else. He was intelligent and creative and a fast learner. In fact, the ostracism hastened the youngster's development. Time that otherwise might have been spent inside pool halls and saloons was used to better advantage, as Ty stared at his hotel room ceiling and dreamed up ways of foiling the opposition. When Ty broke in, he ran the bases "like a fool" and "couldn't hit a left-hander very good," an admiring Ring Lardner once recalled. "That was when he first come up here. But Ty ain't the guy that's goin' to stay fooled all the time. When he wises up that somebody's got somethin' on him, he don't sleep nor do nothin' till he figures out a way to get even. . . . He seen he couldn't hit the curve when it was breakin', so he stood way back in the box and waited till it'd broke. Then he nailed it." Three months into the 1906 season, the Peach was nailing it often enough to challenge for the batting title.

Then, on July 18, Ty mysteriously left the team in Boston and was missing from the Tigers' lineup for several weeks. The newspapers didn't explain or make much fuss over his absence, other than to report that he had been sent back to Detroit because of "stomach trouble." Some speculated that the reason for Ty's "rest" was to remove an ulcer. Many years later it came to light that Cobb's "illness" was a case of physical and emotional exhaustion, brought on by his rugged playing style and compounded by the pressures of dealing with his teammates and his mother's recently concluded trial. "My nerves were shot to hell," Cobb later said of his breakdown. He described himself as being like "a steel spring ... wound too tight" that was ready to "fly apart."

The club quietly arranged for his convalescence at a sanatorium in rural Oakland County, north of Detroit. There, with the aid of medication, he slept long hours, giving his mind and body a chance to rest. He fished, swam, and hiked in the woods, recuperative activities that undoubtedly brought to mind happier moments he had enjoyed as a boy in Georgia and North Carolina. Visitors and newspapers were forbidden, and cooperative sportswriters kept the story to themselves.

There was plenty of time for reflection. Cobb later admitted that he had seriously considered quitting, but "I felt like I was getting close to making a real reputation for myself." Ty, who had "never quit on anything in my life, even

Recuperating from his nervous breakdown in the summer of 1906, Cobb played himself back into shape with the Detroit Athletic Club's amateur nine. He made a couple of valuable and lifelong friends: John Kelsey (fourth from left in the top row) and Ben Guiney (mustachioed player at right in the middle row).

when it looked like the smart play," refused to cave in to his hazers. It was a matter of personal honor, he decided.

After spending several weeks at the sanatorium, Ty played himself back into shape with the Detroit Athletic Club, for years one of the area's top amateur nines. The D.A.C., breeding ground for several major leaguers, including Christy Mathewson's batterymate on the New York Giants, Frank Bowerman, played its games behind a handsome brick clubhouse on Woodward Avenue, about two miles north of downtown. "I can still see Ty getting the opposition up in the air," team captain George McClure remembered years later. "Placing one over third, then over first, and then crossing 'em up by bunting. He was just a boy then. But we knew he had the stuff." According to McClure, Ty played some 40 games in the outfield for the D.A.C. that summer, and the team won them all.

Competing among mature older men and apple-cheeked sandlotters, Ty found the environment friendly and mercifully free of the petty jealousies that had characterized his brief time in the majors. The newcomer made several valuable and lifelong contacts, including men involved with the fledgling auto industry. One was Ben Guiney, a former National Leaguer and a star on the D.A.C's two national amateur championship teams of the early 1890s. Now nearly 50, Guiney was a successful executive with the Kelsey Wheel Company, which provided automakers with wheels and brake systems. In his spare time he still enjoyed playing and coaching the game at the amateur level. It was Guiney—not Ty, as is commonly supposed—who originated an offensive maneuver that became famous as a textbook example of Cobbian baseball.

The tactic was devastatingly simple. Having reached first base, Cobb would flash the "bunt" sign to the batter. Then, as the pitcher went into his windup, Ty would dart for second and, instead of staying there as the ball was bunted toward third base, roar around the bag as the third baseman temporarily abandoned his station to field the ball. Usually Cobb was able to slide safely into third before the fielder could complete his throw to first and hustle back and receive the return throw. The tactic, which required a skilled sacrifice bunter to work, wasn't regularly used by the Tigers until the following season, when Ty teamed with long-armed first baseman Claude Rossman to execute the play to perfection.

Ty returned to the Tigers' lineup on September 3 to find that he was still not free of what was really ailing him. If anything, opposition to him had solidified during his seven-week absence. With McIntyre in left field and Ty back in center, sparks flew when they converged on a fly ball or otherwise crossed each other's path. The smoldering animosity finally burst into flames on the next-to-last day of the season in St. Louis, when George Stone of the Browns slapped an Ed Siever pitch into left-center field. As everyone in the park watched in amazement, what should have been a humble single rolled past Cobb and McIntyre to the flagpole while the two enemies stood planted in the grass yelling at the other one to retrieve it. Stone, on his way to edging Nap Lajoie for the batting championship, gratefully circled the bases for an inside-the-park home run.

The exasperated Siever almost came to blows with Ty in the dugout between innings and again in the clubhouse after the game. Finally, that evening in the hotel lobby, Siever confronted him at the cigar counter. Before anything could happen, Bill Donovan—regarded as the best boxer in the American League—stepped between them. "Let's not have any trouble, boys," he said.

But a short while later, as Ty tried eavesdropping on the murmurings of Siever and a group of his friends, Siever suddenly hurled a curse and a left hook at Ty. Cobb deftly blocked it and returned a right to Siever's jaw. Then, as the pitcher scrambled to get off the floor, Ty punched and kicked him several more times in the face and head until teammates broke up the fight. The ferocity of Ty's counterattack did more than serve notice to the anti-Cobb group to keep their distance. It also underscored an elemental cruel streak in Cobb's nature, a flaw that would create countless unflattering headlines over the coming years.

※※

When Ty arrived in camp the following March, it was not as a high-strung rookie eager to make an impression but as an established, slightly swell-headed lineup regular. His .320 mark in 1906 had not only placed him fifth on the American League batting list, it was 35 points higher than the next nearest Tiger, Sam Crawford, had hit. And although Ty had played in only 98 games, he had still managed to swipe 23 bases and to compile the majors' longest hitting streak, 25 games, since his idol Bill Bradley (a potent hitter for the Cleveland Indians) had hit safely in 29 straight four years earlier. To top it off, Ty was given a raise to $2,400, making him one of Detroit's better-paid players. (Crawford ended a short holdout that spring by signing for $3,000.) Whatever else his teammates thought

One of the leaders of the anti-Cobb faction was Matty McIntyre, a popular veteran whose dislike of the rookie was based on a personality conflict and the fear of losing his outfield job. A .269 lifetime hitter and better-than-average fielder, McIntyre was out of the big leagues by the time he was 32. He died seven years later in Detroit without once shaking Cobb's hand.

of him in the spring of 1907, they had to concede him his obvious talent and his growing popularity with Detroit fans. Although McIntyre and company continued to simmer with hate and jealousy, the hazing gradually disappeared.

The chief reason was a change of managers. Dissension, injuries, and Bill Armour's lackluster bench leadership had led to the Tigers' sixth-place finish in 1906. Armour was replaced by Hughie Jennings, a generously freckled, live-wired disciple of John McGraw's storied Baltimore Orioles of the 1890s. The 37-year-old ex-shortstop was one of the most colorful men ever to don flannel, with a large share of his legend revolving around his periodic brushes with calamity and his everyday antics in the coaching box. As Detroit players would learn over the next 14 seasons, during which Jennings would guide them to three pennants and a couple of near-misses, their noisy manager was a warm but firm boss—firm, that is, except when it came to Cobb. Jennings recognized him as a special talent, someone who exhibited the same fire, grit, and desire that he had had when he was helping the Orioles hip-check, belt-hold, and base-cut their way to three straight National League pennants a decade earlier. Although they often would feud over the years, a mutual respect grew between these two fierce competitors. Jennings decided from the start to allow his young star to do what he wanted on the diamond. There was little, he conceded, that he could teach him about the game.

Ty's off-field deportment, however, resisted instruction. Just four days after the pair met at spring training and went over ground rules for their relationship, Ty chalked up the first in a long line of controversial and embarrassing incidents under Jennings' tenure. This time Ty's bigotry, one of the ugliest parts of his personality, rose to bite him in the ankle. Perhaps he felt emboldened by the race riot in Atlanta a few months earlier, when white Georgians had rampaged through the streets, killing several blacks. The turn-of-the-century South clearly was no place for a black person to challenge a white, which was what happened one March afternoon in 1907, when the Tigers arrived at Augusta's Warren Park for practice. A tipsy Negro named "Bungy," the park's groundskeeper, weaved toward Cobb with an extended hand.

"Hello, you Georgia Peach," said Bungy. Ty, who had known the old man since breaking into pro ball with the Tourists, tried shooing him away. When Bungy persisted, he slapped him and then chased him toward the clubhouse. There Ty ran up against Bungy's large, buxom wife, who started screaming, "Go 'way, white man! We ain't done nothin' to you!" Cobb, his temper boiling, decided to shut the woman up by choking her.

Ty may have felt he was defending the honor of the South, as at least one local paper later proclaimed, but several witnesses saw it differently: as an unprovoked attack on a woman by an out-of-control bully. Charlie Schmidt, a solidly built catcher from Coal Hill, Arkansas, whose past included stints as a miner and a prizefighter, came to her rescue.

"Whoever does a thing like that is a coward," said Schmidt.

"I don't see as it interests you," responded Cobb, who then exchanged some ineffective blows with Schmidt before teammates quickly separated them.

The newspapers played up the feud until Schmidt-Cobb II was a certainty, although the catcher wisely waited until the team had left Georgia before settling the score. The prearranged rematch occurred on an off day at a ball field in Meridian, Mississippi, and judging by accounts Schmidt administered a fearful beating. Rubber-legged and arm-weary, Ty refused to stay down until players finally broke up the one-sided fight. Ty returned to his hotel room with a broken nose and a bouquet of purple and blue bruises. After licking his wounds for several days, during which he missed two exhibitions, he finally emerged for a game against a minor-league team in Little Rock, Arkansas. Displaying his usual zest, Ty stole home—with two black eyes.

By then the Detroit management had tried, and failed, to trade him. The morning after the fracas with the groundskeeper, Jennings offered Cleveland a straight one-for-one swap of malcontents: Cobb for Elmer Flick, a 31-year-old former batting champ who was holding out for more money. But Flick soon signed, squashing any potential deal. Later, Detroit owner Frank Navin received some feelers from the New York Highlanders regarding part-time outfielder Frank Delahanty. "Pudgie," one of the five Delahanty brothers to play in the majors, had hit .238 in 1906. New York insisted the offer was serious.

Navin and Jennings, who weren't conducting a fire sale, resigned themselves to bringing their raccoon-eyed problem child north. For better or for worse, Ty Cobb would remain a Tiger.

The Ty Cobb that infielders came to fear and Detroit fans loved to cheer: clenched teeth, an explosion of dirt, and more often than not, another creatively crafted run or stolen base. Philadelphia shortstop Jack Barry is the infielder in this 1909 photograph.

CHAPTER THREE

The World's Greatest Ballplayer

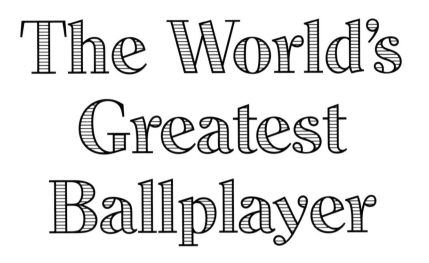

With young Cobb in the game, there's never any telling what might happen: whether he's at bat, on base, or in the field, the fantastic, impossible twist is an easy possibility and we sit there like children wondering what miracle he will perform next. There is an infectious diabolical humor about his coups. Cobb, charging home when he was expected to stay on third, seems to derive much unholy joy at the havoc he causes.

The charm of Cobb lies in his head. His eye and arm, heaven knows, are such as most; but when in addition to directing these against the ball, he directs them against men, then we see more than a game —we see drama. He is a Br'er Fox of baseball, and Br'er Fox, wherever we see him, is a never-failing source of enchantment.

NEW YORK WORLD, 1907

Midway through the 1907 American League season, 20-year-old Ty had served notice on opponents and teammates that he was in the game to stay. More aggressive and imaginative than any other player in recent memory, he exhibited a lethal combination of speed, size, and muscle —all linked to a mind that moved faster than one of Thomas Edison's "flickers" and, as Grantland Rice put it, a determination to "hurl red hell on his way to a score." Inning by inning, game by game, the intense young Georgian was climbing quickly to the top of his profession, his name and antics becoming a familiar topic of conversation in barbershops, schoolyards, and parlors throughout America. "He did not use mystic powers," Harry Salsinger, who launched his 51-year career at the *Detroit News* that year, later wrote. "He had no occult gifts. He simply reduced baseball to a scientific basis and figured it out accordingly."

Another *News* scribe that summer, Malcolm Bingay, delighted in the chaos the Peach caused. "Nobody ever knew what he would do—anywhere or at any time." Many years later, after Bingay had moved to the rival *Free Press* as its city editor and gained a measure of renown as the pseudonymous "Iffy the Dopester," he recalled a game against Philadelphia, when the young and unpredictable Cobb had reached into his bag of tricks to frustrate Connie Mack's Athletics. Ty was on first base when Claude Rossman lined the ball over third base. "Socks Seybold played it like an infielder," wrote Bingay.

> Ty had rounded second with the sweep of a sea gull diving for a fish, and was on his way to third. Home Run Baker, Connie's third-sacker, stood with his back to the plate waiting for the throw from Socks to put the ball on Ty. He knew he was coming. He was always coming.
>
> As the ball shot into Baker's mitt, he swung around to his right to tag Ty. No target. Ty figured that that was just what Baker was going to do and he came into third, sprinting, his body on an angle of 45 degrees. His toe touched the sack with the grace of a Nijinsky—and he was headed for home, without even a change of pace. As always on a close play, he threw himself far away from the plate and swept his hand over it—a swell target for a catcher to tag. He was so safe that the catcher didn't even squawk. Billy Evans was umpiring behind the plate and he was gasping at the daring of it. "Ty," he said, "that looked like suicide."
>
> "Suicide nothing!" snorted the Georgian: "Didn't Baker have to uncross his legs, turn around—and then throw?"
>
> All of which was very true, for Home Run Baker looked like a pretzel out there trying to tag a guy who wasn't anywhere around.

Hughie Jennings' decision to give Ty free rein on the field allowed the Peach to become the catalyst of the Tigers' rise from the second division. By early July Ty had become the first major leaguer to reach one hundred hits, earning him a watch from appreciative fans that was as gaudy as his batting average. Ty's genius at the plate alone would have been enough to warrant the league-wide superlatives over his play. That he also was a rolling ball of hell on the basepaths—"daring to the point of dementia," the *Free Press* said—added to his notoriety and effectiveness. "My whole plan on base was to upset batteries and infields," he would explain years later. "How? By dividing their minds, by upsetting and worrying them until their concentration was affected. I was always looking to create a mental hazard—by, as some writer once put it, the establishment of a threat." That his plays often appeared suicidal or downright stupid bothered Ty not in the least. "All I had to do was make the opposition keep on throwing the ball. Sooner or later, somebody would make a wild throw."

In September, as the surprising Tigers battled Philadelphia and Chicago down to the wire for the pennant, the New York Highlanders got a taste of the mayhem Cobb regularly created on the field. In the ninth inning of the series opener, Ty reached base, then promptly stole second. Seeing that the ball had

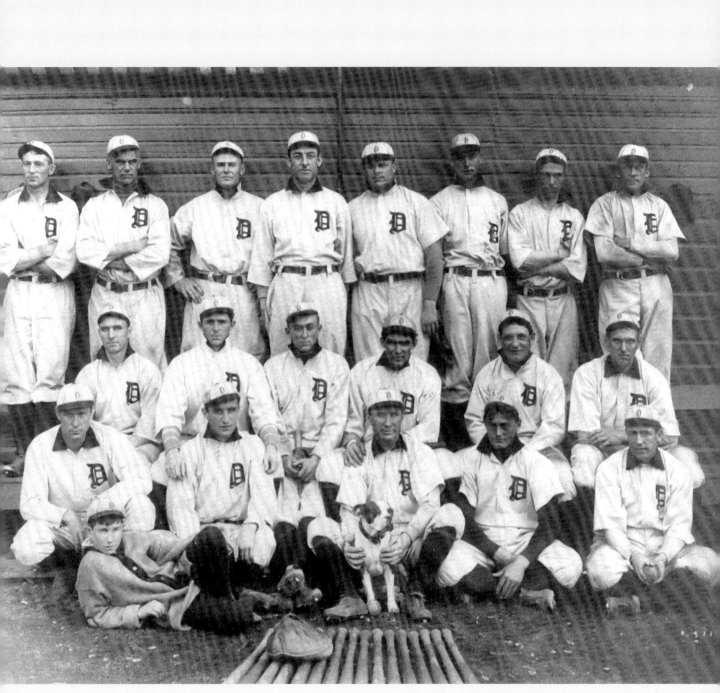

The 1907 pennant winners.

Calamity had a way of finding Hughie Jennings, who survived a near-fatal beaning, a head-first dive into an empty swimming pool, and a car accident that killed two others. Nonetheless, the generously freckled Irishman had a "smile that echoed," said umpire Tim Hurst. Although Jennings was licensed to practice law in his home state of Pennsylvania, he preferred the primitive theatrics of the coaching box, where he entertained the crowd with whoops, whistles, and jigs. He managed the Tigers for 14 years, leading them into the World Series his first three seasons.

rolled a few feet away from the second baseman, Ty jumped up and dashed for third. He was a sure out—except that Cobb contorted his body so that, while sliding, the throw hit him in the back and bounced away. Two outs later, Cobb's repeated dashing up and down the base line caused the pitcher to fumble an easy tap back to the mound. The rattled pitcher finally recovered, but not before the batter had beaten the throw to first and Ty had streaked across the plate with the only run in the Tigers' 1–0 victory.

The war of nerves continued the next day. With Claude Rossman at bat, Ty pulled off the bunt-and-run. Hal Chase, perhaps the finest fielding first baseman ever, made the putout at first—then looked up to see Cobb unexpectedly storming toward third. Chase's hurried throw pulled third baseman George Moriarty off the bag. As Moriarty pirouetted, his back to the play, Ty kept going, flying past Moriarty and sliding safely home a split second ahead of the catcher's tag.

New York's frustration reached a climax in the third game. The Highlanders, vowing that Cobb would not be allowed to repeat his base-running antics of the two previous afternoons, held him at bay until the seventh inning. But upon reaching first base, he again executed the bunt-and-run with Rossman. This time, as Ty stood on third base patting dust off his knickers, the frustrated Moriarty absent-mindedly slammed the ball into the dirt. By the time the bounced ball fell back to earth and Moriarty threw it home, Ty had slid across the plate with another run.

This was thinking man's baseball at its best. Professor Cobb, who had dismissed baseball players as "muscle-workers," would undoubtedly have approved of his son's cerebral style of play. Like a rotating ceiling fan, Ty's mind was constantly humming. With Matty McIntyre sidelined for the year with a broken ankle and the rest of the team channeling its energy into winning instead of bickering, Hughie Jennings' Tigers captured the pennant by 1 1/2 games over Philadelphia.

For all intents and purposes, the race was decided on September 30 with a wild non-decision at Philadelphia, a game that Ty always regarded as the most thrilling of his career. Going into the game the Tigers and Athletics were locked in a virtual tie for first place. After six innings Philadelphia held what looked to be an insurmountable 7–1 lead. But the Tigers chipped away, finally knotting the game at 8–8 when Ty walloped a two-run homer in the ninth inning off ace southpaw Rube Waddell. The blast not only silenced the overflow crowd of 30,000 raucous fans at Columbia Park, it caused the normally taciturn Connie Mack, according to legend, to slide off the bench in shock and into a pile of bats.

The home run was another example of Cobb's heady approach to batting. The eccentric Waddell, a hard thrower who was on his way to leading the league in strikeouts for the sixth straight season, had fired an inside fastball on his first pitch to Cobb. Ty took it for strike one. Figuring Ty was looking for a certain pitch, Waddell decided to "feed this cuckoo one in the same spot and get him in a hole." Instead, Ty turned on the pitch as if he had been expecting it all along—which he had.

"I figured if I let the first one pass and make out I don't notice it and am looking for something else, you'll try to cross me up and shoot the next over the same spot," Ty explained to Waddell after the game. "I feel so sure, when the ball leaves your hand I jump back, take a toe-hold and swing."

"Kid," Waddell replied admiringly, "you had me doped a hundred percent right."

In the tenth the Tigers pushed across a run to go ahead, but the Athletics tied the score in their half of the inning. Then, in the bottom of the 14th inning, all hell broke loose. Philadelphia's Harry Davis hit a long fly ball to center. Just as Sam Crawford was getting ready to make the catch in front of the roped-off over-flow, a pair of overzealous policemen caused him to drop the ball. The umpire ruled Davis out for interference, igniting a brawl among players, fans, and cops. At one point an officer started to arrest Bill Donovan, but after learning that the Detroit pitcher was a Philadelphia native, he took Claude Rossman into custody instead. Despite the commotion and threats, the umpire's decision stood. After order was restored, the next batter followed with a long base hit that would have scored Davis and won the game for Philadelphia. Instead, the teams battled in the dusk until it was declared a 9–9 draw after 17 innings. The Tigers left town with a razor-thin lead that they never relinquished, while Connie Mack complained to the end of his days about being gypped out of a pennant.

The Tigers' opponent in only the fourth modern "world's series" played between the established National League and the upstart American League was the Chicago Cubs, a powerhouse that had won a major-league record 116 games in 1906 before unexpectedly succumbing to the crosstown White Sox in the series. The mighty Cubs had followed up with 107 wins in 1907 and were eager to avenge their embarrassing loss to the junior circuit. The Cubs were led by moundsmen Orvie Overall, Ed Reulbach, Jack Pfeister, and Mordecai "Three Finger" Brown, and an infield soon to be immortalized in verse: shortstop Joe Tinker, second baseman Johnny Evers, and first baseman-manager Frank Chance. Third baseman Harry Steinfeldt, a slugger whose non-lyrical name was left out of Franklin P. Adams' famous ode, rounded out the quartet.

For Tiger fans, all geeked up over the city's first pennant since the National League "Detroits" in 1887, the 1907 World Series was a tremendous letdown. The Tigers, who had led the majors in runs scored, managed but six tallies in five games against the Cubs' staff. Half of those came in the first game, when 25-game-

Herman "Germany" Schaefer was a zany, ruddy-faced alcoholic and one of the few players to unconditionally accept Ty as a teammate.

winner Bill Donovan let a two-run lead slip away in the bottom of the ninth. The tying run scored when Charlie Schmidt dropped what should have been a game-ending third strike on pinch-hitter Del Howard. The game was called a 3–3 tie after 12 innings because of darkness, but they could have just as well canceled the rest of the series for lack of interest. The Tigers went on to lose four straight to the Cubs, with demoralized Detroit fans staying away from Bennett Park in droves for the final two defeats. Cobb hit just .200 with only one run scored, no RBIs, and no stolen bases. Sam Crawford, who had finished second to Cobb in batting during the regular season, was similarly stifled, hitting just .238. But the goat's horns really belonged to the catching duo of Charlie Schmidt and Fred Payne, who between them allowed 18 Chicago stolen bases and the momentum-shifting gaffe in game one.

The five-day Series was an abrupt, dismal climax to an otherwise exciting and stellar season for baseball's brightest new star. In 150 games Ty had hit .350 with 212 hits, 116 RBIs, and 49 stolen bases. All were league highs. He had also signed a contract with Coca-Cola for his first commercial endorsement, a good gauge of his blossoming fame. Had there been a Most Valuable Player award in those days, he would have been the obvious choice. As it was, he was tickled to receive a handsome diamond-studded medal for winning the batting championship—a medal he had coveted since spotting it inside a St. Louis jewelry store window at the start of the season. Two months shy of his 21st birthday, the Peach would remain the youngest man to win a batting title until another Tigers outfielder, Al Kaline, came along a half-century later. Kaline would be exactly one day younger than Cobb when he won the batting championship in 1955.

◎◎

Sportswriters had described the 1907 American League pennant race as "the greatest struggle in the history of baseball," but they nearly ran out of adjectives the following summer, as both leagues featured suffocating races that weren't decided until the final day of the season. Once again the national spotlight fell on Ty, who responded in championship style. In a season dominated by pitchers, he won his second batting title with a .324 average and became the only American Leaguer to knock in more than one hundred runs. He also led in doubles, triples, and hits.

Off the field was another matter. Ty started the season by demanding a three-year contract at $5,000 per season, ending his holdout for a one-year deal at $4,000, plus an $800 bonus if he won the batting championship. In June he managed to get into another racial confrontation, punching a black laborer named Fred Collins after Collins had yelled at Ty for accidentally stepping into freshly poured asphalt outside the Pontchartrain Hotel in Detroit. Cobb was found guilty of assault and given a suspended sentence, and he wound up paying Collins $75 to avoid a civil lawsuit. Then, in early August, with first-place Detroit clinging to a one-game lead in the standings, he impulsively left the team to get married in Georgia. It was a tossup as to who was more surprised: his teammates, who were fighting to get back into the World Series, or management, which had not been informed of the Peach's plans.

The bride was 17-year-old Charlotte Marion Lombard, the quiet, dark-haired daughter of Roswell Lombard, a prominent Augusta businessman. Educated in a convent, "Charlie" nonetheless enjoyed the outdoors, particularly horseback riding. Ty had known her for at least a couple of years and had proposed to her shortly after the 1907 World Series. The ceremony, performed on the afternoon of August 6, 1908, was witnessed by a handful of guests at the Lombard estate. A wing of the sprawling house, known as The Oaks, would serve as the newlyweds' offseason residence until Ty could afford his own place. A luncheon and then an evening banquet at the Hotel Genesta followed the nuptials, after which Ty and his bride boarded a northbound train.

Getting a Grip on Some
Legendary Lumber

An integral part of any hitter's success is his choice of weapon. Ty Cobb broke into the majors using homemade bats that he and his next-door neighbor in Royston, Joe Cunningham, had turned on a lathe in the Cunninghams' tool shed. These were small, heavy clubs made of ash. These favorites, some of which had accompanied Cobb's travels as a Royston Red, Anniston Nobleman, and Augusta Tourist, were sawed in half by malicious Detroit teammates early in the 1906 season. Although the Peach later claimed to have switched to Louisville Sluggers, the famous bats manufactured by the Hillerich & Bradsby Company of Louisville, Kentucky, and used them "exclusively" throughout the rest of his career, he probably experimented with a mix of factory-made bats between 1906 and 1908, winning his first two batting championships in the process. There were, after all, any number of bat manufacturers happy to donate their product for field testing by a budding star. Any Sluggers that Ty did swing during his first four seasons in the American League probably were either unsigned (that is, with no player's signature on the barrel) or Nap Lajoie models.

On October 13, 1908, Ty became the fourth big leaguer (after Honus Wagner, Lajoie, and Harry Davis) to have his decal pasted to the barrel of a Louisville Slugger. The terms of his contract, however, were different from those of the others. Instead of accepting the standard $75 endorsement fee ("a chunk of real money," Ty once reflected), he exchanged the use of his name for a bin of specially constructed bats. Specifically, Ty wanted his bats made of prime ash from Kentucky and Tennessee forests, considering it a stronger wood than the popular hickory and hackberry. He also wanted the wood to have a straight and fine grain, not a heavy grain. "And try to find wood with small whirly knots in it," he instructed. As he explained, this was "indicative of trees that have had a long, slow growth, producing the most resilient and stoutest timber." On his regular trips to the factory Ty would whack each of his finished bats against the ground. "If it rang tenor," he said, "I'd put that one aside to keep. If I got a dull 'thump,' that one I discarded." Some have argued that, in the case of a gifted hitter like Cobb, the effect of a custom-made bat was more psychological than anything else. But in 1909, the first season Ty used his own autograph-model Louisville Slugger, he led all big leaguers in base hits, batting average, total bases, and slugging percentage. He also won the American League's triple crown with nine home runs and 107 RBIs on top of his .377 average.

On September 12, 1911, the Ty Cobb name was registered as a

trademark under certificate No. 83,408. That year his picture started appearing in advertisements in trade journals, most notably *The Sporting Goods Dealer*. In 1921 the company began offering Louisville Slugger bats to the general public. Advertising, coupled with Ty's string of batting titles, made the Ty Cobb model 40Tc bat the company's most popular model through the 1920s.

Ty used the same model of bat from 1911 to 1924. It featured a medium-sized barrel that gradually tapered to a medium handle and knob. (Nobody wore batting gloves during Cobb's era. Because Ty disdained the sticky feel of resin on his hands, all of his bats throughout his career had several twists of tape wrapped about eight to ten inches up the handle to improve his grip.) The length was 34^1/$_2$ inches and the weight, which ranged from 40 to 44 ounces, was evenly distributed. This created a large hitting surface—not that Cobb needed it. Years after Ty retired, an old Hillerich lathe hand named Henry Morrow brought out a bat that showed the Peach's "sweet spot," the place where batters try to consistently hit the ball. "Sure enough," one Hillerich & Bradsby executive recalled, "there was this place on the bat that was a well-worn hollow that showed how Cobb had met the ball squarely over and over." Ty reduced the weight over the years, dropping to a 38- to 40-ounce bat by the time he won his last batting championship in 1919.

On May 5, 1924, Ty ordered a new model. The style was the same, except that this bat was slightly smaller and, at 35 ounces, lighter than his old model. Later that summer Ty returned to a 38-ounce version of his original stick. The following June he placed another order. Again it was similar in style to the 1911 bat, only this time the barrel was slightly smaller and the end had been sawed. The effect was a nearly squared-end bat that was a quarter inch shorter. Cobb used this 34-inch, 40-ounce club for a while, then switched to his lighter 1924 model for the balance of his career in Detroit. He returned to his 1911 bat after he signed with Philadelphia in 1927, typically employing 37- and 38-ounce versions of it for his final two years in the majors.

While many modern ballplayers go through hundreds of bats each season—a result of the trend toward thinner handles and thicker barrels, not to mention wide-open pocketbooks—players in Cobb's day could make a batch of bats last for years. Hall-of-Fame shortstop Joe Sewell, for instance, used the same bat for 14 seasons. Ty wasn't quite as stingy, although he did everything he could to keep his favorite clubs in tip-top condition. To "set" the seams, he would soak them in neat's-foot oil or chewing tobacco, then clamp them in a vise and rub them with a large hollowed-out steer bone.

"My own favorite prescription was a chewing tobacco called Navy Nerve-Cut," he recalled, "the juiciest kind I ever discovered. Using the steer bone, I rubbed in Navy by the hour." Such loving care paid off, as Ty finished his career using a Louisville Slugger that, based on the long discontinued trademark, was judged to be at least 13 years old!

As an outfielder, the Peach put his speed and quickness to good advantage. Until he ruined it by fooling around with pitching, his arm was rated better than average. He threw out 30 base runners in 1907—part of his career total of 392 outfield assists, second only to Tris Speaker. However, Cobb also committed 271 errors, more than any other outfielder in history.

> **"Cobb was born without a sense of humor. He was strictly for himself. He spoiled the game for me."**
>
> —TIGERS OUTFIELDER DAVY JONES

Meanwhile, those back in Detroit pondered the unpredictable behavior of a young man who in just two years had changed from an ostracized rookie into the quintessential 800-pound gorilla. As one local writer rhetorically asked: "What can you do about it? The player is there with the goods on the diamond." When Ty rejoined the team a week later, a fine Sunday crowd at Bennett Park greeted the newlyweds with warm applause and several gifts. Charlie accompanied her husband on the long eastern road trip that followed, during which time Ty was noticeably spaghetti-legged on the basepaths and his batting average dropped about 20 points.

All the same, Ty had enough vim to push the Tigers over the top. Fortified by the addition of rookies Ed Summers, a strapping right-hander who led the staff with 24 wins, and Donie Bush, a pint-sized shortstop who would be a favorite for the next 13 summers, Detroit roared into the final weekend with Cleveland and Chicago clutching its tail. On Friday, October 2, Cobb scored the winning run in a 7–6 victory over St. Louis. Meanwhile, in one of the greatest clutch pitching performances ever, Cleveland's Addie Joss pitched a 1–0 perfect game against Chicago, offsetting "Big Ed" Walsh's brilliant four-hit, 15-strikeout performance. However, Walsh—en route to a 40-win, 464-inning season—returned the next day to beat Cleveland, seriously damaging their chances.

The Tigers then moved into Chicago, losing Sunday to Guy "Doc" White and Monday to Walsh. But Cleveland blew a chance to move into first place when it lost to St. Louis. This set the stage for the final day of the season, with the Tigers up by half a game over Cleveland and Chicago. Because of the uneven number of games the contenders had played (rules then in effect did not require rained-out games to be made up), the winner of the Tigers–White Sox game on Tuesday, October 6, would claim the pennant by half a game; the loser would finish third behind Cleveland.

Earlier in the season, White Sox fans had awarded Cobb a loving cup for being their favorite opposing ballplayer—an irony that undoubtedly troubled more than one disappointed Chicagoan as the Tigers pounded out a decisive 7–0 victory at South Side Park to grab their second flag in a row. Ty was at his best, banging out a triple and two singles, driving in three runs, and annoying the pitcher into making a wild throw that allowed another run to score. Jubilant Detroiters lit bonfires and greeted their conquering heroes the following day with a motorcade through downtown streets.

While the Tigers were being feted, the Chicago Cubs and New York Giants faced off at the Polo Grounds to determine the National League winner. Two weeks earlier, in what remains the most infamous goof in baseball history, young Fred Merkle had cost the Giants a victory, and ultimately the pennant, when he

> ## "Cobb is being criticized, right and left, and being pictured as a murderer of his fellows, mostly by men who have not seen the plays on which he is being attacked."
>
> —DETROIT SPORTSWRITER JOE S. JACKSON

failed to touch second base on what should have been a game-winning hit against these very Cubs. In a storm of controversy, the Giants' victory was rescinded and the tie game was rescheduled for the end of the season. In what amounted to a one-game playoff, the opportunistic Cubs then went on to beat Christy Mathewson, 4–2, for their third straight pennant. Third-place Pittsburgh finished just one game back. Thus ended the two closest three-team races in big-league history.

Unlike the two draining, circus-like pennant races, the World Series between the survivors fizzled instead of sizzled. For the second year in a row it took the Cubs only five days and five games to dispose of the Tigers, although this time Detroit managed a win instead of a tie. That came in the third game, when Ty had his finest postseason game ever: four hits in five at-bats, including a pair of runs batted in. In the ninth inning of the Tigers' 8–3 victory, Cobb put on a show for Chicago fans, announcing beforehand that he would steal second and third, which he did. The Cubs finally quieted Cobb when he was gunned down trying to steal home. Ty's silence grew deeper as the Tigers returned home to suffer consecutive shutout losses to Three-Finger Brown and Orvie Overall, which closed out another disappointing Series. "Don't feel too badly about it," Hughie Jennings told his disconsolate players afterwards. "We were beaten again by a great team. A great team!"

Although the Tigers lost their second fall classic in a row, Ty had a better go of it, hitting .368 against the same Cubs staff that had handcuffed him a year earlier. To Cobb's consternation, however, he could barely touch Three-Finger Brown's fabled bender. When he was seven years old Brown had stuck his right hand into his uncle's corn shredder. The accident left him with a severed index finger, a paralyzed little finger—and a pitch that paralyzed the greatest batters in both leagues. Brown completely mystified the Tigers during the 1907 and '08 World Series, surrendering no earned runs in 20 innings and winning three games. "It was a great ball, that down-curve of his," said Cobb, who in nine plate appearances against Brown struck out three times and got the ball out of the infield only once. "I can't talk about all of baseball, but I can say this: It was the most deceiving, the most devastating pitch I ever faced."

Ty's lack of success against Brown aside, his overall improvement against the Cubs' staff from one World Series to the next underscored what helped make him the hitter he was: the ability to dissect a pitcher's success against him and

then, over repeated encounters, to successfully adjust to that pitcher's style. As Ring Lardner once observed, Ty "don't stay fooled long." In his first 13 at-bats against Doc White in 1905–06, for example, Ty had gone hitless. After White struck him out three times in a Memorial Day game in 1906, prompting Bill Armour to insert a pinch-hitter for him, Cobb experimented with moving to the back of the batter's box and shortening his stride and his swing. These adjustments allowed him to wait until the very last moment to judge the break of the ball. Then, quick as a lizard's tongue, he would flick his bat at the ball and punch it to the opposite field. Having solved White's wicked curve, he went on to extract a .381 lifetime average from the Chicago dentist.

Another example was Cobb's success against the Washington Senators' Walter Johnson, the long-armed Kansan who made his major-league debut against the Tigers in 1907. Ty faced Johnson more often than any other pitcher. Although it was occasionally reported that Johnson, arguably the greatest pitcher of all time, more or less "owned" Ty, Cobb in fact hit .366 against Johnson—just one point under his lifetime average. (The rest of the American League hit a combined .226 against Johnson during his remarkable 21-year career.) Few of Ty's hits off the "Big Train" were for extra bases, but that's because Cobb realized that even a skilled place hitter like himself had an almost impossible task getting around on Johnson's fabled fastball. Ty decided to cut down on his swing and concentrate on spanking the ball to the opposite field. Doubles and triples are nice, he reasoned, but he could always steal his way around to second or third.

The result was a remarkable consistency. Slumps were infrequent; he rarely went hitless for more than two or three consecutive games. His strategy for ending a dry spell was simple. In batting practice he would concentrate on bunting the ball back to the mound, gradually increasing the arc of his swing until he was whistling hard ground balls and line drives up the middle. "After a few such sessions," he explained, "my timing returned and my slump went away." Ty compiled the league's longest hitting streak on five occasions, the most ever by any player: in 1906 (25 games), 1911 (40), 1917 (35), 1926 (21), and 1927 (21). For his career Ty batted .370 at home and .363 on the road, and he hit southpaws at a .347 clip. No matter how one twists and folds the numbers, the simple, unavoidable fact that pitchers had to deal with for so many years was that the Peach could flat-out hit —against left-handers, right-handers, speedballers, curve-ballers, spitballers, at home, and on the road.

᠅

In 1909 the Tigers, hungry to erase their two postseason blemishes, roared to an unprecedented third straight American League pennant, winning a then league-record 98 games in the process. They ultimately beat out Philadelphia by three and a half games, thanks to a revamped infield, George Mullin's major-league-leading 29 victories, and Ty's Triple Crown season. Ty hit .377 with nine home runs and 107 RBIs. But, as rattled pitchers, befuddled infielders, and nervous catchers were learning, a base hit usually was just the start of their problems with Cobb. Once Ty arrived at a base, the odds were excellent that he wouldn't stay long. "Infielders didn't know what the hell he'd do next," said Philadelphia catcher Rube Bressler, "and neither did he until the last split second. You couldn't figure Cobb. It was impossible."

That year Ty fully arrived as a base runner and a base stealer, leading the circuit in runs scored and setting a modern individual record with 76 stolen bases. All of his home runs were inside-the-parkers, putting his distinctive running style on display for the 15 or so seconds it took him to circumnavigate the bases. "He ran like a pacer," Ken Smith wrote, "never lifting his knees much, his body weaving from side to side and his hands standing out like fins. He could run like a streak with his head over his shoulder, watching the ball, and he never needed a coach." In his prime Cobb exhibited close to Olympics-caliber speed, once touring the bases in cut-down uniform pants and spikes in thirteen and a half seconds. His time going from home to first base was a sizzling three and a half seconds.

Ty's scorched-earth approach to base-running featured an assortment of slides, including his famous "fadeaway." Before Cobb, runners typically had slid straight into a bag. Ty perfected the art of pulling his body away from an infield-er's tag and tucking his toe into a distant corner of the base as he slid past. At other times he used the "down-and-up" slide, hitting the dirt and then bounding up, running. He was a wonder to watch, unless you happened to be the poor soul he was bearing down on. "Hold onto your pants," Germany Schaefer would yell out, "or he'll steal those too!"

According to catcher Henry Beckendorf, who joined the Tigers in 1909, his contortionist teammate was "the hardest man in the league to get. He is fast and he can throw his body like an eel. You can't figure on what side he is coming. It seems as though he can throw his body while he is diving at the base. You can make a pass for him on one side and he simply jerks by on the other. I really do not think that Ty ever tried to spike a baseman intentionally. He comes in so

fast and throws his body so quickly that he cannot figure on the position of the baseman."

That was Ty's argument after one of the most controversial episodes of his career: the spiking of Philadelphia's Frank Baker on August 24, 1909. That afternoon the first-place Athletics, who led the Tigers by a single game, began a crucial three-game set at Bennett Park. In the bottom of the first inning, Ty walked and stole second. As Sam Crawford took a fourth ball, Ty suddenly lit out for third. The catcher's throw to third baseman Frank Baker had him easily. When Cobb hook-slid to his left in an attempt to avoid Baker's bare-handed tag, his right foot flashed out and nicked the infielder's forearm. Baker's wound was little more than a scratch and he stayed in the game, but Connie Mack and all of Philadelphia went ballistic. Mack called Cobb the dirtiest player in the history of baseball, while others talked of running him out of the league. Although a photograph clearly showed Baker awkwardly leaning over the bag, and league president Ban Johnson declared Ty to have been within his rights on the play,

According to Detroit catcher Henry Beckendorf, his contortionist teammate was "the hardest man in the league to get. He is fast and he can throw his body like an eel."

When the Tigers next played Philadelphia after the Baker incident, hundreds of policemen were on hand to guard Cobb from venomous fans. Despite the death threats, Ty played with customary gusto, at one point cutting Jack Barry's leg with a hard slide into second. As Barry left the field for stitches, the Athletics shortstop indicated to fans that the spiking was not intentional. This cartoon in *Detroit Saturday Night* would have readers believe that Cobb later blubbered over the episode in his hotel room.

Cobb Wept Because He Had Spiked Barry.

Philadelphia sportswriters didn't let the issue die. A minor scrape quickly evolved into a case of felonious assault. What really upset Baker's supporters was that the Tigers had swept the series, capturing a lead they never surrendered. The controversy produced an outpouring of letters with Philadelphia postmarks, many threatening death and dismemberment when Ty next visited the City of Brotherly Love.

The Baker spiking once again focused attention on Ty's spirited play, which disgruntled opponents were increasingly often describing as dirty. It was, complained many, of a piece with his abrasive personality. "His trouble is he takes life too seriously," complained the venerable Cy Young. "Cobb is going at it too hard."

Ty never made any apologies about his aggressiveness or intimidating tactics. "When I played ball," he stressed in his autobiography, "I didn't play for fun. To me it wasn't Parcheesi played under Parcheesi rules. Baseball is a red-blooded sport for red-blooded men. It's no pink tea, and mollycoddles had better stay out. It's a contest and everything that implies, a struggle for supremacy, a survival for the fittest. Every man in the game, from the minors on up, is not only fighting against the other side, but he's trying to hold onto his own job against those on his own bench who'd love to take it away. Why deny this? Why minimize it? Why not boldly admit it?"

Ty had displayed much the same Darwinian philosophy as a minor leaguer in Augusta and Anniston, and no one had complained. Then again, no one really cared about the bushes. It was a different story in big-league cities, where dozens of sportswriters, eager to beat deadlines and the competition, daily manufactured reams of copy out of whole cloth. The most damaging of these tales was the allegation that Ty filed his spikes.

According to Cobb, the story was fabricated by New York writers in 1908 when a couple of Detroit pranksters—very likely Germany Schaefer and Charlie O'Leary—joked around on the bench before a game with the Highlanders. Subscribing to the prevailing journalistic philosophy of never letting the truth get in the way of a good story, popular writers such as Bugs Baer used the spike-filing fiction as an example of Cobb's take-no-prisoners approach to the game. When Ty clipped Baker a year later, it was already an article of faith among many that he sharpened his spikes to a razor's edge before each game, which presumably made it easier for him to disembowel innocent infielders. "Complaints that Cobb uses his spikes to injure and intimidate infielders are so common that his mere denial will not relieve him of the odium that attaches to a player of this infamous practice," *The Sporting News* editorialized in the midst of the Baker controversy. "The list of his victims is too long to attribute the injury of all concerned to accidents. Down with this Cobb!"

Although Ty appreciated the psychological effect of the sharpened-spike stories, choosing not to discount them until after he had retired, he always bristled when described as a dirty player. He played hard, as did most players, albeit with more flair and effectiveness. Like any player protecting his place on the diamond, he settled quarrels in time-honored fashion. Head-hunting pitchers like Carl Mays and Dutch Leonard might suddenly find themselves fielding a drag bunt along the first-base line, giving Cobb a clear shot at stomping on their toes or hip-checking them into the stands. Or, on plays at the plate, catchers who strategically placed their iron masks in the base path might one day have their vital organs squeezed into pulp by a pair of scissored legs. Cobb, who admitted to spiking only two men deliberately in 24 years, normally didn't go out of his way to hurt anyone. But he also knew the rules of the game, both written and unwritten, and played accordingly.

"They always talk about Cobb playing dirty, trying to spike guys and all," said Sam Crawford. "Cobb never tried to spike anybody. The base line belongs to the runner. If the infielders get in the way, that's their lookout. Infielders are supposed to watch out and take care of themselves."

Opponents echoed Crawford. "Despite what has been said, Cobb never went out of his way to spike people," insisted Billy Rogell, who broke in with the

"I'll be on a roof across from the park with a rifle and in the third inning I'll put a bullet through your heart."

—ONE OF THE THREATS MAILED BY PHILADELPHIA FANS TO COBB, 1909

Red Sox in 1925, by which time Cobb's nefarious reputation had long been set in stone. "Since I was a shortstop, he slid into me quite a few times but he never tried to spike me. Others would come in with their damn feet in your face. They always made a big deal out of him sharpening his spikes." Most players of the time did, noted Rogell. "You had to sharpen your spikes with those infields or else you couldn't dig in."

"I wouldn't say Cobb played dirty," said "Smokey Joe" Wood, who entered the big leagues with the Boston Red Sox in 1908. "Cobb always told me and other fellows he played against, 'All you've got to do is give me room to get in there and it'll be all right, but if you don't give me room I'll cut my way in.' Fair enough." Jimmy Austin, the longtime third baseman of the St. Louis Browns, described Cobb as "fair enough on the bases. He nicked me a couple of times, but it was my fault. I don't blame him." Ray Fisher, a Vermont farm boy who joined the New York Highlanders in 1910, also remembered Cobb as a tough but fair competitor. "I pitched against him a lot," he said. "I know one time I had to cover first, and I had trouble getting my foot on the bag. I had my leg out. He jumped over the bag. He could've stepped on me. He had a perfect right to." Of course, avoiding a confrontation didn't make for good copy, so innocuous but telling episodes like this never made it into the papers.

After the Baker spiking, Ty needed more controversy like he needed an extra set of elbows. But less than two weeks later, he got into a late-hours argument with a black elevator operator inside Cleveland's Hotel Euclid. Thinking the man was "uppity" and "insolent," Ty slapped him in the face, which prompted a black night watchman named George Stansfield to join the fray. After Stansfield hit him with his nightstick Ty pulled out a knife and slashed at him. Badly cut, Stansfield managed to knock Cobb silly with a blow to his head, at which point hotel employees moved in. By the time the incident came to light, the Tigers had left town. Cobb faced a civil lawsuit and criminal charges whenever he returned to Cleveland. Frank Navin's attorneys got Stansfield to settle out of court and, in late November, plea-bargained Cobb's case down to the lesser charge of assault and battery, for which he was fined $100. But for the rest of the regular season and the World Series, Ty had to avoid traveling through Ohio for fear of being arrested.

Death threats in Philadelphia and an arrest warrant in Cleveland—now *this* was the Ty Cobb the press and the public loved to hate. But, as he would so many times during his career, Cobb used the mounting controversy as a form of amphetamine. Nothing stirred him to the heights of his ability more than the

idea that the world was against him. That September in Philadelphia, with hundreds of policemen on hand to protect him from the record number of fans, some of whom were reportedly there to shoot him dead, Ty played with his customary fervor as the Tigers escaped town with their lead—and necks—intact. On the evening following the first game, Ty emerged from the hotel lobby, looking to take his usual after-dinner walk. Before he knew it, he was surrounded by scores of angry Philadelphians. Rather than retreat, Ty lit his cigar and slowly strolled down the sidewalk, parting the hostile crowd down the middle as casually as he parted his already thinning hair. Despite the mumbling and curses in his wake, no one dared touch him. It was quite an exhibition of bravado, the kind Cobb excelled at staging throughout his life. You didn't have to like the cocky son of a bitch, some in the crowd grudgingly agreed, but you had to admire his style. Before the series ended Cobb had won over the fans, diving over the outfield rope into the overflow crowd to make a circus catch of a fly ball, then offering five dollars to the man whose straw boater he had crushed. He even shook hands with Baker after stealing third base.

Cobb scores against the Cubs in the opening game of the 1908 World Series as Chicago catcher Johnny Kling looks helplessly on. It was a rare moment of triumph for the Tigers, who for the second straight October were steamrollered by the Cubs.

Lou Criger of Boston was one of the few catchers who generally held his own against the game's most aggressive base runner. In this shot from the 1909 season, however, Ty has managed to slide in safely under Criger's unprotected shins while umpire Billy Evans rushes in to make the call.

That October the Tigers faced the Pittsburgh Pirates in one of the most eagerly anticipated World Series ever, giving the country a chance to see the game's two greatest players go head-to-head. In one corner, of course, was Cobb, the American League's top batsman, base stealer, and headline maker. In the other was his National League counterpart, shortstop Honus Wagner.

Wagner was a veteran of the first modern World Series in 1903, when Pittsburgh was upset by the Boston Pilgrims. The 35-year-old "Flying Dutchman," who in 1909 won his seventh of an eventual eight batting championships, was an unlikely looking hero. He was squat, chunky, and extremely bowlegged. His large hands hung like baked hams from his long limbs, but he had tremendous range and a powerfully accurate throwing arm. Wagner also ran the bases with as much success as Cobb. In fact, Wagner would retire in 1917 with 722 career steals, a National League mark that would stand until Lou Brock broke it in 1967. Almost everyone had a good word to say about Wagner, a good-humored, sociable man who enjoyed drinking beer and spinning stories.

It was a rugged Series. At one point George Moriarty, the fearless third baseman whom Detroit had acquired at mid-season from New York, snatched the hat off Pittsburgh's Tommy Leach and unaccountably started whacking him over his bald head with it. And game six, which Detroit won in dramatic fashion to knot the Series at three games apiece, featured several spikings and collisions. But the most enduring episode was one that, like many stories involving Cobb, is more imagination than fact.

According to legend, Ty reached base in the first inning of the first game and immediately yelled to Wagner: "Hey, Krauthead, I'm coming down on the next pitch!" Then, the story continues, Ty set off for second, where Wagner impassively put the young pup in his place by slapping the ball into his face and knocking out a couple of teeth.

Such braggadocio certainly wouldn't have been out of character for Cobb, who during his short career had already endeared himself to the opposition by often broadcasting his intentions before stealing a base. But, like Babe Ruth's famous "called shot" in the 1932 World Series, the incident was a postgame invention, something that its authors decided would help illustrate the "comeuppance" the brash and controversial young star was expected to receive from the beloved Pittsburgh paterfamilias.

According to contemporary newspaper reports, the truth was more prosaic. In the fifth inning of the first game, Ty successfully stole second, with Wagner's sweeping tag of a low throw innocently nicking him in the face as he hook-slid into the bag. Afterward, Detroit trainer Harry Tuthill sewed three stitches into Ty's lip. Compared to the bruises, blisters, scars, cuts, and strawberries that typically covered Ty's hands, arms, legs, and hips at the end of the summer, his split lip was as inconsequential as the nick on Frank Baker's forearm. Significantly, there were no contemporaneous reports of the "Hey, Krauthead!" story in either the Detroit or Pittsburgh papers. Cobb later claimed it was an invention of the press and Wagner agreed, though both players were guilty of muddying the issue when they repeated the yarn as old men. So the story lives to this day.

Wagner indisputably outplayed Cobb in the Series. Wagner hit .333 and stole six bases, while Ty was held to a .231 average and two stolen bases, including a theft of home in the second game. Unlike the two previous Octobers, though, the Tigers managed to be competitive, taking the Pirates to a seventh game. However, for the third straight year the Tigers ingloriously closed out the postseason by getting shut out at home. Babe Adams, a 12-game winner in the regular season, spun a six-hitter to win his third game of the Series, 8–0, on a blustery Saturday afternoon in Detroit.

Hughie Jennings' team remains the only American League club ever to lose three World Series in a row. Viewed objectively, however, the Tigers of 1907–08–09 were not a great squad but rather a collection of scrappy ballplayers taking their lead from two big cats. That Cobb and Crawford were toothless at the plate accounted in part for Detroit's sorry postseason record of just four wins (and a tie) in 17 outings, but unreliable pitching and pitiful catching were just as much to blame. "I was too young when that part of my career happened," Ty later said. "I regret I never got a crack at a World Series during my peak years." As the stately trees arching Detroit's cobblestoned streets changed colors in the autumn of 1909, the Georgia Peach helped overcome his annual postseason disappointment by doing what every American with enough money was doing. He bought a new car.

Series of Disappointments

Much to the chagrin of teammates, fans, sportswriters–and most of all himself–Ty Cobb never was able to break loose and dominate play in a World Series in the same fashion that he did during the regular season. Still, his composite performance in three dead–ball World Series–a .262 average in 17 games–compares favorably with those of fellow Hall of Famers Stan Musial (.256 and one homer in 23 games), Ted Williams (five singles and a .200 mark in his lone World Series), and Willie Mays (.239, no home runs, and only six RBIs in 20 games).

Why the relatively lackluster numbers for Cobb? Beyond the obvious fact that in two of the three Series the Tigers were facing one of the truly great pitching staffs of all time in the Chicago Cubs, Ty always maintained that his lack of experience and maturity contributed. After all, he was just 22 when he played in his last World Series game. Even a storied postseason performer like Babe Ruth (.326 with 15 home runs in 41 games) needed time to find his stride. Ruth, in his first 17 World Series games (as a pitcher with Boston in 1915–16 and 1918, and then as an outfielder with New York in 1921–23), hit a collective .188 with just one home run and 15 strikeouts in 48 at–bats. However, Ruth did star on the mound during this stretch, winning all three of his Series starts.

After Detroit dropped its third straight World Series in 1909, the Peach would play 19 more seasons without gaining a shot at postseason redemption. As soon as he retired, however, the team he left–the Philadelphia Athletics–immediately began its own streak of three consecutive pennants, winning the World Series in 1929 and 1930. As some reporters observed, Ty Cobb seemed to be "Series–jinxed."

Cobb and Honus Wagner before the start of the 1909 World Series.

TY COBB, DETROIT

HANS WAGNER, PITTSBURG

PHOTO FROM

CHAPTER FOUR

Foot to the Pedal

*Fortunes were made overnight in early Detroit. You could toss
your money in almost any direction and not miss.*

TY COBB

◯◯

"My godfather was in Detroit and wrote me that he had paper on the walls,
shoes, meat every day, fresh bread, milk, water in the house, beer on the corner,
soup and plenty of money. From that time I was crazy to come." Those words,
written by a Polish immigrant the same year Ty Cobb broke in with the Tigers,
reflected the wonder with which the rest of the world regarded the city in the
early part of the century. The generator of such wonder and enthusiasm was the
automobile, which by 1910 was lifting the world into the modern age and radi-
cally altering the face of Detroit.

The first person to drive an automobile on city streets had been Charles
Brady King. "Turn that peanut roaster off before it spooks my horses!" a startled
brewery teamster yelled as King maneuvered his contraption through downtown
streets one nippy March evening in 1896. Three months later, Henry Ford, the 33-
year-old chief engineer of the Edison Illuminating Company, got into his "quadri-
cycle" and chugged straight into the history books, becoming in time one of the
most recognized names in the world and the acknowledged architect of the greatest socio-economic revolution ever.

As the Tigers started their pursuit of an unprecedented fourth straight pennant in the spring of 1910, Ford's brand-new Highland Park plant began full production of the Model T. The ungainly but dependable vehicle had captured the
public's imagination and a good share of the marketplace since its debut 18
months earlier. Ford didn't invent the assembly line, but he did perfect its use. As
the time required to build Ford's "tin lizzy" continued to drop, so did its price—
from $850 in 1908 to a mere $290 in 1924. By the First World War half of all cars
in use were Model Ts. The mammoth electric sign atop the Temple Theatre on
Monroe Street, where Ty often went to see the country's top vaudeville acts, asked

Opposite: In the
driver's seat. The
free-wheeling Cobb
was a perfect symbol
of the Motor City.

Detroit, circa 1915.

people to "Watch the Fords Go By." As if they had any choice. By the time the folk-hero industrialist discontinued production in 1927, more than 15 million of his beloved "flivvers" had rolled onto America's primitive, pot-holed roads.

Cobb's career as a Tiger coincided with the city's dynamic transformation into the "Motor City." When he arrived in 1905, Detroit was a tranquil, conservative, mid-sized community of 300,000 souls, its commercial and political affairs dominated by the scions of 19th-century lumber and railroad tycoons. At the time, it was still very much a horse-and-buggy town. Within five short years, however, fashionable residential districts along Woodward and Cass avenues had changed irreversibly. Gas stations and car dealerships sprang up, and stately homes were sold and subdivided into boarding houses. Factory smoke, exhaust fumes, noise, dirt, and overcrowding characterized Detroit's emergence as a major manufacturing center. By the time Cobb left in 1926, Detroit had exploded in size from 26 to 139 square miles; its population had passed the 1.5 million mark (only New York, Chicago, and Philadelphia were more populous); and its factories were spitting out several million cars a year. Life in this clangorous, confusing, polyglot urban colossus was far from perfect.

> "It is undoubtedly true that more than one little missus escaped from having her teeth knocked out or her eyes punched black and blue because her loving husband could go to a ballpark to insult Ty Cobb."
>
> —JAMES T. FARRELL, *MY BASEBALL DIARY*

Workers constantly suffered from the "boom-or-bust" vagaries of a one-industry town. Acute shortages of housing, health care, schools, and basic services plagued the city. But life here for newcomers was still better than what it had been in Russia, Armenia, Poland, Italy, Lebanon, or Greece. A colorful floral display in Grand Circus Park spelled out this optimism: "In Detroit Life Is Worth Living." Regardless of one's language, few could argue with that assessment. Detroit, a place that to this day remains inextricably linked with the automobile, offered many opportunities, especially for those with gasoline in their veins.

In 1910 the informal headquarters for the automobile set was the elegant oak and brass bar in the lobby of the Pontchartrain Hotel, which had opened in the fall of 1908. Located at the southeast corner of Michigan and Woodward avenues, the hotel was for several years the starting point for the famous Glidden Tour, an annual cross-country car rally that did much to convince a skeptical public that, thanks to the internal combustion engine, horsepower no longer had to mean horse apples. Here the aroma of cigar smoke mingled with the smell of opportunity. Although he was beginning to stake out a reputation as a ballplayer, Ty kept his ears open, his mouth shut, and what little money he had in his pocket. He went to the Pontchartrain Hotel bar after games and listened to the architects of the new industrial age wheel and deal and argue the relative merits of the new machines. Engaged in these conversations were men like David Buick, a plumbing contractor who thought of cars as bathtubs with engines and wheels; the two-fisted Dodge brothers, John and Horace, who had started out as uneducated factory hands and now built car bodies for Henry Ford; and others whose names were becoming associated with their products: Louis Chevrolet, the Fisher brothers, and the Stanley twins. And as countless stockowners were learning, you didn't have to be a manufacturer to make it big. James Couzens, a bookkeeper who had invested $2,500 in Ford stock in 1903, cashed out in 1919 for $29,308,857. His sister's original $100 investment paid off $355,000 in just a few years.

Ty became close to two men who were classic success stories. One was Walter O. Briggs, who started off as a young man checking coal cars in the Michigan Central Railroad yards for five dollars a week. He later joined a boyhood friend in a trim and painting shop, buying the business in 1909. The rough-hewn

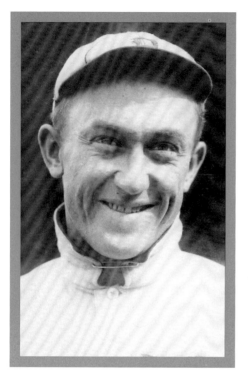

The Tigers were the last major-league team to abandon the once popular Byron collar, finally changing their uniform style in 1915. Unlike most players, who folded down their collars or tucked them in at the neckline, Ty always wore his tunic-style, fastening the ends at the throat with a large safety pin. Fashion considerations aside — Ty was a big admirer of Napoleon and other military figures — the upright collar also had a practical purpose, keeping the brutal summer sun off Ty's fair skin.

entrepreneur renamed it the Briggs Manufacturing Company and won contracts to build car bodies for Ford, Hudson, Packard and other automakers. In time the Briggs empire would include 16 plants and 40,000 employees. Ty liked Briggs, "his interest in baseball, also his rugged outspoken ways," he said years later. "While I liked Walter I would have to say I loved John Kelsey."

Cobb and Kelsey had become acquainted on the Detroit Athletic Club baseball team when Ty was recuperating from his breakdown during the 1906 season. Kelsey, a third baseman on the D.A.C.'s 1892 national championship nine, subsequently gained considerable adulation as a financial angel, spending tens of thousands of dollars to keep the aging club alive even as his own business ventures were failing. Kelsey spearheaded the effort to build a magnificent seven-story D.A.C. clubhouse on Madison Avenue. When it opened in the spring of 1915 (taking the auto crowd away from the Pontchartrain bar), many naturally thought its initials stood for "Detroit Automobile Club." Kelsey, elected president of the august group, never strayed far from his workbench beginnings. One of the many anecdotes illustrating his unaffectedness concerned a trip to New York, years after he had made his fortune producing wheels and brake systems for the auto industry. When businessmen dropped by Kelsey's hotel room to finalize a multi-million-dollar transaction, they discovered the wealthy owner of the Kelsey Wheel Company in his underwear, washing his socks in the bathroom sink.

Because of their love of the game and their close friendship with Cobb, Briggs and Kelsey bought quarter-shares of the Tigers for $250,000 apiece in 1920. After Kelsey died in 1927, Briggs purchased his stock and became half-owner of the club. Upon Frank Navin's death eight years later, Briggs bought out his widow to become the sole owner. He then spent more than one million Depression dollars converting Navin Field into Briggs Stadium, a 52,000-seat all-purpose sports facility that was one of the finest in the country. Not bad for someone who used to self-consciously sip ten-cent sherry flips at the lower end of the Pontchartrain bar with his ballplayer friend "because we could not afford [to] buy drinks for a number of them, though we would accept their proffer if they asked us," recalled Cobb.

By the winter of 1909–10 Ty was financially able to follow up on several tips—and, despite his well-deserved reputation as a nickel-nurser, presumably pick up a tab or two himself. After the World Series with Pittsburgh he had signed

a new three-year contract for $9,000 a year, a salary second only to Honus Wagner's. (By comparison, the hourly wages in auto plants ranged from 9 cents for unskilled labor to 40 cents for experienced hands.) Perhaps taking a cue from Wagner, who owned a Regal Motor Car dealership in Carnegie, Pennsylvania, Cobb opened a small showroom, Ty Cobb Motors, in Augusta. He also started buying stock in General Motors, which had just been organized in 1908. In 1915 his Detroit connections allowed him, for a $2,500 stake, to open a Hupmobile dealership on Augusta's Broad Street. Trading in on his famous name, Ty sold about 125 vehicles his first two years. Hupmobile was destined to go under as the auto industry continued its shakeout in the 1920s, but by then Ty's General Motors stock had already climbed nicely in value.

More immediate rewards, however, were right down the road. Hugh Chalmers, president of the fledgling Detroit auto company that bore his name, announced before the start of the 1910 season that the winner of the batting championship in each league would receive a new Chalmers "30," a luxury car that normally retailed for a cool $2,700. This kind of promotion would cause barely a ripple of excitement today, of course, but in 1910 the opportunity to win an exotic prize worth what many ballplayers made in a year had fans, players, and sportswriters handicapping the contenders all season. Philadelphia outfielder Sherry Magee wound up winning the Chalmers in the National League without much suspense. But in the junior circuit, what some called "The Great American Automobile Race" developed between Cobb and Cleveland's Napoleon "Nap" Lajoie, throwing much-needed drama into an otherwise ho-hum year.

A mixed bag of major and minor leaguers gather around Ty during spring training in Augusta in 1910. Standing at far left is Nap Rucker of Crabapple, Georgia. Cobb's old Augusta teammate won 134 games during a 10-year career with Brooklyn.

Despite leading the league in scoring for the fourth year in a row, the Tigers never contended, finishing in third place. Unlike the hungry Athletics, who rode the arms of Jack Coombs and Chief Bender to the pennant and a World Series win over the Cubs, the Tigers too often resembled placated pussycats. One of the few times the team showed its teeth all summer occurred not long after the city had finally removed its ban on Sunday ball, which allowed Detroit to join Chicago, Cincinnati, and St. Louis as the only major-league towns where the cries of "Kill the umpire!" could legally disturb the sacred air of the Sabbath. Bluenoses, who considered it a sacrilege for a working man to visit Bennett Park on his only day off, had their worst fears realized during a Sunday game with Boston. George Moriarty attempted to steal home in the bottom of the ninth, resulting in some banging and bruising at the plate. Red Sox catcher Bill "Rough" Carrigan responded by squirting tobacco juice into the prone base runner's eye. Moriarty slugged Carrigan in the jaw, and within seconds the two clubs were a knot of windmilling fists. Players and fans battled all the way to the clubhouse. As Navin stood on top of the dugout shouting in vain for order, a small army of Detroit cranks laid siege to the Boston dressing room, pounding on the door and threatening to lynch Carrigan. After about an hour, the Boston backstop escaped by slipping into a groundskeeper's overalls and boots, smearing his face with mud, and walking unmolested through the unsuspecting mob.

This was excitement, of a sort. But the real race, the one that captivated baseball fans, and whose result remained undecided until long after the season ended, was just heating up. At the beginning of September, Cobb led Lajoie by just three percentage points, .362 to .359. Through October the two jockeyed for the lead, with the nation's newspapers reporting various "official" and "unofficial" averages. Most days it was a tossup as to who was on top. The American League office didn't help the confusion, issuing a notice that "the result probably will not be known until [league secretary] Rob McRoy gives out his figures."

Ty gambled that the figures showing him holding an eight-point lead as of October 6 were correct. He decided to sit out the final two games of the season against Chicago. Lajoie figured he needed a herculean effort to pass Cobb. What he didn't expect was an unprecedented level of help from the opposition.

If someone had polled American Leaguers on whom they wished to see win the Chalmers, the 35-year-old Lajoie would have won hands down. The graceful

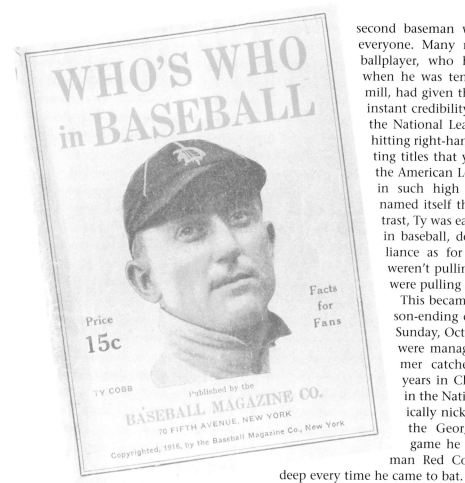

WHO'S WHO in BASEBALL

Price
15c

Facts
for
Fans

TY COBB

Published by the
BASEBALL MAGAZINE CO.
70 FIFTH AVENUE, NEW YORK
Copyrighted, 1916, by the Baseball Magazine Co., New York

During his career Ty's familiar face was seen on such items as magazine covers, tobacco cards, candy bar wrappers, and paper fans.

second baseman was well-liked by practically everyone. Many remembered how the gifted ballplayer, who had dropped out of school when he was ten to work in a Rhode Island mill, had given the fledgling American League instant credibility when he jumped over from the National League in 1901. The line-drive-hitting right-hander won his first of three batting titles that year with a .422 average, still the American League record. Lajoie was held in such high esteem the Cleveland club named itself the "Naps" after him. By contrast, Ty was easily the most unpopular man in baseball, despised as much for his brilliance as for his disposition. Many fans weren't pulling for Lajoie as much as they were pulling against Cobb.

This became obvious in Cleveland's season-ending doubleheader in St. Louis on Sunday, October 9. The last-place Browns were managed by Jack O'Conner, a former catcher who had played several years in Cleveland when the team was in the National League. O'Conner, ironically nicknamed "Peach Pie," despised the Georgia Peach. Before the first game he instructed rookie third baseman Red Corriden to play Lajoie extra deep every time he came to bat.

In Lajoie's first at-bat, he hit a long drive to center field that some observers claimed was misjudged deliberately by outfielder Hub Northern. It was scored a triple. In his next seven trips to the plate, Lajoie—noticing that Corriden was playing on the fringe of the outfield grass— bunted down the third-base line. The first six times the slow-footed Lajoie beat them out for hits, Corriden not even making a throw on some, and the seventh time he was credited with a sacrifice. In his final at-bat Lajoie grounded to shortstop Bobby Wallace, long considered the league's finest glove man at that position. Wallace threw wildly to first and Lajoie was awarded a hit by the official scorer, who explained that even a good throw wouldn't have retired him.

Lajoie finished the doubleheader with eight hits in eight at-bats. "Larry Does Great Work at St. Louis," one out-of-town paper reported. Afterward Lajoie received several congratulatory telegrams, including one signed by several Tigers.

The transparent strategy enraged those writers on the scene. The five St. Louis dailies spoke of an "open scandal," whereby "certain St. Louis players allowed Napoleon Lajoie to obtain base hits with the aim of letting him beat out Cobb for the batting title. . . . Lajoie and others say there was no trickery—just cleverness and misjudgment combined."

The misjudgment turned out to be on the part of O'Conner, who explained,

"Lajoie outguessed us." American League president Ban Johnson didn't buy that. As the public waited for the official averages to be computed, new information about Lajoie's final-day performance came to light. During the doubleheader St. Louis coach Harry Howell had repeatedly visited the press box, asking how Lajoie's bunts were being scored. At one point a note arrived in the press box promising a new suit of clothes to the scorer if he would be lenient toward the Cleveland batter. After holding hearings and absolving Lajoie and the rookie Corriden of any blame, Johnson had O'Conner and Howell thrown out of the league.

On November 21 the league office released the final official averages. According to its statistician, Cobb had won the batting title by the slimmest of margins:

	At-Bats	Hits	Avg.
Cobb	509	196	.3851
Lajoie	591	227	.3841

Lajoie went to his grave insisting he had won the disputed batting championship, a belief proved correct long after all the principals in the controversy were dead. In 1981 Paul MacFarlane of *The Sporting News* reconstructed the 1910 batting race game by game. He reported that, among other minor errors in both players' records, the American League had mistakenly credited Cobb with an additional 2-for-3 performance on September 24. The recalibrated figures revealed that Lajoie had actually outhit Cobb:

	At-Bats	Hits	Avg.
Lajoie	591	227	.3841
Cobb	506	194	.3833

Despite then-commissioner Bowie Kuhn's decision not to alter the record book, some revisionists have since credited Lajoie, not Cobb, with the 1910 batting title, tainted "hits" and all. As it turned out, neither Lajoie nor Cobb lost anything of real value at the time. Hugh Chalmers, delighted with the windfall of free publicity the controversy had brought his product, awarded both men a new Chalmers before the final results were released. Perhaps the most sporting gesture of the whole affair was Ty giving his loyal friend, Germany Schaefer, his old car "in appreciation of the many kindnesses he has shown me."

Despite the aroma surrounding it, the first Chalmers Award (it would continue in a revised format for three more years) highlighted the growing association between ballplayers and motor cars. The automobile had replaced the diamond stickpin as a symbol of status and conspicuous consumption. Sam Crawford was an impressive man-about-town in his polished Cadillac, while several Pittsburgh players used their $1,825 winning shares to purchase new Regals after the 1909 World Series. Club owners were ambivalent about what the new machine age meant for the game. They feared many fans would decide to motor

"My father liked Cobb but he also thought he had some disagreeable qualities. He could be quick-tempered and a bully at times. They used to have their outs. Once my father scored a ball an error instead of a hit. He told Cobb, 'If our friendship isn't based on anything stronger than a dispute over a base hit, it's really not worth continuing.' Ty came to agree."

—EDDIE BATCHELOR JR.

off in search of love, adventure, or other attractions outside of the ballpark. They also worried about their star players getting injured in an accident. After Honus Wagner crashed into a railroad crossing gate, *The Sporting News* urged owners to "forbid this fad, a result of players' natural craving for speed and undue risk."

For true adventure, nothing could compare with motoring. However, only a small percentage of Americans owned an automobile in 1910. It was still an expensive, unreliable machine, though sales were climbing steadily, prices were coming down, and mechanical advances were being made almost daily. The field was wide open. In 1911, 270 manufacturers were producing 400 models, including such exotic-sounding vehicles as the Grabowsky "Power Wagon" and Faulkner-Blanchard "Gunboat Six." These early vehicles could be dangerous. Until the widespread use of Charles Kettering's electric self-starter (introduced on the 1912 Cadillac), motorists had to turn a crank to start the engine, a muscle-numbing procedure that could easily snap a forearm, shatter a jaw, or rip an arm out of its socket. Tires blew frequently. A set of four cost several hundred dollars but typically lasted only a few hundred miles. In 1909, a mile-long stretch of concrete highway, the country's first, was laid on Woodward Avenue in Highland Park, but only a tiny fraction of the country's other two million miles of rural roads were paved, some with nothing more than crushed seashells. Rain and snow made them impassable, forcing more than one stranded motorist to endure the barb "Get a horse!" while some amused farmer pulled him out of the mud.

Driving conditions were scarcely better in the city. One of the great untold stories of early-20th-century America was the absolute chaos caused by the coming of the automobile. Cars, trucks, buggies, horses, wagons, streetcars, pushcarts, bicycles, pedestrians—all were knotted at intersections like balls of hopelessly tangled yarn. Despite the soaring number of accidents and fatalities, traffic control was practically nonexistent in 1911. Years later Detroit's mayor admitted the city

had been purposely lax on traffic offenders. The rea-
soning: since its citizens were putting the world on
wheels, they deserved some slack. Thus the driving, unimpeded by traffic signals, patience, or
common sense, often resembled a thrill show.

Ty, frequently spotted tooling around
town in a succession of luxury models, was
a regular offender. During the 1911 season, on one of the few occasions when a
patrolman actually issued him a ticket
for speeding, Ty received a suspended
sentence from a sympathetic judge. "He
told the judge he wasn't going any faster
than when he steals second base," a local
paper reported.

As more and more Americans were
learning, an automobile created a previ-
ously unheard-of freedom. Out of uniform
and behind the wheel of his 1910 Owen, Ty
could even achieve some welcomed anonymity.
"More than 500,000 people saw Ty Cobb perform in
Bennett Park this summer," observed the *Detroit News*.
"Daily, when the team is home, Cobb drives about the streets
in his automobile and not one person out of 100 ever gives
him a second look."

Young, vibrant, self-made, and adventurous, Ty and the
automobile seemed to personify America in these throttle-
down, big-shouldered years before the First World War. Even Ty's early diamond
exploits coexisted on the same page as the motor car, as most papers published
box scores and the latest auto news in an "Automobile and Sports" section.
Throughout his twenties, Cobb caused Frank Navin fits by regularly taking laps at
speedways in Atlanta, Indianapolis, Savannah, and elsewhere, sometimes exceed-
ing speeds of 100 miles per hour. Navin once had to step in at the last moment
to cancel a heavily promoted ten-mile race in Atlanta between his star ballplayer
and Brooklyn pitcher Nap Rucker.

In 1911, Barney Oldfield, the veteran driver who had set several early speed
records, announced he was considering retirement. Exploding tires, failed brakes,
and other mechanical or human failures had caused more than two hundred drivers and mechanics to die in the previous seven years. The famous racer's nerves
were frayed almost beyond repair. "The motor racing game has outlived its useful-
ness," he said. "The science of speed has reached a point where any manufacturer can produce a car which will satisfy any buyer."

Cobb's response, in effect, was to take several bone-jarring laps around a
racetrack, wipe the bugs off his teeth, and just laugh. To him, auto racing was simply another expression of virility. "The point was: they'd never strapped themselves behind the wheel of a powerful Mercedes, Pope-Toledo, White Streak,
Thomas Flyer, Lozier or Fiat and experienced the hair-raising thrill of mastering
the roaring beasts," is how he once explained his fascination with speed. "Those

Cleveland's "Shoeless Joe" Jackson, flanked by Cobb and Sam Crawford in 1911. One of the more enduring Cobb myths has Ty purposely ignoring Jackson in the latter stages of the 1911 season, so confusing the illiterate Jackson that he fretted and stopped hitting, allowing Ty to overtake him for another batting title. Ty and sportswriter Grantland Rice repeated this tale in their autobiographies, using it as an example of Cobb's prowess in psychological warfare. But Jackson biographer Donald Gropman has pointed out that Jackson never led Cobb during the 1911 season; actually, Jackson *gained* ground in the last week. Although his .356 career average is third best of all time, trailing only Cobb's .367 and Rogers Hornsby's .358, the unlucky Jackson never won a batting title, finishing runner-up to the Peach for three straight seasons beginning in 1911.

who feared for my life were the pedestrian type. You have to do it to appreciate it." Cobb's personal best for a "flying kilometer" was a 45-second mile at the brickyard in Indianapolis, driving a National "40." He once drove umpire Brick Owens around "the greatest race course in the world" at breakneck speed. Owens released his white-knuckled grip only long enough to lean over the side of the car and throw up. Despite the protestations of those close to him, Ty didn't ease his foot off the pedal until wrecks killed race drivers Bill McNey and "Wild Bob" Burman, both of them friends.

Cobb's heavy foot was the perfect metaphor for the 1911 edition of the Tigers, who won their first 12 games and accelerated to a blistering 21–2 start. Ty's 40-game hitting streak was finally stopped by Chicago's Ed Walsh during a sweltering Independence Day doubleheader at Bennett Park. That was just a momentary setback. One week later, in an important series against the Athletics, Ty kicked his competitive zeal into overdrive. On July 11 he scored from second on a fly ball, and the following day he made the veteran Philadelphia battery of Harry Krause and Ira Thomas look like helpless rookies as he swiped second, third, and home on consecutive pitches in the first inning.

Such exploits had fans talking of another World Series with the Chicago Cubs, who were setting the pace in the National League. However, like the Cubs, the Tigers faded badly and finished runner-up. Injuries to such key players as rookie first baseman Del Gainor and continued dissension over Jennings' preferential treatment of Cobb caused the huge early lead to dissipate. On the field, Cobb and Crawford presented the most feared one-two punch in the game, a threat to bang out back-to-back triples or pull off a double steal. Off the field they refused to speak to each other. Before the season Jennings and team captain George Moriarty had implored the two to bury the hatchet. Crawford figured he knew the perfect spot—Ty's swollen head—but the two agreed to shake hands, although friction in the clubhouse never disappeared. Meanwhile, Philadelphia passed Detroit for good on August 4, finishing thirteen and a half games in front. Connie Mack's white elephants then went on to stampede the New York Giants for their second straight championship.

Thanks in part to the introduction of a more lively cork-centered ball, averages and home runs jumped noticeably that summer. Several players, including Crawford and Cobb, enjoyed their finest all-around seasons. Wahoo Sam posted career highs in hits (217), runs (109), and batting average (.378). He also knocked in 115 runs, second in the league, and stole 37 bases.

But those numbers paled alongside Cobb's. Ty won his fifth straight batting title, hitting .420 with 248 hits, 47 doubles, and 24 triples. He scored 147 runs and knocked in 127. Not only were these all league highs, they would turn out to be personal bests. Ty, who also led in total bases and slugging, swiped 83 bases, easily outdistancing Clyde Milan to capture his third stolen base crown. In addition, he hit eight home runs, second only to Philadelphia's Frank Baker (who would earn his sobriquet as "Home Run" Baker after hitting two more against the Giants in the World Series). He struck out swinging only twice all season.

All in all, it was an extraordinary season statistically for Ty, one of the finest individual performances ever put together. Before the season the Chalmers Award had been restructured. Now a committee of sportswriters representing all major-league cities voted an automobile to the player in each league who "should prove himself as the most important and useful . . . to his club and to the league at large in point of deportment and value of services rendered." With 64 points, Ty easily outdistanced Ed Walsh (35 points) and Eddie Collins (32) for the American League award. There was no doubt about the value of his "services rendered," and the voters apparently didn't attach much weight to the issue of deportment. For temperamentally, Ty remained as unstable as a feather in a tornado, with an almost uncanny ability to get under the skins of all those around him. Exactly how much of the abuse Cobb inspired was deserved was open to debate. New York sportswriter Heywood Broun, for one, thought it was a case of small minds attached to feeble limbs:

> Whether you like or dislike this young fellow, you must concede him one virtue: what he has won, he has taken by might of his own play. He asks no quarter and gives none. Pistareen ball players whom he has "shown up" dislike him. Third basemen with bum arms, second basemen with tender shins, catchers who cannot throw out a talented slider—all despise Cobb. And their attitude has infected the stands. Why do they so resent Cobb when he plays the game at every point on the field, giving his best at every moment, and makes life miserable for those less willing?

Cobb may have pondered that question as he drove away yet another new Chalmers in the fall of 1911. Given his "vying nature" and his age—he was only 24—long stretches of rough road loomed. However, his approach as he embarked on the most tumultuous seasons of his career would remain that of the speedway and the basepaths: full-bore and straight out, leaving detractors to choke on his dust.

Amanda Cobb visited her famous son in Detroit in the summer of 1911. Ty holds Ty Jr., while Charlie humors their second child, Shirley, who had been born that June.

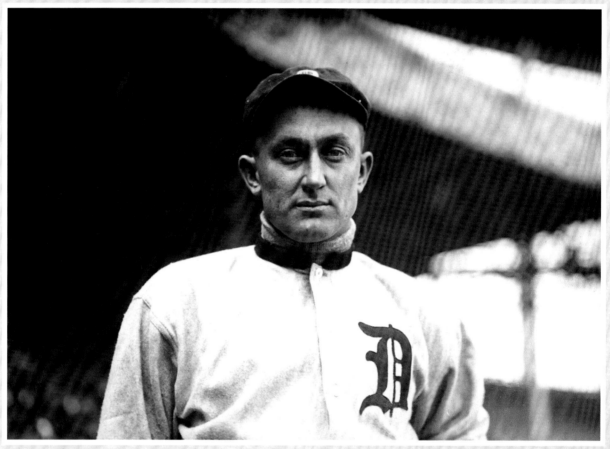

Cobb in his prime. "He was possessed by the furies," wrote Bozeman Bulger.

CHAPTER FIVE

Glory Days and Others

A swing—and a smash—and a gray streak partaking
Of ghostly manoeuvres that follow the whack;
The old earth rebounds with a quiver and quaking
And high flies the dust as he thuds on the track;
The atmosphere reels—and it isn't the comet—
There follows the blur of a phantom at play;
Then out from the reel comes the glitter of steel—
And damned be the fellow that gets in the way.

A swing and a smash—and the far echoes quiver—
A ripping and rearing and volcanic roar;
And off streaks the Ghost with a shake and a shiver,
To hurdle red hell on the way to a score;
A cross between tidal wave, cyclone and earthquake—
Fire, wind and water all out on a lark;
Then out from the reel comes the glitter of steel,
Plus ten tons of dynamite hitched to a spark.

GRANTLAND RICE, "COBB"

Nobody in New York City in 1912 hated Ty Cobb more than Claude Lucker, a rabid Highlanders fan whose favorite pastimes included screaming slurs at the Detroit star whenever the Tigers visited Hilltop Park. The exact roots of his hostility remain unknown, but it probably was nothing more than a case of one of life's victims venting his frustrations and bitterness at a convenient target—a thin-skinned ballplayer whose slow burn made for great sport.

Lucker, a former printing press operator, undoubtedly thought he had a right to be bitter. A year earlier an accident had severed one of his hands and lopped three fingers off the other. Forced to quit his printing job, the middle-aged Lucker found work as a flunky for a minor political official. His friends were the

Contrary to what some might have believed, Cobb didn't eat his young. Offered as proof is a shot of the proud papa and his first-born, Ty Jr., prior to a game in Detroit.

low-rent cronies at downtown Tammany Hall, the center of New York's corrupt Democratic machine. Enduring stares and barbs, Lucker wasn't above using his handicap as an excuse for his churlish behavior.

Louts like Claude Lucker have always been a staple of sporting events. However, player abuse was worse at the turn of the last century. In the absence of ushers and security guards, spectators exercised little restraint. Police were always on hand, but they usually were highly partisan and—especially in New York—frequently joined in the fun. Catcalls, insults, threats, and an occasional thrown bottle or seat cushion were accepted hazards of the ballplayer's trade. There were legions of Cobb-haters in every park, and Ty dealt with them the only way he could—by embarrassing the home nine to the best of his ability. But on the afternoon of May 15, 1912, Claude Lucker outdid himself, pushing Cobb over the edge and setting in motion one of the wildest chain of events in sports history.

The trouble started shortly after the opening pitch of the Wednesday game between the Tigers and the Highlanders. Lucker, seated about a dozen rows behind the visitors' dugout, directed an unceasing stream of invectives at Cobb. After Ty muffed a fly ball in the bottom of the first inning, Lucker screamed, "You look a little dopey. Hey, Cobb, are you doped up?"

"**I don't think there's anybody that ever saw Cobb play in his heyday who wouldn't say, without a doubt: Cobb. If there'd been a higher league, he'd have been the only one in it.**"

—BOSTON PITCHER "SMOKEY JOE" WOOD, ASKED IN RETIREMENT TO NAME BASEBALL'S GREATEST PLAYER

Although Ty traded insult for insult with his antagonist, he did his best to avoid a physical confrontation. In the bottom of the second inning he lingered in the outfield area rather than go back to the dugout and endure another point-blank blast of taunts and insults. After New York was retired in the bottom of the third, Ty swung by the first-base stands, looking to ask New York officials to have Lucker removed from the park. Unable to find anyone, he returned to the Tigers' bench, yelling at Lucker, "I was out with your sister last night." Lucker yelled something back.

"You going to let that bum call you names?" asked Sam Crawford.

"I don't know how much more I can take," admitted Cobb, who sat there simmering as epithets rained down. Newspapers delicately avoided the exact wording of Lucker's razzing, but it's known that less-than-flattering comments about the morals of Ty's mother finally set him off. Hughie Jennings later explained that, among other things, Lucker had called Ty a "half-nigger," an insult Jennings knew no Southerner would tolerate.

"I heard the remark," said Jennings, "but I knew it would be useless to restrain Ty, as he would have got his tormenter sooner or later. When Ty's Southern blood is aroused he is a bad man to handle." The unlucky Lucker would quickly discover that. As the Tigers trotted out to take the field in the bottom of the fourth, Ty suddenly turned on his heel, vaulted over the grandstand railing, and rushed up several rows to confront his nemesis. As the crowd stood to get a better view and Detroit players stepped outside their dugout brandishing bats, Ty went to town on the astonished Lucker.

"Everything was very pleasant," the *New York Times* reported, "until Ty Cobb johnnykilbaned a spectator right on the place where he talks, started the claret, and stopped the flow of profane and vulgar words. Cobb led with a left jab and countered with a right kick to Mr. Spectator's left Weisbach, which made his peeper look as if someone had drawn a curtain over it…. Jabs bounded off the spectator's face like a golf ball from a rock." Lucker's account to police was more prosaic. "He struck me with his fists on the forehead over the left eye and knocked me down. Then he jumped on me and spiked me in the left leg and kicked me in the side, after which he booted me behind the left ear."

Park police finally broke up the assault. Lucker was led away, bloodied and sputtering, while Ty was tossed from the game. Despite the shocking nature of the beating, which made headlines across the country, the main working press defended Ty's actions. The reaction of Hugh S. Fullerton, who noted that the police in New York's three major-league parks were "among the violent rooters," was typical. Cobb, he wrote, "goes around the circuit year after year, singled out as the special mark by every violent fan, and he has learned to endure almost any kind of abuse possible. If the epithets and accusations made by the Highlander fan towards Cobb was half as bad as the Detroit players claim, it was a case for violence. The wonder to me is that other spectators could sit and listen without taking a hand in it and beating up and throwing out the person using such language."

Unfortunately for Cobb, the league president didn't agree with the Peach's hands-on method of conflict resolution. Ban Johnson, who happened to be in the stands that day, suspended Ty immediately without hearing his side of the story.

The following afternoon's game in Philadelphia was rained out, which gave the Detroit ballplayers plenty of time to grouse about Johnson's high-handed decision. On Friday the Cobbless Tigers dropped a 6–4 decision to Philadelphia, after which they displayed a rare show of solidarity with their temperamental teammate by sending a telegram to Johnson at his Chicago office. It read:

> Feeling Mr. Cobb is being done an injustice by your action in suspending him, we, the undersigned, refuse to play in another game until such action is adjusted to our satisfaction. He was fully justified, as no one could stand such abuse from anyone. We want him reinstated or there will be no game. If players cannot have protection, we must protect ourselves.

To the press, Cobb maintained his right to defend his person and his honor. Although Lucker was physically handicapped, he got what he deserved, Ty said. "When a spectator calls me a 'half-nigger' I think it is about time to fight." Atlanta's mayor agreed, congratulating one of Georgia's favorite sons for upholding "the principles that have always been taught to Southern manhood."

Meanwhile, in Detroit, Frank Navin fretted over the automatic $5,000 fine he would have to pay if he didn't field a team for Saturday's game. He instructed Jennings and his coaches, Joe Sugden and Jim "Deacon" McGuire, to fan out over Philadelphia and gather a squad of substitutes, in case they were needed. As Bugs Baer later put it, any sandlotter who could "stop a grapefruit from rolling uphill or hit a bull in the pants with a bass fiddle" was given a chance. The scrubs were signed for $10 apiece and hustled out to Shibe Park, where a large crowd was gathering to see if the Tigers were really going to follow through on their threat to strike.

They were. When informed that Cobb's suspension stood, Sam Crawford, George Mullin, Donie Bush and company marched off the field, turned in their uniforms, and joined the amused Philadelphia bugs in the stands to watch the raggedy band of sandlotters battle the two-time champion Athletics.

The game of May 18, 1912 remains the most absurd big-league contest ever played. Twenty-year-old Aloysius Travers, who like most of the scrubs was recruited from nearby St. Joseph's College, volunteered to take the mound when he learned the pitcher was to receive an additional $15—combat pay, as it were. As

No one took greater advantage of basic base-running principles than Cobb. Instead of circling bases in a wide arc, Ty pushed his left foot against the inside of the bag, then crossed over with his right leg. The pivot, executed at full speed, saved precious seconds and made him appear faster than he really was.

Mullin surrendered his uniform to Travers in the clubhouse, he said, "Kid, you can steal anything, but don't steal the glove." Mullin didn't know his man. Travers was a theology student who later became a Catholic priest.

Nothing short of divine intervention could have saved these ersatz Tigers. Aware of what awaited them, they had to be coaxed from the dugout and onto the field. Travers' only pitch was a roundhouse curve that "was not fast enough to dent butter," observed one writer. He did attempt one fastball in the first inning—to Frank "Home Run" Baker, of all people—and Baker sent it rocketing toward Opal Street, three blocks away but foul. This prompted Deacon McGuire, who at age 48 found himself pressed into duty behind the plate, to rise from his creaking knees and visit the mound.

"You wanna get killed, kid?" McGuire asked. "Just throw your regular stuff. It ain't good enough to hit."

It was a beautiful day for a game: sunny and about 75 degrees. Buoyed by the weather and the spectacle on the field, the crowd cheered the misfits on. One of the scrubs fielded a ground ball with his face, losing two teeth in the process.

Ty, home in Georgia after the 1914 season, posed with Charlie, little Ty, and Shirley.

> **"The whole secret of sliding is to make your move at the last possible second. When I went in there I wanted to see the whites of the fielder's eyes."**
>
> —TY COBB ON THE ART OF SLIDING

"This ain't baseball," he sputtered. "This is war." Travers staggered the distance, giving up 26 hits and 24 runs. He walked seven and struck out one. To add to the merriment, his teammates chipped in with nine errors. "It's a circus," declared Donie Bush, sitting in the upper pavilion. "I'm glad I came."

The third baseman, a 30-year-old semipro named Ed Irvin, accounted for half of the strikebreakers' four hits. Irvin made the most of his abbreviated major-league career, cracking two triples in three at-bats before falling back into obscurity with a lifetime .667 batting average in the record books. Neither of Irvin's three-baggers did any damage. In fact, the scrubs' only runs came in the fifth inning on a throwing error by shortstop Jack Barry.

Bill Leinhauser, a slightly built 18-year-old, wore Cobb's uniform and played his position. There the comparison ended. Leinhauser went hitless in four at-bats and got conked on the head with one of several fly balls driven his way. At one point during the fusillade Jennings called time to give his distraught center fielder advice. "Forget about catching them, son," he said. "Just play them off the walls." Leinhauser later became a cop in Philadelphia, and until his death in 1978 he never tired of telling people of the time he had filled in for the great Georgia Peach.

With minimum effort the Athletics chalked up an official win, 24–2. Jennings, pinch-hitting for one of his shell-shocked troops, drew the curtain on this theatre of the absurd by taking a called third strike from Herb Pennock for the final out.

Ban Johnson exploded when he learned of the farce. He and Navin hurried to Philadelphia for a conference. Meanwhile, Ty urged his striking teammates to go back to work. "You've made our point," he said. "With the publicity we've received, the facts are now on record with the public. I don't want you paying any more fines. You've got to go back on the field sooner or later, so do it now. I'll be all right. Johnson will lift my suspension soon."

Which he did. Each of the striking Tigers was fined $100. Ty paid $50 and sat out the balance of his ten-day suspension.

As ugly and ludicrous as the Lucker beating and its aftermath were, the episode was perhaps the only time during Ty's long career when he had the almost universal approval of his teammates. Asked about the Lucker incident some 80 years later, Red Hoff—then a 21-year-old pitcher sitting on the Highlanders' bench—spoke for most ballplayers when he said simply, "He went into the stands and did his duty." The most significant development to come out of the affair was that ushers eventually were installed inside all big-league parks.

☾☽

Lost in all of the commotion over the Lucker affair was another superb offensive season for Ty, who hit .410 in 1912 to capture his sixth straight batting title. On April 20, he had christened Frank Navin's new $300,000 concrete-and-steel ballpark by scoring the Tigers' first-ever run there. He did it in typically dramatic style, swiping home in the bottom of the first inning against Cleveland's Vean Gregg. It was the first of a record eight steals of home he would pull off that summer.

Pilfering the plate had turned into a specialty. During his career he stole it 54 times (plus one World Series theft), far outdistancing runner-up Max Carey, who had 33 during his 20 seasons with Pittsburgh and Brooklyn. To put Ty's feat in perspective, consider that the two players ahead of him in career steals, Rickey Henderson and Lou Brock, stole home only seven times between them.

Larry Amman of the Society for American Baseball Research has tracked all of Cobb's attempted steals of home and discovered some interesting figures. Of the Peach's 98 regular-season dashes for home, two-thirds occurred with two outs. Of these 66 all-or-nothing attempts, he was successful exactly half of the time. Cobb made an additional 28 attempts with one out and was successful 18 times—a commendable 64 percent. Only four of his attempts were with none out. This has always been considered a bad tactic—why risk having the first out of the inning occur at home?—but Ty was successful the first three times he tried it.

Analyzing Cobb's attempts further, we find that he was far more likely to pilfer home with his team ahead (28 steals in 53 attempts) than with his club behind (14 steals in 27 attempts). With the score tied, he was able to dramatically deliver the go-ahead run 12 of 18 times. He also was more aggressive in the early innings, stealing home 24 of 46 times in the first three innings of a game. From the seventh inning on he was more responsible, with 14 steals in 19 attempts—a sterling 74 percent.

Conventional wisdom holds that stealing home should be attempted with a poor hitter at the plate because a weak hitter is less likely to drive in the runner from third. Moreover, that batter should be right-handed so as to obscure the view of the catcher's view of the runner. Once again Cobb turned baseball logic on its ear. He was more likely to break from third with Bobby Veach, a left-handed hitter who was one of the game's most productive RBI men, at bat than any other player. "Cobb was using the element of surprise," a writer noted after one of the Peach's successful swipes. "No one thought he would try for home with a left-handed hitter up." Which, of course, is exactly why he did it.

No one will ever approach Ty's record for stealing home. Today's big-bang offense has cheapened the importance of a single run, and modern teams are smarter about defending against the maneuver. Third basemen play closer to the bag, while pitchers long ago abandoned the windup in favor of the set position. Both reduce the big lead a runner needs to get a jump on the ball as it's being delivered to the plate. Additionally, in this era of astronomical contracts, few base stealers are willing to risk a career-ending injury through a home-plate collision.

"Ty Cobb would get on and beat you alone," said Joe Wood. "He had every catcher in the league crazy." Here the Peach artfully kicks the ball out of St. Louis catcher Paul Krichell's mitt on July 4, 1912, one of four times during his career when he stole second, third, and home in the same inning. The only other player in baseball history to steal his way around the bases as many as three times was Honus Wagner.

Cobb vs. the American League

The following list shows Ty Cobb's lifetime batting average against all American League pitchers that he had at least 20 at-bats against. In the case of a Hall of Famer (identified by an asterick), Cobb's performance is included regardless of how few at-bats he may have had against him. Note that the teams and years following each pitcher's name include only those seasons when he might have faced Cobb.

Pitcher (Team–Years)	AB	Hits	Avg.
Nick Altrock+ (Chi 1905–09, Was 1909–24)	49	18	.367
Doc Ayers (Was 1913–19)	66	25	.379
Jim Bagby (Cle 1916–22)	118	47	.397
Bill Bailey+ (StL 1907–12)	66	18	.273
Stan Baumgartner+ (Phi 1924–26)	23	4	.174
Bill Bayne+ (StL 1919–24, Cle 1928)	36	5	.139
Hugh Bedient (Bos 1912–14)	28	16	.571
*Chief Bender (Phi 1905–14, Chi 1925)	82	30	.366
Joe Benz (Chi 1911–19)	51	14	.275
Heinie Berger (Cle 1907–10)	20	9	.450
Fred Blanding (Cle 1910–14)	38	17	.447
Ted Blankenship (Chi 1922–28)	50	17	.340
Joe Boehling+ (Was 1912–16, Cle 1916–20)	38	17	.447
Garland Buckeye+ (Was 1918, Cle 1925–28)	26	6	.231
Fred Burchell+ (Bos 1907–09)	20	5	.250
Joe Bush (Phi 1912–17, Bos 1918–21, NY 1922–24, StL 1925, Was 1926)	152	58	.382
Ray Caldwell (NY 1910–18, Bos 1919, Cle 1919–21)	120	45	.375
*Jack Chesbro (NY 1905–09, Bos 1909)	54	23	.426
Eddie Cicotte (Bos 1908–12, Chi 1912–20)	143	54	.378
Ray Collins+ (Bos 1909–15)	112	35	.313
Rip Collins (NY 1920–21, Bos 1922, Det 1927)	33	12	.364
Sarge Connally (Chi 1921–28)	42	14	.333
Jack Coombs (Phi 1906–14)	73	29	.397
Fritz Coumbe+ (Bos 1914, Cle 1914–19)	30	13	.433
*Stan Coveleski (Phi 1912, Cle 1916–24, Was 1925–27, NY 1928)	163	59	.362

Pitcher (Team–Years)	AB	Hits	Avg.
Dave Danforth+ (Phi 1911–12, Chi 1916–19, StL 1922–25)	77	22	.286
Dave Davenport (StL 1916–19)	35	12	.343
Dixie Davis (Chi 1915, StL 1920–26)	57	13	.228
Jimmy Dygert (Phi 1905–10)	41	14	.341
Howard Ehmke (Bos 1923–26, Phi 1926)	28	11	.393
*Red Faber (Chi 1914–28)	164	55	.335
Cy Falkenberg (Was 1905–08, Cle 1908–13, Phi 1917)	58	23	.397
Alex Ferguson (NY 1918–21, 1925, Bos 1922–25, Was 1925–26)	50	26	.520
Ray Fisher (NY 1910–17)	59	16	.271
Russ Ford (NY 1909–13)	71	32	.451
Rube Foster (Bos 1913–17)	49	15	.306
Curt Fullerton (Bos 1921–25)	23	8	.348
Bert Gallia (Was 1912–17, StL 1918–20)	58	20	.345
Milt Gaston (NY 1924, StL 1925–27, Was 1928)	40	15	.375
Fred Glade (StL 1905–07, NY 1908)	30	5	.167
Bill Graham+ (StL 1908–10)	41	13	.317
Dolly Gray+ (Was 1909–11)	57	21	.368
Sam Gray (Phi 1924–26)	30	13	.433
Vean Gregg+ (Cle 1911–14, Bos 1914–16, Phi 1918, Was 1925)	68	25	.368
*Clark Griffith (NY 1905–08, Was 1912–14)	4	1	.250
Bob Groom (Was 1909–13, StL 1916–17, Cle 1918)	95	26	.274
*Lefty Grove+ (Phi 1925–26)	15	5	.333
Rip Hagerman (Cle 1914–16)	24	10	.417
Sea Lion Hall (Bos 1909–13)	26	11	.423
Earl Hamilton+ (StL 1911–17)	100	38	.380
Harry Harper+ (Was 1913–19, Bos 1920, NY 1921)	75	28	.373
Slim Harriss (Phi 1920–26, Bos 1926–28)	88	31	.352
Bob Hasty (Phi 1919–24)	45	11	.244
Fred Heimach+ (Phi 1920–26, Bos 1926, NY 1928)	36	13	.361
Otto Hess+ (Cle 1905–08)	43	12	.279
Bill Hogg (NY 1905–08)	39	17	.436
Ken Holloway (Det 1927–28)	21	9	.429
Harry Howell (StL 1905–10)	47	11	.234
*Waite Hoyt (Bos 1919–20, NY 1921–28)	98	26	.265

George Sisler made his mark as one of the game's greatest hitters, twice topping .400 in a season, but the former University of Michigan standout began his career on the mound. He split eight decisions with the St. Louis Browns in 1915 before shifting full time to first base. In one of those games he held Cobb hitless in five at-bats. As a gimmick Sisler and Cobb pitched against each other in the final game of the 1918 and 1925 seasons.

At the plate, Cobb's chief nemesis during the 1920s was an obscure pitcher named Bill Bayne. The little southpaw lost one more game than he won during his nine-year career, the bulk of it spent with the Browns. But he limited Ty to a puny .139 average, the Peach's worst performance against any pitcher he had at least 30 at-bats against. Bayne's handling of Cobb, much like teammate Hub Pruett's well-publicized success with Babe Ruth, defies easy explanation. One theory is that Bayne was a lefty with good control–the kind of pitcher that gave Ty the most fits–and that he was used primarily in relief, denying Ty the extra at-bats it often took him to solve a pitcher during a game.

Pitcher (Team–Years)	AB	Hits	Avg.
Willis Hudlin (Cle 1926–28)	21	5	.238
Tom Hughes (NY 1906–10)	53	20	.377
*Walter Johnson (Was 1907–27)	328	120	.366
Sam Jones (Cle 1914–15, Bos 1916–21, NY 1922–26, StL 1927, Was 1928)	121	38	.314
*Addie Joss (Cle 1905–10)	94	25	.266
George Kahler (Cle 1910–14)	37	12	.324
Ray Keating (NY 1912–18)	24	8	.333
Dickie Kerr+ (Chi 1919–25)	47	16	.340
Ray Kolp (StL 1921–24)	22	6	.273
Dutch Leonard+ (Bos 1913–18)	67	25	.373
Dixie Leverett (Chi 1922–26)	30	14	.467
Glenn Liebhardt (Cle 1906–09)	27	7	.259
*Ted Lyons (Chi 1923–28)	75	24	.320
Firpo Marberry (Was 1923–28)	26	8	.308
Carl Mays (Bos 1915–19, NY 1919–23)	116	39	.336
Jake Miller+ (Cle 1924–28)	25	6	.240
Willie Mitchell+ (Cle 1909–16)	58	20	.345
George Mogridge+ (Chi 1911–12, NY 1915–20, Was 1921–25, StL 1925)	137	47	.343
Cy Morgan (StL 1905–07, Bos 1907–09, Phi 1909–12)	32	10	.313
Guy Morton (Cle 1914–24)	71	19	.268
Rollie Naylor (Phi 1917–24)	64	33	.516
Doc Newton+ (NY 1905–09)	25	10	.400
Buck O'Brien (Bos 1911–13, Chi 1913)	22	9	.409
Al Orth (NY 1905–09)	23	9	.391
Frank Owen (Chi 1905–09)	20	7	.350
Casey Patten+ (Was 1905–08, Bos 1908)	24	11	.458
Barney Pelty (StL 1905–12, Was 1912)	43	20	.465
*Herb Pennock+ (Phi 1912–15, Bos 1915–22, NY 1923–28)	142	52	.366
Scott Perry (StL 1915, Phi 1918–21)	34	17	.500
Bill Piercy (NY 1917–21, Bos 1922–24)	33	14	.424
*Eddie Plank+ (Phi 1905–14, StL 1916–17)	201	69	.343
Jack Powell (NY 1905, StL 1905–12)	70	24	.343
Jack Quinn (NY 1909–12, 1919–21, Chi 1918, Bos 1922–25, Phi 1925–26)	91	43	.473

> **"Every great batter works on the theory that the pitcher is more afraid of him than he is of the pitcher."**
>
> -TY COBB

Pitcher (Team–Years)	AB	Hits	Avg.
Bob Rhoads (Cle 1905–09)	79	24	.304
Eddie Rommel (Phi 1920–26)	89	31	.343
Dutch Ruether+ (Was 1925–26, NY 1926–27)	28	11	.393
*Red Ruffing (Bos 1924–28)	26	6	.231
Allan Russell (NY 1915–19, Bos 1919–22, Was 1923–25)	69	23	.333
Reb Russell+ (Chi 1913–19)	60	23	.383
*Babe Ruth+ (Bos 1914–19, NY 1920–28)	67	22	.328
Jim Scott (Chi 1909–17)	64	28	.438
Joe Shaute+ (Cle 1922–28)	64	19	.297
Jim Shaw (Was 1913–21)	61	28	.459
Bob Shawkey (Phi 1913–15, NY 1915–27)	140	59	.421
Urban Shocker (NY 1916–17, 1925–28, StL 1918–24)	95	35	.421
Ernie Shore (Bos 1914–17, NY 1919–20)	52	22	.423
*George Sisler+ (StL 1915–22, 1924–26)	6	0	.000
Charlie Smith (Was 1905–09, Bos 1909–11)	29	14	.483
Frank Smith (Chi 1905–10, Bos 1910–11)	74	22	.297
Allan Sothoron (StL 1914–21, Bos 1921, Cle 1921–22)	56	28	.500
Jesse Tannehill+ (Bos 1905–08, Was 1908–09)	27	10	.370
Tommy Thomas (Chi 1926–28)	48	16	.333
Hank Thormahlen+ (NY 1917–20, Bos 1921)	31	9	.290
Sloppy Thurston (StL 1923, Chi 1923–26, Was 1927)	68	26	.382
George Uhle (Cle 1919–28)	101	37	.366
Elam Vangilder (StL 1919–27, Det 1928)	81	32	.395

The Cobb cut.

Pitcher (Team–Years)	AB	Hits	Avg.
*Rube Waddell+ (Phi 1905–07, StL 1908–10)	76	27	.355
Dixie Walker (Was 1909–12)	32	15	.469
*Ed Walsh (Chi 1905–16)	123	42	.341
Jack Warhop (NY 1908–15)	110	49	.445
Carl Weilman+ (StL 1912–20)	97	23	.237
Doc White+ (Chi 1905–13)	139	48	.345
Lefty Williams+ (Chi 1916–20)	59	15	.254
Hal Wiltse+ (Bos 1926–28, StL 1928)	26	13	.500
Ernie Wingard+ (StL 1924–27)	37	18	.486
George Winter (Bos 1905–08)	28	14	.500
Joe Wood (Bos 1908–15, Cle 1917–20)	70	30	.429
John Wyckoff (Phi 1913–16, Bos 1916–18)	38	13	.342
*Cy Young (Bos 1907, Cle 1909–11)	97	33	.340
Tom Zachary+ (Phi 1918, Was 1919–25, 1927–28, StL 1926–27, NY 1928)	111	37	.333
Paul Zahniser (Was 1923–24, Bos 1925–26)	24	7	.292

+ Left–handed pitcher

* Hall of Famer

For these reasons this once-popular offensive maneuver is virtually obsolete. This particular record of Ty's is as safe as his .367 lifetime batting average.

After five straight seasons as a top contender, the Tigers dropped to sixth place in 1912. Despite the team's fall in competitiveness, a growing population base and a new ballpark helped Frank Navin once again turn a nice profit. Ty, whose contract ran out out at the end of 1912, thought he was entitled to a larger share of the purse. When Navin rejected his demand for a three-year deal at $15,000 a season, Ty stubbornly held out through the following April. Because of organized baseball's unique reserve clause, Cobb was legally bound to play for the Tigers—or no one. Displaying his usual tenacity, he vowed to enter the business world rather than accept a lower figure. Navin and his star attraction finally came to terms on a one-year deal for $14,000 (which included a face-saving $2,000 bonus), but only after Ty's old Georgia friend, U. S. Senator Hoke Smith, made noises about launching an investigation into whether baseball violated federal antitrust laws. "He threw more curves in money negotiations than a whole tribe of Arabs," Navin later said. "He would hold out until hell froze over or until he got what he demanded."

Ty hit a major-league best .390 in 1913 as the Tigers once again finished sixth, then watched with satisfaction as a heretofore closed market suddenly offered baseball's rank and file fresh opportunities to improve their financial lot. The reason was the formation of the Federal League, which remains the only serious challenge to the established major leagues since the turn of the last century. The Feds started 1914 with franchises in eight cities, many in direct competition with major-league teams. Before the league went belly-up after three seasons, its owners had succeeded in signing 172 players from American and National League rosters and driving up the game's salary structure.

Navin was so afraid of losing the game's number-one gate attraction to the Federal League that he had Cobb's telegrams intercepted in an attempt to keep abreast of any developments. Although the Peach received overtures from Chicago manufacturer James Gilmore and oil magnate Harry Sinclair, two of the new circuit's wealthiest backers, he never seriously considered jumping. Instead he used the threat to leverage a $15,000 contract for the 1914 season from Navin. The following year he signed a three-year pact for $20,000 per annum.

Twenty thousand dollars was a tremendous amount of money, and thus a point of considerable pride to Cobb, whose obsession with being the best included being the best paid. In early 1914, Henry Ford shocked the world by introducing the Five Dollar Day for his unskilled workforce. As unbelievable as that figure seemed to the tens of thousands of laborers hurrying to Detroit, it was but a fraction of the $130 or so baseball's highest paid performer made every time he played a two-hour game of baseball.

The Peach was worth every penny. He was the unquestioned king of the diamond, the master of the unexpected, though the audacity and cunning that made him so great can be difficult to convey today. One of the biggest regrets of modern sports historians is the lack of game-action film footage and radio play-by-play recordings from this period of "small ball" that Cobb so dominated. Still, contemporary news accounts and the memories of those he played with and against provide a sense of the mayhem Cobb regularly generated on the field.

Following the 1916 season, Cobb became the first professional athlete to star in a commercial motion picture. He played a small-town bank clerk in *Somewhere in Georgia* and Elsie MacLeod played his girlfriend.

Ty didn't take up cigarettes until late in his career, believing they cut down his wind. But he saw nothing wrong with chewing tobacco, snuff, and cigars, all of which he used freely during his playing days.

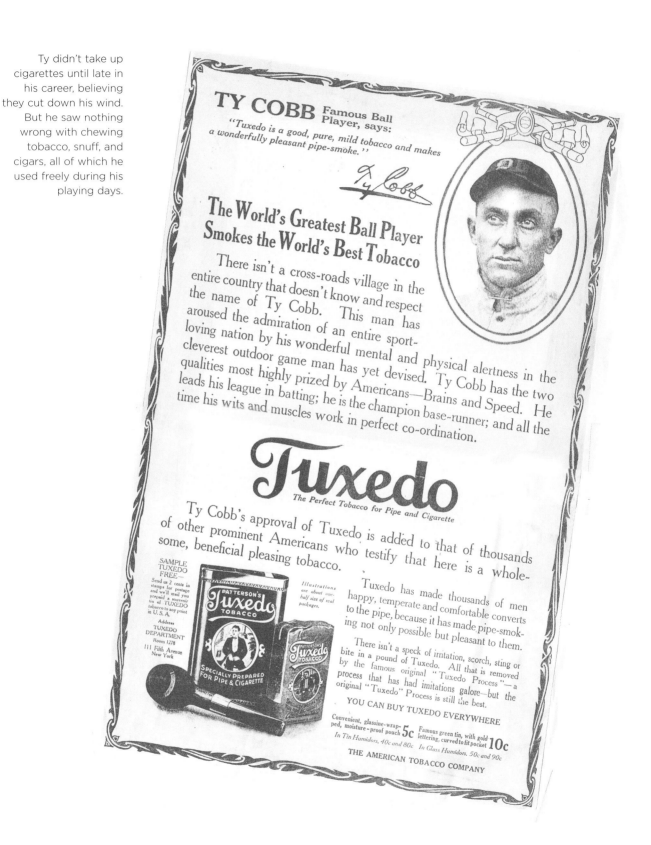

"A lot of times Cobb would be on third base and I'd draw a base on balls," said Sam Crawford, speaking into the microphone of Larry Ritter's tape recorder one day in 1964, "and as I started to go down to first I'd sort of half glance at Cobb, at third. He'd make a slight move that told me he wanted me to keep going—not to stop at first, but to keep on going to second. Well, I'd trot two-thirds of the way to first and then suddenly, without warning, I'd speed up and go across first as fast as I could and tear out for second. He's on third, see. They're watching him, and suddenly there I go, and they don't know what the devil to do.

"If they try to stop me, Cobb'll take off for home. Sometimes they'd catch him, and sometimes they'd catch me, and sometimes they wouldn't get either of us. But most of the time they were too paralyzed to do anything, and I'd wind up on second on a base on balls. Boy, did that ever create excitement. For the crowd, you know; the fans were always wondering what might happen next."

Branch Rickey, then managing the St. Louis Browns, told of an incident that began innocently enough—then quickly exploded into full-blown mischief that allowed Ty to single-handedly snatch a victory from the Browns. "One day he was on first base against us. The pitcher threw over to first and Cobb got back in time. But as the first baseman lobbed the ball back to the pitcher, Cobb was off in a flash streaking for second. The pitcher hurried his throw and it went into center field. Cobb popped to his feet and headed for third. The throw had him beaten, but the third baseman dropped the ball. Cobb slid for the ball and kicked it into the dugout, then got up and jogged home with the winning run. It was a clear case of interference, but the umpires said it must have been an accident. They could not believe that any player could perform such a stunt on purpose."

⚆⚆

The years from 1911 through 1919 were Cobb's salad days. After years of living in rented apartments and houses, he bought a spacious two-story home at 2425 William Street in Augusta's fashionable Summerville neighborhood. There he and Charlie and their children shared space with several domestic servants and pets. Life was comfortable. In addition to his regular-season salary Ty drew endorsement fees from the manufacturers of such products as underwear, suspenders, chewing gum, Coca-Cola, motor parts, cigarettes, chewing tobacco, and a nickel candy bar that was named after him. He was the most famous and recognizable ballplayer in the country, his name and face appearing on bats, magazine covers, tobacco cards, gum tins, sheet music, paper fans, and a patent medicine called Nuxated Iron, which—if the ad copy was to be believed—rescued baseball's number-one star from his early-season listlessness. It's hard to believe that Ty could be ever so afflicted. Always restless, he spent his off-seasons barnstorming, hunting, golfing, and motoring. He followed the progress of his stock investments and engaged in a wide range of entrepreneurial activities, including car dealerships and real estate.

Like other famous athletes of the time, Ty took a turn on the vaudeville circuit. During the off-season of 1911–12 he signed a $10,000 contract to star alongside actress Sue MacManamy in a touring comedy called *The College Widow*. Cast as gridiron hero Billy Bolton, Ty nearly drowned in flop sweat, but he

"I'm a better actor and ballplayer than you—where do inferiors get off criticizing their superiors?"

—COBB'S RESPONSE TO AN ALABAMA REPORTER WHO PANNED HIS STAGE PERFORMANCE IN *THE COLLEGE WIDOW*

gamely delivered such lines as "Marry me and we'll live happier than any lovebirds" before abruptly quitting halfway through the scheduled three-month run. At the end he was gulping bourbon between acts to help him get through each performance.

Despite his less than satisfying experience as a stage actor, Ty five years later became the first professional athlete to star in a commercial motion picture. It was a forgettable two-reeler called *Somewhere in Georgia*. The film was shot in New York in two weeks—and looked it. The story, written by Grantland Rice, had Ty playing a small-town bank clerk who is signed to a contract by the Detroit Tigers. Homesick for his girlfriend (played by actress Elsie MacLeod), Ty returns to Georgia, where he is kidnapped by villains. Not to fear. Ty escapes, commandeers a mule wagon, and arrives at the park just in time to win the game. Much to the relief of Detroit fans and noted critic Ward Morehouse, who called the production "absolutely the worst movie I ever saw," the Peach didn't quit his day job.

In an era where debt was still abhorred and frugality was widely admired, Ty displayed a miserliness that became the stuff of legend. "Two stories have been told and retold of his lack of generosity," said sportswriter Edgar Hayes, who grew up near the Detroit ballpark in the 1910s.

> The head groundskeeper, who was named Neal Conway, thought all baseball revolved around Cobb. Neal saw that his clothes were pressed, his shoes were shined, and everything else that could be done was done. One year, the day after the season ended, Neal was invited to meet Cobb in a downtown office building to accept a small token of Cobb's appreciation. The ballplayer presented his admirer with an oblong box that was just about the size of a wrist watch. After bidding a tear-filled farewell to Cobb, who was on his way to Georgia, Neal hastily opened his gift—and found a tube of Colgate toothpaste!
>
> On another occasion, Cobb was invited to Malcolm Bingay's wedding. Bingay was about to become the editor of the *Detroit News*. On returning from his honeymoon, Bingay took the gift—a cigar stand—to Traub's, the leading Detroit jeweler. When informed that the gift came with a purchase of White Owl cigars, Bingay said, "Throw it in the alley." Mr. Traub replied haughtily, "Not in our alley."

Ty didn't care what anybody thought about his hoarding and the long line of waiters, porters, and cab drivers he left grumbling in his wake. The nickels and dimes he saved piled up. By the time he was 30 he was bragging to friends that

Tris Speaker was a gambler, outdoorsman, Southerner, and consistently spectacular performer. Small wonder that he and Cobb were good friends. Speaker, who broke in with the Red Sox in 1907, snapped Ty's string of batting titles at nine in 1916, the year he was traded to Cleveland. An outstanding center fielder who hit—and prevented—more doubles than anybody else in history, Speaker had the misfortune to play during Cobb's era. "Good as I was," he once admitted, "I never was close to Cobb, and neither was Babe Ruth or anybody else." Nonetheless, Speaker was good enough to join Ty in the Hall of Fame's inaugural class of inductees.

The famous Detroit outfield of 1915: Bobby Veach (left), Cobb, and Sam Crawford. The trio dominated the league's batting lists that summer, capturing the top three positions in base hits, RBIs, and total bases. The RBI title was the first of three in four years for Detroit's "other" outfielder, Veach, who for a dozen productive summers labored in the shadow of Cobb, Crawford, and later, Harry Heilmann. A lifetime .310 hitter, the colorless left fielder from Kentucky also at various times led the junior circuit in doubles, triples, and base hits.

he was worth $200,000—nearly enough to buy some big-league franchises of the day. Within a few short years his assets would total well over $1 million. So much for Professor Cobb's worry that his son would amount to nothing better than a muscle-worker.

As Cobb's wealth grew, so did the size of his family. In addition to Ty Jr. and Shirley, he and Charlie had three more children. Herschel was born in 1916, followed by Beverly in 1918 and Jimmy in 1921. Ty admittedly lacked patience with people of all ages—the modern term "zero tolerance" leaps to mind—but his affection for children was the same as his father's: genuine, if often awkward. He frequently brought his frustrations home with him. He had a short fuse and could be bitingly sarcastic. As the children grew, his high and often unrealistic expectations for them created tension within the household. His youngest child, Jimmy, always insisted that although his dad was a strict disciplinarian, he never physically mistreated them. Others who knew the family disagreed.

Cobb's relationship with children has taken its own beating, with one author maintaining that only a couple of photographs of him with children exist. Actually, there are many, not all of them posed. Some images survive only in the memories of old men who knew him as more than the one-dimensional devil of popular lore.

"This man had the most compacted muscles in his thighs and legs than any human I have ever seen. When I placed my hand on his thigh it felt like a ham of a hog. He was just that firm. His legs should have been attached to a man of 250 pounds instead of 187 pounds. No wonder he is the base runner he is."

—ASSISTANT TRAINER ELY GREEN AFTER GIVING COBB
     A RUBDOWN IN 1917

"I know people say Cobb was mean and rotten on the baseball field and off," said Jim Cullen, whose family lived in an apartment building on Woodward Avenue in Detroit, close to where Ty and Charlie rented during the season. "But he was always great with us. He would play with all the little kids whenever he was in town." When he was about 25, Ty joined the Masonic Order, the ancient society that his father had belonged to. He regularly visited Masonic temples in American League cities and participated in the Shriners' many charitable activities for handicapped children.

William McBrearty, another Detroit boy of the period, wasn't handicapped, not even particularly star-struck. But he did have a handsome Irish setter named Jesse, which attracted Cobb's attention one spring day in 1913 as McBrearty walked the dog a few blocks from Navin Field. Ty, a dog lover who honestly believed that his four-legged friends had souls, stopped his car and asked the 12-year-old boy how much he wanted for him. "Of course," McBrearty recalled many years later, "I wouldn't sell that dog for anything."

The compromise was for Ty to drive the youngster and his dog to the ballpark, where Jesse entertained Tigers players by running down fungoes in the outfield. For a while it became a routine, every Saturday being picked up and dropped off by the Peach. "It was just a very pleasant experience with this fearsome guy who loved dogs," said McBrearty, who grew up to be an attorney. "I realize he wasn't exactly the fourth person of the Blessed Trinity, but he did right by me. He couldn't have been all bad."

Jasper Miner, the sweet-tempered grandson of famed Canadian naturalist Jack Miner, remembered Ty as "a man's man" who took an interest in earnest youths. Today the Miners still operate a bird sanctuary in Ontario, Canada, across the river from Detroit. The grounds include a ball field named after Cobb and a couple of dusty display cases of photos and memorabilia dedicated to him. Starting in 1917 and continuing for nearly a decade, Ty and his family often

> **"I have observed that baseball is not unlike a war, and when you come right down to it, we batters are the heavy artillery."**
>
> —TY COBB

visited the Miner sanctuary, with Ty Jr. often spending summers there. Knowing Jack Miner, a man he often went on moose hunting expeditions with, "was one of the finest things that happened to me," said Cobb.

As regular hosts to Ty's family, and as frequent guests of Ty at Navin Field, the Miners were witnesses to more than one Cobb outburst. But like others who spent much time with Ty away from the diamond, the Miners considered his radical mood swings one of those unfortunate prices of friendship and moved on from there. Jasper was impressed enough with the Peach to try his hand as a catcher. Ty, knowing Jasper had a snowball's chance in Arizona of making a living playing pro ball, nonetheless arranged a tryout for him with the Philadelphia Athletics. "You don't hear at all about the good things that Ty did," said Miner. "As far as this family goes, he'd give you the shirt off his back."

Unfortunately for the Peach's reputation, thoughtful interactions like these have been crowded out of public memory by the infinitely more rousing tales of confrontations and bloodlettings. One of his most dramatic encounters—especially as Cobb liked to tell it—came on the heels of the Lucker incident. One August day in 1912, as Ty and his wife were driving to catch a train in Detroit, three men jumped on the running board of their car. Although their identities were never established, Cobb came to believe they were thugs hired by Tammany Hall to avenge the Lucker beating. A stronger theory is they were friends of a newsstand worker nicknamed "Scabby," whose vendetta against Cobb stemmed from a recent incident in which he had been thrown out of the clubhouse for shooting craps with some players. In a follow-up altercation, Ty then punched out the newsie on a downtown street. A more prosaic conjecture is that the assailants were just three inebriated lowlifes who happened to pick the wrong fellow to try to rob.

Whoever they were, one knife-wielding attacker was able to slash Ty's back before Cobb finally fought them off with the .32-caliber automatic pistol he often carried. Leaving a terrorized Charlie behind, Ty then chased one of the men down an alley. He caught up with his assailant and then, flush with anger, pistol-whipped him until his face resembled hamburger. As an old man Cobb liked to brag that he may have killed the man, though no evidence to support that boast has ever been found in the appropriate police files or coroner reports. In fact, one diligent researcher, Doug Roberts, has argued persuasively that the alley chase and pistol whipping never even happened. According to Roberts, the attack was real enough, but the men fled unharmed. Also, the wound young Ty suffered was far less serious than the life-threatening one a much older Cobb described in bull sessions with friends. He was healthy enough to make his scheduled train trip to Syracuse, New York, where he had his wound cauterized and bandaged by a local doctor before collecting two hits in an exhibition game. While in Syracuse he talked of the assault for the first time, making no mention to a reporter of pursuing and beating one of his attackers. For whatever reason Ty later felt the need to embroider the incident, which, like most involving Cobb, was extraordinary enough without jazzing up the facts.

A couple of years later, in June of 1914, the same Luger pistol figured prominently in another row. This time the affair revolved around twenty cents' worth of spoiled fish that a Detroit merchant supposedly sold Ty's wife. Coming home with Washington manager Clark Griffith after a Saturday game with the Senators, Ty was told of an argument Charlie Cobb had had with William L. Carpenter, the owner of a local butcher shop. Carpenter asserted that Mrs. Cobb was mistaken, that the three pieces of perch he had delivered earlier in the day to the Cobbs' rented home on Longfellow Avenue had been fresh.

More unsavory than the fish in question was Cobb's reaction. Ty phoned the merchant and, convinced that he had insulted his wife, marched out the door, revolver in hand. As crimson-faced Charlie stayed home with several dinner guests, Ty drove to the Progressive Meat Market at 1526 Hamilton Boulevard and forced Carpenter at gunpoint to phone Charlie and apologize.

"Cobb acted like a maniac," the shaken Carpenter told the press. "He certainly should be restrained until he learns to control himself. When I said no one had insulted his wife, he demanded who had talked with her. I said I had. He leveled the revolver straight at me and walked around behind the counter. He was glaring like one insane. In self defense, I grabbed my cleaver. I did not raise it from the block, though, for it came to me in an instant that if I aggravated him further he would shoot me. He backed me all around the store at the point of that revolver until, to pacify him, I called up Mrs. Cobb. And we had precisely the same conversation as we had had during the afternoon. She said she wouldn't argue, and I said I didn't care for their account. Then Cobb thanked me for my 'apology.'" All the while Ty carried on a wordfest with Carpenter's 20-year-old brother-in-law, Harold Harding, who finally got Cobb's goat by calling him a coward. As the papers later reported, the ensuing "fist mill was interrupted by two policemen, who, with great reluctance, called the patrol wagon" and delivered Ty to the Bethune Avenue station.

At the station, Ty nursed a fractured thumb and declared his reputation ruined. "I'll be joshed out of Detroit and sent to the Federal League," he moaned. Instead he spent the night in jail, was found guilty of disturbing the peace, and paid a $50 fine. The injured thumb limited him to just 97 games in 1914, but he still hit .368 to once again lead all major-league batters.

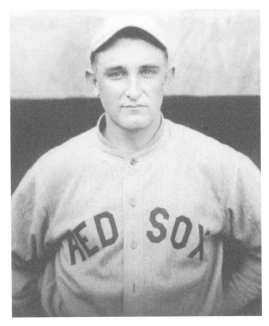

A thorn in Ty's side — or, more accurately, a fastball in the ribs — was Carl Mays. The surly, submarining right-hander pitched on six pennant winners with the Red Sox and Yankees between 1915 and 1923 but is best known as the man who killed Ray Chapman with a pitched ball. Mays hated Cobb. The feeling was mutual.

Such shameful episodes added to Ty's reputation as a social miscreant and placed additional strains on his marriage. Charlie shunned public life, but her husband's periodic run-ins aimed the spotlight indirectly on her and the children. Soon Charlie and the kids were living most of the year at their Augusta home, where the results of Ty's propensity for violence and embarrassing confrontations could be mitigated by distance.

American Leaguers weren't as fortunate. By 1915 the Tigers had been rebuilt into a contender, and for the next two summers they battled the Boston Red Sox for the pennant. "Battle" was indeed the operative word, as Detroit-Boston contests typically featured slurs, beanballs, locomotive-style slides, and all the other weapons of intimidation available to hard-nosed competitors hungry for a post-season check. The Red Sox, world champions in 1912, were just setting out on a run that would produce three more titles in the next four years. Boasting the greatest defensive outfield of all time in Harry Hooper, Duffy Lewis, and Tris Speaker, the Sox also featured one of the era's best mound staffs in Ernie Shore, "Smokey Joe" Wood, Babe Ruth, Hubert "Dutch" Leonard, and Carl Mays. Although everybody on the staff regularly aimed a few pitches each game at Ty's noggin, it was Mays—a surly, submarining right-hander most famous for throwing the pitch that killed Cleveland shortstop Ray Chapman—whom Ty most detested on the Boston club.

Matters came to a head in the opener of a four-game series in Boston on September 16, 1915. Mays threw at Cobb each time he came to the plate. Finally, in the eighth inning, Ty responded by firing his bat at Mays and calling him a "yellow dog." Ty stepped back into the batter's box after order was restored—and was hit on the wrist with Mays' next pitch. As Cobb took first base the Fenway Park faithful showered him with pop bottles.

The Tigers retired the Red Sox in the ninth to preserve a 6-1 victory, the final out coming on a fly ball to Cobb. Immediately, thousands of angry, frustrated fans carpeted the field. They surrounded Ty, who coolly walked in from center field as curses, paper wads, and bottles filled the air. "None of the mongrels in the crowd had the nerve to attack him," marveled Eddie Batchelor, "each waiting for somebody else to strike the first blow." Cobb's remarkable show of courage, however, couldn't prevent Boston from taking the next three games and the pennant.

Hughie Jennings later labeled 1915 his biggest disappointment. The Tigers, propelled by 20-game winners George "Hooks" Dauss and Harry Coveleski and outfielders Sam Crawford and Bobby Veach (who tied each other for the league lead with 112 RBIs), became the first team to win 100 games but not the pennant. Ty, his competitive instincts kicked into overdrive by a pennant race and the pursuit of personal glory, was more brilliant than ever. He scored 144 runs, won his ninth straight batting title with a .369 mark (breaking Honus Wagner's record of eight), and set a single-season base-stealing mark of 96. Cobb, who typically stole second base for the team and third for himself, departed from tradition and played every game of the schedule, seeking to rack up as many steals as possible. "I've always regretted I didn't make it a hundred steals that year," he later reflected. "With a little greater effort, I believe I could've gotten those four additional bases." As it was, the record—which seemed invincible—wound up standing for nearly a half-century.

In 1916 the Tigers again made a serious bid for the pennant, and again they

A bat-throwing altercation with Carl Mays produced this remarkable scene at Fenway Park on September 16, 1915. After catching a fly ball for the last out of the game, Cobb slowly walked in from center field, through a crowd of several thousand infuriated Red Sox fans. They pelted him with bottles and paper wads and hurled insults and curses—and wisely kept their distance.

In 1918, Ty exchanged his flannels for khaki. As was the case with many gung-ho Americans, Cobb was shipped to France too late to participate in the fighting. This was a shame, said Hughie Jennings, who considered him "the most fearless man I have ever known. He was afraid of nothing." Jennings always thought it was the North's good fortune that Cobb hadn't been born 40 years earlier. "He would've been a whole Confederate army," he said.

fell just short, finishing in third place, four games behind Boston. To top off his disappointment, Ty saw his string of batting titles snapped at nine. Tris Speaker, who had been dealt from Boston to Cleveland before the season, bested Cobb's .371 average with a .383 effort. Ty's stolen base total dropped to 68, but he easily outdistanced runner-up Armando Marsans of St. Louis, a refugee from the Federal League.

The following April the United States finally entered the war that had been draining Europe of its young men for nearly three years. As if to warm up for the real thing, Ty got involved in one of his most widely publicized frays. That spring the Tigers trained in Waxahachie, Texas. On March 31, 1917, the club traveled to Dallas to open a series of exhibitions with the New York Giants, managed by the feisty John McGraw. Ty, who had played 18 holes of golf that morning, arrived just before game time. This earned him an earful from the Giants' Art Fletcher and Charles "Buck" Herzog, who shouted that the Detroit star was a "showoff" and a "swellhead."

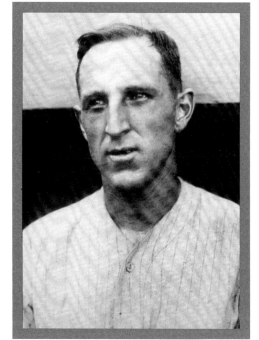

Buck Herzog was involved in one of Cobb's most vicious altercations during spring training in 1917.

Ty singled his first time up and yelled to second base-man Herzog that he was coming down on the next pitch. The throw had him easily, but Cobb was more concerned about delivering a message. His spikes sliced Herzog's trousers and drew blood. As the two thrashed about in the dirt, Fletcher ran over from his shortstop position to get in his licks. Within seconds, Giants, Tigers, and park policemen were knotted around second base, but order was quickly restored. Ty was ejected from the game, a decision that brought a storm of protest from the 5,500 fans who had come to see a favorite son of the South.

Both teams were staying at the Oriental Hotel. That evening, Herzog interrupted Ty's dinner and challenged him to finish their business in one hour inside Ty's room. This was enough time for Cobb to clear away the rugs and furniture and to sprinkle the floor with water. Herzog, who boxed some in the army, arrived at the appointed time wearing tennis shoes. Several players from both teams jammed the fourth-floor hallway to get a better view of the show, but only the Giants' Heinie Zimmerman and Detroit's Oscar Stanage, serving as seconds, were allowed into the room. Detroit trainer Harry Tuthill refereed the match, which according to everyone present was won by Cobb. As he had planned, the slippery floor negated Herzog's superior boxing skills. Ty, who was wearing leather street shoes for a better grip, had his opponent stretched backward over the bed and was hammering him with blow after blow when Tuthill finally declared the affair finished.

But it wasn't. McGraw, enraged when he discovered the condition of his badly mauled infielder, accosted Cobb the following morning in the lobby. As a crowd of stunned hotel guests looked on, McGraw "became so vituperative that I had to restrain myself from repeating the performance of Room 404," said Ty. The two men nearly came to blows. "If you were a younger man," Ty told McGraw before walking away, "I'd kill you."

"Anyone who calls me a slacker is dead wrong. That I am going in as a captain will be criticized ... but none can say that I will be protected from danger more than the humblest private in the trenches."

—TY COBB UPON ENTERING THE ARMY IN 1918

Ignoring the pleas of local chambers of commerce and the taunts of the New York team, Ty then refused to take the field for the rest of the Tigers-Giants tour. Instead he traveled to Cincinnati, where he continued his conditioning with the Reds. The Giants and Tigers finally parted company in Kansas City, where McGraw and Company dashed off a telegram to Cobb: "It's safe to rejoin your club now. We've left."

"That was the one way the Giants could have the last word," Cobb retorted in his autobiography. "By mail."

The Peach reclaimed the batting championship in 1917, hitting a resounding .383, which was 30 points higher than anyone else in the majors. He also easily outdistanced everybody in hits, doubles, triples, total bases, and slugging percentage. He added his sixth, and final, stolen-base crown with 55 thefts, though his days as a dominant base-stealing threat were just about at an end. To use an automotive metaphor, at 30 his wheels simply had too many miles on them. "The shock when he hits the dirt is terrific, especially in mid-season when the ground is hard," observed Vic Tomlinson, the physical director of the Detroit Athletic Club. "Anyone who wants to get an idea of the bump that a man sliding to a base receives can easily do so by running at top speed and then jumping with all his might flat on the ground." After averaging 61 stolen bases during his first dozen full seasons, Ty would slip to 34 steals in 1918, then average but 15 steals a season for the final decade of his career.

Cobb's last two batting titles bracketed an abbreviated military career. As hundreds of thousands of Yanks went "over there" during 1918, the provost marshal of the armed forces issued a "work or fight" order for all men of draft age. Baseball players were classified as nonessential to the war effort, and the regular season ended a month earlier than usual. Ty batted .382 in the curtailed 1918 campaign (once again outdistancing his closest competitor by 30 points), then joined the scores of current and former professional ballplayers serving in the military in France.

Given his combative personality, Ty and the military seemed a perfect fit. Hughie Jennings considered him the most fearless man he had ever known, the kind of warrior who would have personally impaled the Kaiser on a *picklehauser* if he'd gotten to Europe in time to do some real fighting. As it was, Ty arrived overseas as a captain in the Chemical Warfare Service less than three weeks before the armistice ended the shooting.

"Gas and flame" service was hazardous duty. After receiving just a week of instruction at a base near Claumont, France, Cobb and his fellow CWS officers—including former pitching great Christy Mathewson—were expected to train enlisted men in the proper use of their gas masks. During one training exercise, poison gas was inadvertently released into a chamber before he and Mathewson, the officers in charge, had given the signal that it was safe to do so. Panic broke out in the room. By the time the chamber door was finally yanked opened, several men had inhaled a lethal dosage. "When it was over there were sixteen bodies stretched out on the ground," Ty recalled. "Eight men died within hours of lung damage ... others were crippled." Ty was mildly sick for a week and then recovered, but the accident was widely blamed for the tuberculosis that killed Mathewson seven years later.

The botched training exercise was not the only eventful experience of Ty's three-month hitch. A few days later he survived another near-miss. He was leaving an outdoor latrine when a German shell exploded nearby, sending metal fragments whizzing through the air. A sliver skimmed his head, just missing an eye. Musing over his close call, Ty couldn't decide what would have been worse: the tragedy of being half-blinded by a Boche shell, or the ignominy of getting killed while leaving the crapper.

His martial duties done, Captain Cobb caught the first troop ship home from France and arrived in New York on December 16, 1918. On the cusp of turning 32, he told reporters on the dock that he was tired of baseball and wished "to quit while I'm still good."

Instead he held out almost all of spring training in a dispute with Frank Navin, who saluted his returning doughboys by trying to force pay cuts on them. Cobb refused, finally signed his sixth straight $20,000 contract, then went on to notch the last of his dozen batting titles with a .384 average. Also making 1919 a memorable year for Cobb were a postgame confrontation at Navin Field, where one afternoon he kicked a mouthy fan in the groin and then faced down several of the victim's pals, and the insatiable demand for American cotton, which allowed Ty to sell his futures for a whopping $155,000 profit.

The most momentous event of the 1919 season took place that fall in Chicago, where gamblers and eight disgruntled players conspired to throw the World Series to Cincinnati. Ty, who prided himself on always having inside information, be it baseball or stocks, strongly suspected the games weren't being played on the square. But word of the "Black Sox scandal" wouldn't surface until the following year. For now baseball fans couldn't stop talking about the game's newest sensation, a converted pitcher who had just set a new season's home run mark with 29. George Herman "Babe" Ruth, the *New York Times* declared, had "supplanted the great Ty Cobb as baseball's greatest attraction." Although followers of thinking-man's baseball disagreed, their protests were already being drowned out by the din of shouting headlines and the jazzed-up pace of American life.

CHAPTER SIX

Damn Yankee

How dear to my heart was the old-fashioned batter
Who scattered line drives from the spring to the fall.
He did not resemble the up-to-date batter
Who swings from his heels and then misses the ball.
The up-to-date batter I'm not very strong for;
He shatters the ozone with all of his might.
And that is the reason I hanker and long for
Those who doubled to left, and tripled to right.

The old-fashioned batter,
The eagle-eyed batter,
The thinking-man's batter,
Who tripled to right.

GEORGE E. PHAIR

Despite the Tigers' unexciting prospects in 1920, Ty went into the new season confident of adding another batting title to the dozen he already owned. There was no change in his routine, even as the club dropped its first 13 games en route to a seventh-place finish. As he had for each at-bat throughout his career, Ty would approach the plate, tap each foot with his bat, then yank the peak of his cap low over his forehead. His eyes, thus shielded, would dart around the field until he had determined the opponent's defense and settled on a strategy. The shortstop shading toward second base? Perhaps he would punch the ball through the hole between third and short. The right fielder playing too far off the line? Maybe he should try to pull the pitch. A tough lefty on the mound? Okay, maybe a drag bunt was in order…. "I'd say he was the greatest all-around batter," Ted Lyons, Chicago's ace pitcher of the 1920s, would tell an interviewer years later. "He could hit the ball anywhere he wanted to, and he'd hit it wherever you pitched it." Tris Speaker, himself a career .345 hitter, also marveled at how Cobb handled a

Opposite: Cobb and Ruth, circa 1924. "We are alike in only one way," said Cobb. "We're both hard losers."

Babe Ruth surrounded by admirers in 1922. "God, we liked that big son of a bitch," said one teammate. "He was a constant source of joy."

Louisville Slugger as if it were a wand. "There's no doubt in my mind that Ty is the best all-around hitter who ever lived. He can bunt, chop-hit, deliver long drives, or put balls out of sight."

What Ty didn't fully appreciate as his mind whirred and clicked and processed information was that his cerebral style of place-hitting was endangered. The "old-fashioned batter," that favorite of Grantland Rice, Ring Lardner, George E. Phair, and other press-box poets, would soon be shoved out of the spotlight and into the orchestra pit by a muscular stagehand named George Herman Ruth.

The phenomenon who came to be known as Babe Ruth was one of those unforeseen marriages of man, moment, and media with which modern American cultural history is rife. Ruth, the son of a Baltimore saloonkeeper, was born in 1895 and consigned to an orphanage when he was seven. An incorrigible schoolboy and a natural athlete, he moved from the playground to the International League's Baltimore Orioles, who in turn sold the talented pitcher to the Boston Red Sox in 1914. According to teammate Harry Hooper, Ruth by 1916 was "already the best lefty in the league." A batter's reputation meant nothing to him, Hooper added. "He was probably too dumb to know the difference. But he was one of the few men who could throw a fastball past Cobb with any regularity." In a 1917 game against Detroit, Ruth fanned Bobby Veach, Sam Crawford, and Cobb in the ninth inning to preserve a 1–0 shutout—a moment Babe would long rate as his greatest thrill in baseball.

But forget the glittering pitching stats: 23 wins and a league-low 1.75 ERA in 1915, 24 wins in 1916, and a record 29²/₃ consecutive scoreless innings in World Series play. It was Ruth's bashing—home run titles in 1918 and 1919 while still taking a regular turn on the mound—that turned heads and caused Yankees owner Jacob Ruppert to write the cash-strapped Red Sox a check in excess of $100,000 for Ruth's services before the 1920 season.

Aiding Babe and all hitters were significant rule changes. Prior to 1920, in the so-called dead-ball era, a ball was kept in play until it practically disintegrated in a pitcher's hand. By the middle innings it was a dark, lopsided sphere with the resiliency of squash, making power hitting next to impossible. Now a fresh ball was introduced into play several times a game, handing batters an unprecedented advantage. In addition, trick pitches such as the spitter and emery ball were outlawed starting in 1920 (although a grandfather clause allowed a few veteran pitchers to continue throwing them). Adding to the mayhem were the new smaller parks being built. Their inviting fences tempted even longtime choke hitters to pull and uppercut the ball. The ball soared, and so did attendance. The infusion of power in the 1920s opened the door for one-dimensional players— "professional hitters" like Dale "Moose" Alexander—who ordinarily never would have been allowed to don a big-league uniform. It was all too much for old-school types like Ring Lardner:

> A couple of yrs. ago a ball player named Baby Ruth that was a pitcher by birth was made into an outfielder on acct. of how he could bust them and he begins breaking records for long distance hits and etc. and he becomes a big drawing card and the master minds that controls baseball says to themselves that if it is home runs that the public wants to see, why leave us give them home runs, so they fixed up a ball that if you don't miss it entirely it will clear the fence, and the result is that ball players which use to specialize in hump back liners to the pitcher is now amongst our leading sluggers when by rights they couldn't take a ball in their hands and knock it past the base umpire.

Even without Ruth the changes eventually would have killed the place-hitting and base-stealing game Cobb had dominated for so long. But Ruth's remarkable performance his first summer in New York accelerated the pace of change. In 1920 he slugged a staggering 54 home runs (including 10 against Detroit), more than any other *team* hit. Each seemed to soar farther than the last. Moreover, he hit .376 (fourth in the league) and broke existing records for runs scored, walks,

"Cobb couldn't understand why anybody who had a good enough physique to be in the major leagues couldn't do approximately the things he did. He found that some of the fellows who could hit, field, and run the bases almost as well as he could didn't have the 'will to win' nor the interest in the game which made him great."

—DETROIT SPORTSWRITER EDDIE BATCHELOR

and RBIs. His .847 slugging percentage would remain the single-season standard for the next eight decades. That August, as the dreary and punchless Tigers fought to stay out of the basement, Ruth checked into Navin Field and poled three long home runs in two days, prompting the record number of Tigers fans to go wild. Detroiters gave the new superman of baseball "the welcome due a conquering hero," observed Harry Salsinger. "He got the applause, the shrieking adoration of the multitude, in Cobb's own city. Cobb, standing aside, could feel deeply how fickle the adoration of the sport-loving public is. He saw before him a new king acclaimed."

King, indeed. Helped substantially by modern myth-making machinery—mass-circulation magazines, radio, movies, sophisticated national advertising, countless daily newspapers—Ruth became one of the beneficiaries of postwar America's fascination with the cult of personality. He joined Valentino, Grange, Dempsey, and Lindbergh as heroes whose fame fed on itself. In this league of media superstars, the Babe rose to the top. His breathtaking metamorphosis into the country's foremost cultural icon flabbergasted even those who knew him well.

"You know, I saw it all happen, from beginning to end," Harry Hooper recalled years later. "But sometimes I still can't believe what I saw: this 19-year-old kid, crude, poorly educated, only slightly brushed by the social veneer we call civilization, gradually transformed into the idol of American youth and the symbol of baseball the world over—a man loved by more people and with an intensity of feeling that perhaps has never been equaled before or since. I saw a man transformed from a human being into something pretty close to a god. If somebody had predicted that back on the Boston Red Sox in 1914, he would have been thrown into a lunatic asylum."

Ruth more than personified the shift from skill to power in the national pastime. His storied hedonism embodied the entire Roaring Twenties, a decade he and his fellow free-swinging Yankees were to dominate. There was that one April

This gag shot of two Tigers at spring training in San Antonio in 1921, Ty's first as manager, could serve as a metaphor for the lack of communication between the players and their demanding boss.

evening in 1924 when a teammate wandered into Rose Hicks' brothel in Philadelphia to find Babe, a girl on each knee, having his hair shampooed with a bottle of champagne. "Anybody who doesn't like this life," roared Babe, "is crazy!" Later in the decade Ruth kicked off a pennant-clinching victory celebration by ordering a piano and a boatload of premium booze up to his Detroit hotel room. "Anyone who doesn't want to fuck," he announced to the assembled merrymakers, "better leave now!" Millions of Americans vicariously joined the Babe in his spree. Disillusioned by the "war to end all wars" and only spurred on by Prohibition, they rejected longstanding standards of social behavior in favor of dancing the Charleston, getting "blotto" on a hip flask of bathtub gin, and taking a joyride into the countryside—ideally in an automobile with removable seat cushions. Women, that forgotten half of Victorian society, were especially shocking as they joined in the revolt. They bobbed their hair, shortened their skirts, jammed cigarettes into their painted mouths, and in 1920 even voted for the first time. The pace of change was breathtaking, the once quiet air choked with the sounds of progress. Radios spit out jazz, silent movies turned into "talkies," jackhammers heralded the coming of the latest skyscraper, airplanes roared overhead, and each month hundreds of thousands of honking Chevys, Dodges, and Ford "flivvers" poured off assembly lines and onto the country's already overwhelmed streets. The cultural quick-step of the Twenties took in the national pastime, whose signature dead-ball image—a blurry newspaper photo of Ty Cobb, gritted teeth and all, jamming his spikes into a bag—was replaced by the enduring newsreel footage of a spindly legged, moon-faced man-child taking mincing steps around the bases as another of his wallops landed a Pullman's jump from the plate.

If there was an upside
to missing out on
another World Series,
it was that Ty could
get a jump on his
annual postseason
hunting expedition.
This time Tris Speaker
(far right) joined him.

"You might have fellows today hitting more home runs than Babe Ruth," one veteran player of the Twenties reflected a half-century later, "but you still don't have Babe Ruth. To me it was remarkable what a drawing card that man was. The fans—grown-ups as well as kids—would ache just to touch him." Added a sportswriter from the period: "If you weren't around in those times, I don't think you could appreciate what a figure the Babe was. He was bigger than the President." As for Cobb, he remained, in the words of Grantland Rice, "an extremely peculiar soul, brooding and bubbling with violence, devious, suspicious and combative all the way."

The reminiscences of Bill Kennedy, a young scorecard seller at Cleveland's Dunn Field in the 1920s, capture the essence of the two superstars' disparate public images. "When the Tigers played the Indians we scorecard sellers would see Ty Cobb coming into the park around noon or so," said Kennedy.

Cobb was always indifferent to us, striding by us as though we weren't there. But Babe Ruth? We loved him. The proudest day of my life was when he gave me a pat on the back. A thrill supreme! And he would always say, "Hello, kid." He called everybody "kid." He had a deep, wonderful, masculine voice, a la Wallace Beery, who could have played the Bambino in a movie.

Anyway, the Babe always would go directly to Lefty Weisman, the Indians' trainer, for a rubdown before the game. While waiting for the scorecards to be printed one day, I opened the door to the locker room. There was the Babe, lying flat on his back on the massage table, his giant body completely naked. And Lefty slapping his hands, smacking them against the Babe with some kind of bottled lotion.

There were about 12 or 13 reporters, all with notebooks. They were asking the usual routine questions—but only half-heartedly. They were staring at another Ruthian achievement—his giant penis! Erect!

I, too, was nonplussed. It reminded me of a tennis match, with reporters' heads turning with the gyrations of Lefty's skilled hands, resulting in the Babe's Tower of Pisa leaning in north and south directions. All the time the Babe was roaring with laughter at the embarrassment of the fourth estate. He just didn't give a damn! He was like a giant infant.

Cobb initially paid little attention to Ruth, stating that he and most others in baseball "figured he'd eat and fuck himself right out" of the American League. Much later, the Peach analyzed his rival's development as a slugger. He came to the conclusion that starting off his career as a pitcher had aided Ruth immensely. "He could experiment at the plate," Ty explained. "He didn't have to get a piece of the ball. He didn't have to protect the plate the way a regular batter was expected to. No one cares much if a pitcher strikes out or looks bad at bat, so Ruth could take that big swing. If he missed, it didn't matter. And when he didn't miss, the ball went a long way. As time went on, he learned more and more about how to control that big swing and put the wood on the ball. By the time he became a fulltime outfielder, he was ready."

All of Ruth's infantile charm and superhuman ability could not put the Yankees in the World Series in 1920. Instead the Cleveland Indians, overcoming the accidental death of shortstop Ray Chapman in August, grabbed the pennant and beat Brooklyn in the Series. For Ty, it was a bittersweet win. He was happy for Cleveland manager Tris Speaker, but envious of his old friend's participation in one more fall classic.

That opportunity seemed more distant than ever to Ty, who was now nearly 34. Hobbled by a knee injury, he wound up hitting a mere .334 in 1920, his weakest performance since 1906. More discouraging were the Tigers' prospects for a turnaround. The pitching staff was thin and the middle infield played as if in a

"I've seen him at midnight, propped up in bed, order six club sandwiches, a platter of pigs' knuckles and a pitcher of beer. He'd down all that while smoking a big black cigar. Next day, if he hit a homer, he'd trot around the bases complaining about gas pains and a bellyache."

—TY COBB, DISCUSSING BABE RUTH'S LEGENDARY APPETITE

trance. Ty, financially set, made some noises about retiring. Then in November, while he was duck hunting and barnstorming in California, he received word that Hughie Jennings had been fired. After 14 years, the club would have a new manager. Frank Navin called Cobb. Would the Peach be interested in the job?

Ty said no. Throughout his career he had stated time and again that the headaches of managing held no appeal for him. And Jennings, who at the end was a burned-out alcoholic, was a fresh warning of what could happen to even the best of them.

But trusted friends and members of the press wore Ty down. Walter Briggs and John Kelsey, old buddies from early days at the Pontchartrain Hotel who had recently bought quarter-shares of the team, wanted Cobb. And sportswriter Eddie Batchelor warned Ty that if he didn't take the job, he might find himself playing for an alternate candidate, Clarence "Pants" Rowland. Ty considered the former Chicago White Sox skipper an incompetent fraud. Mulling over Navin's offer, Ty finally met with the Detroit owner on December 18 at the Hotel Vanderbilt in New York. It was Ty's 34th birthday, but it was Navin who emerged from the four-hour meeting with the biggest present: a new manager.

Ty was hardly celebrating. A huge pay raise to $35,000 made him the best-paid player in the game, but he always regretted his decision. "Rowland or no Rowland," he later said, "I wish now I'd never stuck my neck in the noose that the Tiger management represented."

No rope was present as Cobb officially took over the club in a civic lovefest on February 1, 1921. The decision was extremely popular in Detroit. Many assumed Ty's brilliance as a player would naturally translate into success as a manager. Fans, players, and reporters would soon find out differently.

Ty's managerial debut was a soggy 6–5 win over Chicago at Navin Field on April 14, 1921. From there the pitching-poor Tigers went into a tailspin that landed them in sixth place at season's end. The low point for Ty came June 13 at the Polo Grounds, when the versatile Ruth returned temporarily to the mound. He pitched five innings to get credit for an 11–8 Yankees victory, hit two home

runs—including a monstrous 460-foot drive to right center field—and struck out Cobb. While the Tigers floundered near the bottom of the standings, Ruth led the Yankees to their first pennant with another astonishing year: a .378 average, 59 home runs, 177 runs, 171 RBIs. Only the efforts of Harry Heilmann, who hit .394, and Cobb, who hit .389, kept Ruth from capturing the Triple Crown.

Heilmann's unexpected batting title illustrated Cobb's chief managerial quality. "In all modesty," Ty later admitted, "I could teach hitting." The first edition of the "Cobbmen" hit a blistering .316, still the American League record. Heilmann, a slow-footed first baseman who had hit a composite .282 in his first six big-league seasons, blossomed under Cobb's tutelage. Ty tinkered with Heilmann's stance and swing, moved him to right field permanently, then watched him emerge as the most feared right-handed hitter in the junior circuit. "Ol' Slug" would go on to win three more batting championships, in 1923 (.403), 1925 (.393), and 1927 (.398).

Ty always had all sorts of dogs around the house—hunting, show, and domestic. "You will find qualities in a dog that you can't find in a human," he insisted. "No man ever had a friend as honest or faithful as a dog."

Ty and family posed for this portrait in March of 1923. From left: Shirley, Ty, Jimmy, Ty Jr., Charlie, Beverly, and Herschel.

"You should have seen other teams' before a game … They'd circle around to cross his path, to give him the 'How are you, Ty? How's the Peach?' Oh, how they sucked around! The idea was to keep him friendly and in no mood to go on one of his wild sprees and beat the hell out of you."

—LU BLUE, TIGERS FIRST BASEMAN OF THE 1920S

Ty used psychology to motivate some players. Looking to impel Bobby Veach to greater heights, he instructed Heilmann to start insulting the easygoing left fielder from the on-deck circle. The manufactured feud worked, up to a point. Looking to show up his tormentor, Veach had career highs in home runs and RBIs in 1921. However, at the end of the season, Cobb returned to Georgia without explaining the strategy to Veach, as he had promised Heilmann. When Heilmann tried to apologize, Veach waved him away. "Don't come sucking around me with that phony line," he said. The two outfielders remained on the outs until Veach left the team three years later.

A more appreciative pupil was Fred Haney, a hustling infielder whom Ty reluctantly left behind in spring training in 1921. Cobb worked as mightily on the young man's confidence as he did his stroke. He encouraged Haney, who was no bigger than a plug of tobacco, to continue to work hard in the minors and to use his small size to his advantage by crouching at the plate. Haney came north with the Tigers in 1922 and surprised everyone, except Cobb, by batting .352.

For the rest of his life the feisty Haney generally had nothing but good things to say about his mentor. Haney was a case study in what Cobb was looking for in a player. Ty felt a professional owed it to his owner, his manager, his fans, and his teammates—but most of all, to himself—to constantly strive for perfection. You may fall short, Ty would instruct, but it shouldn't be for lack of effort. Cobb had few complaints, even with a utility player with minimal ability, as long as he hustled, hollered, and otherwise gave the game his all every moment he was on the field. But if a player's effort was lacking or his work habits were sloppy, he could be unduly harsh in his criticism. Players came to resent Cobb's tirades, which after several frustrating seasons often degenerated into biting sarcasm.

Eddie Forester, who lived three blocks from Navin Field, worked in the Tigers' organization for 53 years. He started off as a bat boy in 1919, then took care of Cobb's locker when he was manager. He remembered the Peach as "one of the crabbiest people I've ever met," a mentor to some, a tormentor to most.

He'd call all those players all kinds of names—and not nice names, either. He was tough. "I'm the manager, you do what I tell you," he used to say. "I send you up there to bunt, you bunt." He was always mad. He was the meanest man I ever met. He'd swear all through the place, and some of the players told him, "We play ball for you, but we don't have to take this stuff." He'd just walk away and wouldn't pay much attention to them. When he said he wanted you to do something, you'd do it. "It's a baseball game," he'd say, "and you play to win."

Cobb would say, "Cut the inside of the base," and he'd go out there and show them. He'd get a tape measure and show them where they were way out of line. He'd run the bases himself and then show them. I never saw any other manager do that.

"He was good," concluded Forester, "but he had his faults."

Cobb's approach to the game was considered outdated, even then. He complained that players who were supposed to be fighting each other tooth-and-nail on the diamond had had their competitive drive dulled by indiscipline and off-field fraternization, which had become a real problem in the wide-open 1920s. For nowhere was the exaggerated motion of the decade more pronounced than in Detroit, a boom town whose growing pains were exacerbated by Prohibition. The Motor City, described by one national publication as "soused and serene," had an estimated 25,000 speakeasies doing their best to quench the public's thirst. An unknown number of amateur and professional bootleggers found it a simple matter to smuggle Canadian booze across the mile-wide Detroit River.

The Detroit clubhouse had its share of rounders, whose escapades tried Ty's patience. Heilmann was a regular man-about-town, as were promising outfielder Heinie Manush and star pitcher George "Hooks" Dauss. Once a drunken Heilmann drove his Austin roadster down the steps of a basement speakeasy and up to its bar, whereupon he casually ordered a drink. On another occasion, following a long night of drinking rotgut, Heilmann legged out a triple, then vomited all over the bag. Ty, unmoved by Ol' Slug's misery, left him in the game. In fact, having a hung-over player take his medicine under the hot summer sun was a favorite disciplinarian tactic. When Dauss reported red-faced for a 1924 start in New York, Ty sent him to the mound anyway. Dauss was pounded for seven runs before he was yanked.

Aside from Ty's old-school ways, there also was the problem of the material he had to work with. "Some of the young men that he expects to manipulate subtleties are better equipped for the use of the broad-axe than the rapier," observed a writer close to the team. "Instead of comparing a player's brains with the average, Ty insists upon comparing them with his own. Naturally the player suffers in the comparison, since there are few so fast and original in their baseball thinking as the Georgia phenomenon."

Cobb, like his predecessor, Hughie Jennings, was an early believer in platooning his players—usually with mixed results. With pitchers he almost made a mockery of the practice. Long before baseball had heard of middle relievers, set-up men, and stoppers, before pitchers were routinely yanked after facing one batter, Cobb often used four or five hurlers a game. He thought nothing of calling

time and trudging in from the outfield to offer pitching advice. "Golly, he wore a path from center field to the pitcher's mound," recalled one Tigers infielder. During each of Ty's first four seasons at the helm, the Detroit staff had the most relief appearances and fewest complete games in the league. The Peach even took a turn on the mound himself. On the final afternoon of the 1925 season he tossed an inning of perfect relief against the Browns and decades later was officially credited with a save.

"The way he treated pitchers was awful," said Al Schacht, a Washington pitcher who moved to the Senators' coaching box in 1922. "I remember one day Howard Ehmke was pitching for the Tigers. He was getting hit, and Cobb called time to go to the mound and talk to him. Well, Cobb stood there on the mound showing Ehmke up in front of the whole ballpark. I mean Cobb was holding the ball demonstrating the grip, the stride, the release, and everything else. Imagine that! Talk about ruining a pitcher's confidence! I don't think Ehmke ever was the same after that."

One day in New York, Eddie Wells, a young southpaw in a slump, found himself alone in the clubhouse with Cobb.

"Ty," he said, "I'm having a tough time."

"I know it," said Cobb.

"What in the name of sense do you think my trouble is?" asked Wells. "I can't seem to figure out what's wrong."

"Ed," replied Cobb, "that's something I know nothing about—pitching."

"And that was the truth," added Wells years later.

This lack of expertise helped cost pitching-poor Detroit the future Hall of Famer Carl Hubbell, whose screwball failed to impress Ty in a pair of spring training camps. Upon Cobb's advice, the slim left-hander was assigned to Detroit's farm club in Toronto. "The best thing that ever happened to me was when that son of a bitch released me," Hubbell, who went on to stardom with the New York Giants, said later. Hubbell's memory was flawed. It was Frank Navin who finally sold Hubbell to the Giants in 1928, after the club had exhausted its options on him. By that time Cobb had been out of the Detroit organization for two years.

Ty had promised to quit managing if he couldn't better the Tigers' seventh-place finish of 1920. The '21 squad moved up only one notch in the standings in Cobb's first year at the helm, but he was encouraged enough by what he saw to come back for more. In 1922 the Tigers improved all the way to third, the wrecking crew hitting a composite .305. Leading the way was Cobb, whose .401 mark was aided by a controversial scoring decision. During a midsummer game in New York, Ty's grounder was misplayed by shortstop Everett Scott. The official scorer, Fred Lieb, scored it an error. The Associated Press scored it a hit. No one cared until the final averages showed Ty batting .399. American League president Ban Johnson, with a vested interest in promoting his circuit's marquee player, retroactively overruled the official scorer and gave Ty an unprecedented third .400 season, a gift that still kept him runner-up to George Sisler's .420.

The following season the Tigers finished a distant second with an 83–71 record. The Yankees, playing in their new stadium in the Bronx, won a third straight pennant and their first World Series. Once again the headlines screamed Ruth's name. In 1923 the free-swinging Falstaff rang up his usual power numbers and, just to prove he could hit for average, stroked the ball at a .393 clip. Only Heilmann's .403 was better. "The Ruth is mighty," wrote Heywood Broun, "and shall prevail." The following year Babe won the batting title. Watching his undisciplined rival trespass on what had once been his exclusive domain galled Cobb, for whom Ruth had become flypaper for all that was wrong with the modern game. That Babe's ceaseless wenching and drinking was being rewarded with universal public adoration was almost more than his Spartan counterpart could stand.

One of the great ironies of the Cobb-Ruth rivalry is that despite Ty's reputation as a villain, Ruth had as many run-ins with authority. During his career he punched umpires, bullied managers and teammates, regularly reported for spring training out of shape, charged into the stands after hecklers, and was named in several paternity suits. He was suspended four times in 1922 alone and five more times in 1925, the year he had to cough up a record $5,000 fine. But while the world frowned at Cobb's indiscretions, it winked at Babe's indulgences.

Cobb's bench jockeying grew more vicious as Ruth's popularity grew. One of his favorite tactics was to call Ruth "nigger," a dig at his broad nose and dark complexion. (Actually, for years players around the league had referred to Ruth by the nickname "Nig," a corruption of Cobb's insult.) A typical exchange between

"When the Detroit Tigers came to town we hated them. Ty Cobb was a dirty word in New York."

—PAUL GALLICO, *NEW YORK DAILY NEWS* SPORTSWRITER
IN THE 1920S

the two rivals occurred in early 1923, with Ruth coming off a second straight miserable World Series performance against the Giants the previous fall.

"We hear that little Johnny Rawlings ran you out of the Giant clubhouse," Ty said. "Is that true?"

"It ain't a goddamned bit true," Ruth retorted, "and you sons of bitches can go fuck yourselves."

For all his bravado, Babe was more lover than fighter. All things considered, he would much rather expend his mental energy mapping out a swell time at his favorite brothel, the House of the Good Shepherd in St. Louis, than debate his contemptuous rival. In the final analysis it was pennants that counted, and in this Ruth and the Yankees had the last laugh. During Cobb's six seasons as manager, New York won four pennants, Detroit none.

The Tigers' best chance came in 1924. That year Detroit beat the Yankees in 13 of 22 meetings, including a final-week sweep that kept the Bombers from a fourth straight pennant. The most memorable contest between the two occurred June 13 at Navin Field, when their festering feud exploded into full fury.

That afternoon the first-place Yankees took a 10–6 lead into the ninth. As usual, the air had been turned blue with profanity and taunts. In the top of the inning, the Tigers' Bert Cole first fired a fastball at Ruth's head and then drilled Bob Meusel in the back with a pitch—both presumably on Cobb's orders. Meusel flung his bat at Cole and then charged the mound. Both benches emptied, and according to one report Cobb and Ruth plowed into each other like a pair of runaway trains at home plate. Before they could settle their differences once and for all, about a thousand spectators joined in the melee, including several Neanderthals who tore seats loose from the concrete floor and tossed them onto the field. When order still hadn't been restored after a half-hour of fighting, umpire Billy Evans forfeited the game to New York.

The fired-up Tigers stayed in the race until the end, ultimately finishing third, six games behind Washington. This despite a season-ending leg injury to first baseman Lu Blue in August and Heilmann's summer-long bout with sinusitis. Ty, smelling a pennant, ignored his own aches and pains and played the full schedule of 155 games. He piled up 211 hits and 23 stolen bases (including three steals of home), admirably robust numbers for a 37-year-old man.

"I knew Cobb was a pretty tough hombre during his stormy career," a St. Louis physician who examined Ty told Fred Lieb. "But, when I saw him stripped, my admiration for him increased manyfold. His legs from his feet to his hips were a mass of scars and bruises, new ones and old—souvenirs of years of play. In some

This studio portrait of Ty dates from about 1920.

places, there was a new scar over an old one. I decided then and there that Ty Cobb could take it as well as dish it out."

What Ty couldn't take was Frank Navin's perceived indifference to winning. He bemoaned to the end of his days how the penurious owner's refusal to shell out $5,500 to buy Johnny Neun from Minneapolis as a replacement for the injured Blue had cost Detroit the 1924 flag. As it was, Navin, who had added an upper-deck grandstand to push his park's capacity to forty thousand, seemed pleased enough with how the year had gone. His team had won 86 games, its most since 1916, and the excitement of the pennant race, coupled with the park's increased size, had allowed the Tigers to join the Yankees as the only teams in the league to draw a million fans at home. And on the road, the heavy-hitting Detroiters—who led the circuit in batting and runs—remained the league's top-drawing attraction, outside of the Yankees.

Ty figured to improve on the near miss of 1924. Instead the "Tygers" (as newspapers had inevitably dubbed them) sank into fourth place in 1925, despite batting a collective .302 and averaging a league-high six runs per game. Ty was drained, both physically and mentally, by the twin demands of playing and managing. The dual responsibilities meant he took each loss twice as hard. At night he lost sleep replaying that afternoon's game, second-guessing the moves he had made and agonizing over the ones he hadn't.

The manager of the "Tygers" exchanges idle talk with actress Hope Hawthorn in 1925.

Dissension was rampant, with players regularly grousing behind closed doors to Navin. They had cause to complain, for Ty had grown increasingly bitter, sarcastic, and thin-skinned. "Nobody liked him as a manager," said second baseman Charlie Gehringer, who signed with Detroit in the fall of 1923. "He was such a great player himself, he figured that if he told you something, there was no reason why you couldn't do it as well as he did. But a lot of guys don't have that ability. He couldn't understand that."

Gehringer's quiet nature exasperated Cobb, who expected incessant chatter from his infielders. Nonetheless, Ty spent considerable time with the future Hall of Famer on train rides and inside hotel lobbies. "He even made me use his own bat, which was kind of a thin little thing," said Gehringer. "I said, 'Gee, I'd like a little more batting space,' but I didn't dare use another one. He would've shipped me to Siberia." Or the Tigers' farm-team equivalent, Oklahoma City.

Bill Moore, a big right-handed pitcher with control problems, had a confrontation with Cobb in 1925 that he always felt cost him a big-league career. One day in spring training the nervous rookie was erratically pitching batting practice to the regulars when Ty suddenly grabbed a bat and jumped into the box. After Moore delivered two across the plate, Cobb asked, "What would you do now with a couple of strikes?" Intentionally or not, the next pitch sent him sprawling into the dirt.

Navin Field in 1924. A high-octane offense made Cobb's "Tygers" the top draw in baseball, outside of the Yankees.

"Cobb got up spluttering, 'You son of a bitch!'" Moore recalled. "All sorts of words. I turned around to get another ball and I could just feel the hair rising on the back of my neck. I got so mad, I took the ball and threw it over the grandstand and yelled, 'Stick the ball up your ass!'"

Moore stormed into the clubhouse. Despite the dust-up, he made the trip north in April. Considering Detroit's weak staff, Moore figured to get plenty of opportunities to prove himself. On the second day of the season, during a lopsided loss to Chicago, Ty sent Moore to the mound. "Go in there and try to throw strikes," he instructed. Instead Moore walked the first three men he faced and pitched a ball to the fourth before he was yanked.

"Cobb didn't even come out to the mound," he said. "He just hollered for me to get out of there." Moore was immediately dispatched to the Tigers' farm club in Rochester, New York. He languished in the Detroit system for several years, finally quitting during the Depression to become a policeman in his native Corning, New York. He always blamed Cobb's capricious, vindictive nature as much as his inability to throw strikes for his truncated major-league career. "From that day I told Cobb to stick that ball up his ass," he said, "I think I was cooked."

Ty never really cared what Moore or anybody else in the dugout thought of him. "The great trouble with baseball today," he complained, "is that most of the players are in the game for the money that's in it—not for the love of it, the excitement of it, and the thrill of it. Times seem to have changed since I broke in more than a generation ago."

Although the team was going nowhere, Ty could still rise to the occasion. Of course, the ever-scientific Peach knew when to pick his spots—such as May 4, 1925, when he brashly announced to Harry Salsinger and Sid Keener of the *St. Louis Star* that he was going to try for home runs for the first time.

Even allowing for the short right-field fence at Sportsman's Park and a strong wind blowing out from the plate, as well as for the more lively "cushioned cork center" ball introduced that season, the results were astonishing. In six at-bats Cobb collected two singles, a double, and three home runs, as the Tigers swamped the Browns, 14–8. All three round-trippers were pulled to right, the last one clearing the bleachers and landing on Grand Avenue. The 16 total bases set a big-league record while the three homers tied a mark shared by four others. Scanning that evening's sports pages, Cobb must have been pleased to learn none of them was named Babe Ruth.

The following afternoon Ty continued his apple-slapping ways by cracking out a single and two more home runs, giving him nine straight hits and five home runs in two days. Satisfied he had made his point, Ty returned to "nipping" at the ball, finishing the 1925 season with a .378 average and 102 RBIs in 121 games.

Cobb's time in uniform coincided with a dramatic change in the ethnic makeup of Detroit, Chicago, Cleveland, and other big cities in the North. The "Great Migration" of blacks from the South, which began during the war as industrialists looked for unskilled labor to man their factories, continued unabated after peace came. Nowhere was the percentage of increase greater than in Detroit, where the black population grew sevenfold between 1910 and 1920, from less than 6,000 to more than 41,000. Most of these single young men from Mississippi, Alabama, Georgia, Louisiana, and the Carolinas were recruited by agents of Henry Ford. The city's biggest employer, a social thinker by inclination, put them to work at the massive Rouge complex and did his best to improve their lot in what was undeniably still a racially polarized society generations after emancipation. During the 1920s tens of thousands of additional blacks flocked to the Motor City, so that by the end of the decade some 120,000 were squeezed into the dilapidated east-side ghetto known as Black Bottom.

The Negro Leagues, a symbol of growing black pride and entrepreneurship, flourished in these years before the Great Depression. Their number included the Detroit Stars, whose lineup during the '20s featured such players as center fielder Norman "Turkey" Stearnes, destined for the Hall of Fame, and catcher-manager Bruce "Buddy" Petway, who many feel deserves his own plaque at Cooperstown.

Baseball's color bar denied some of the finest ballplayers the game has ever known their opportunity for fame and fatter paychecks. However, the races did commingle in hundreds of exhibition matches over the years, including a three-game set between the Tigers and the Chicago American Giants at the end of the 1922 season. "Of course," observed one black weekly, "old Ty Cobb of Georgia won't show up." The paper knew its man, for Cobb had played in only one series against blacks during his entire career. That was in 1910 in Cuba, a favorite off-season destination for barnstorming major leaguers, when he arrived midway through the Tigers' series against a pair of all-star teams featuring black and Cuban players.

The Peach batted .371 in five games, but he had his pride stung when he was thrown out attempting to steal by Bruce Petway and was struck out by the mighty Cuban fastball pitcher Jose Mendez. Cobb swore never to take the same field with men of color again, and he remained as good as his word. Deference, not chumminess, was what kept the social order to his liking, and his run-ins with blacks even as manager underscored that thinking. One May afternoon in 1924, for example, he grew impatient with a black man using a pay phone under the stands at Philadelphia's Shibe Park. "You'd think this was the only phone in the park the way you hang around," the man angrily told Cobb after hanging up. The next day's headlines spelled out what happened next: **COBB IN FIST FIGHT AT PARK Twice Knocks Down Negro Patron; Spectators Absolve Tyrus.**

The Ku Klux Klan enjoyed a huge revival during this period, partly thanks to D. W. Griffith's 1915 film *The Birth of a Nation*, arguably the most racist movie ever made and certainly one of the most inflammatory. Assuming that Cobb, who was a big movie buff, saw this silent film about the Civil War and the defeated South, he undoubtedly left the theatre with his feelings about the perils of "racial pollution" and the nobility of the Lost Cause reinforced by Griffith's cinematic stereotypes. Superheated controversy over the film incited deadly racial violence across the country, especially in urban areas, where growing numbers of blacks competed for jobs and housing with native whites and European immigrants. The Klan's ranks swelled in the South, with huge rallies held outside Atlanta and at other locations throughout the former Confederacy. In Detroit during the early 1920s, the KKK recruited several thousand members (including many policemen), burned a cross on the steps of city hall, and just narrowly missed placing a Klan-

The Cobb home in Augusta, pictured in 1924.

backed candidate in the mayor's office. It was whispered that major-league stars Tris Speaker, Rogers Hornsby, and Gabby Street belonged to the Klan; several players admitted as much to New York sportswriter Fred Lieb. Given Ty's prejudice and love of intrigue and ritual, Lieb suspected the Tiger star may very well have been a member for a time, either in Detroit or Georgia, though it seems improbable that Cobb would have been foolish enough to slip his famous face inside a pillowcase at a rally. Certainly no evidence exists that Cobb ever belonged to the Klan, just speculation fueled by his demonstrated hostility.

As in so many other aspects of his life, Cobb was self-contradictory when it came to matters of race. He was capable of befriending individual blacks. One was a homeless youngster nicknamed "Li'l Rastus," whose real name was Ulysses Harrison. Halfway through the 1908 season, some Detroit players discovered Harrison trying to find shelter inside Bennett Park. When the slumping Tigers then unreeled a long winning streak, the superstitious Cobb kept him around as a good-luck charm, lodging him in the clubhouse and sneaking him aboard trains and into whites-only hotels during road trips. Harry Salsinger observed that Ty was the "Ethiopian's main defender and patron." Cobb took Harrison home to

Cobb with Alex Rivers,
his personal "batman"
of many years.

> "He expected everybody to strive and play the way he did. That just wasn't possible. His players could not do the things that he did. Nobody could. He got tired of it after 1926 and didn't pursue managing any more."
>
> —DETROIT CATCHER RAY HAYWORTH

Augusta after the 1909 season, promoting him from mascot to domestic servant. Harrison returned to Detroit early the following year, to be replaced by a young black man, Alex Rivers, who Ty approached during an exhibition game in New Orleans. Cobb asked if he'd like to come north with the club. Rivers didn't like cold weather, but he wound up being Ty's personal "batman" and assistant for as long as Ty played in Detroit. Among his varied duties was keeping on top of all of his and Cobb's superstitions, including massaging good luck into bats and banning peanuts from the dugout. "If a cross-eyed man or woman dared look at Mr. Cobb on Monday, he would have dead bad luck all week," he explained. Rivers married and raised four children in the Black Bottom neighborhood, including a son he named after his benefactor.

Curiously, many black players, acclimated to the world of prejudice they had lived in since birth, were able to take a step back and objectively assess Cobb simply in performance terms. Blacks were not barred from major-league parks, so the Peach was as much a box-office attraction to Negro Leaguers on their off days as he was to white fans. While Ty certainly was not alone in his refusal to play against blacks, he stood out as "the only white ballplayer that we observed who played somewhat like we played on the American Giants," said Dave Malarcher, who played with and managed a generation of black stars. "None of the teams in the major leagues in those years ... really concentrated their attack against the opposition. The batters come up and they swing away and okay, it's ... a home run. But as often they fail." Daring base running was always a feature of black baseball, even as it languished in the big leagues in the 1920s. But as Negro League great Walter "Buck" Leonard admitted, "We never did have a Ty Cobb."

On August 29, 1925, Ty was feted by thirty thousand fans at Navin Field in ceremonies marking his 20th anniversary as a Tiger. He contributed a couple of hits in a 9–5 win over Philadelphia, then changed into formal attire for that evening's banquet at the Book Cadillac Hotel. Among the gifts were a $1,000 grandfather clock and a check from the ball club for $10,000. Frank Navin was all smiles when he presented the check. But Ty had to hold back from decking his

August 29, 1925: Cobb shakes hands with some young admirers at Navin Field in ceremonies marking his 20 years in baseball.

boss. Unbeknownst to the six hundred guests inside the banquet hall, Navin's magnificent "gift" was in reality the balance of Ty's $50,000 salary. During contract negotiations before the season, Ty had agreed to a lump-sum payment in order to hide the fact that he was making as much as the president of the American League. Navin's "phony act," Ty said many years later, had soured one of the finest evenings of his life.

Although Navin was making a handsome profit off his one-dimensional but still competitive team, the overly cautious and close-fisted owner regularly refused to buy the players Cobb recommended. "No one understands what a sincere manager suffers when he lacks just a few of the tools necessary to make a strong contender a champion," Ty moaned. That winter Navin said no to a $45,000 purchase of San Francisco Seals outfielder Paul Waner, "who single-handed could have brought us two and maybe three pennants," Cobb argued in retirement. Waner, a future Hall of Famer, thus joined infielder George Grantham, pitchers Jim Bagby and Flint Rhem, and a host of other promising minor leaguers and available veterans that slipped through Ty's fingers. "It got so I couldn't stand to look at Navin," said Cobb. Nonetheless, he returned in 1926 for a sixth season as manager.

Exactly why isn't clear. He certainly didn't need the money and he didn't welcome the aggravation. And he had to be realistic about the Tigers' pennant chances. One guess is that he looked forward to finishing the development of young players like Heinie Manush and Charlie Gehringer. Even that small pleasure was muddled by a severe case of "proud flesh," an eye condition that required surgery and caused him to wear smoked glasses at the start of the season. He took them off in time to see Babe Ruth smite what may have been the longest home run ever—a clout off Hooks Dauss on June 8, 1926, that soared beyond Navin Field's right-field wall and traveled an estimated 626 feet before coming to rest on Brooklyn Avenue, two blocks away.

About this time Ty's vantage point shifted from the outfield to the bench. He installed Manush in center field, and the 25-year-old Alabaman responded with a .378 average. Much of the credit went to Cobb, who worked to level his swing. Ty whistled from the dugout whenever he noticed Manush holding the bat below his waist, an arm position that caused him to uppercut the ball. "He ran things like a dictator," Manush would later say of Cobb. "But as a teacher he was the best." Manush was one of the few bright spots in the Tigers' sixth-place season. Although the Yankees finished on top of the standings, Manush did his whistling mentor proud by going 6-for-9 in a season-ending doubleheader to edge Ruth for the batting title. It was the third time in Cobb's six seasons as manager that a Tiger batting champion had prevented Ruth from capturing batting's Triple Crown, one of the few accomplishments that would elude him during his career.

For the year Ty appeared in only 79 games, 61 as a starter, and most of those before July. He hit .339 in just 233 at-bats, content to watch while the starting outfielders—Manush, Heilmann, and Bob Fothergill—finished first, third, and fourth, respectively, in the batting race. "I'd call that hitting, wouldn't you?" Chicago pitcher Ted Lyons said to Donald Honig a half-century later. "Keeping Cobb on the bench! Fothergill came over to the White Sox a few years later, and he'd love to tell about that. 'Remember the time Cobb couldn't get into the lineup?' he'd say, and he'd laugh and laugh."

It went deeper than that. Throughout the summer Navin Field fans lustily booed Cobb, who spent less and less time on the field. Some cranks, straining for symbolism, even threw rotten peaches. More worrisome to longtime observers was that Ty's familiar all-consuming drive to excel seemed to have faded. As Ty explained to Eddie Batchelor, forcing himself to make that extra effort had indeed become more and more of a chore. "You might say that I am slowing up, not so much physically in that my muscles aren't capable of their former performance, or slowing up mentally in that my brain hasn't the same command over my muscles, but slowing up in my desire to force myself to the utmost to attain success that I already have achieved."

Cobb understood that it was human nature to try harder to reach the peak than to stay there. He had not only climbed to the top of his profession, he had stayed there for the better part of two decades. Now, having grown round, bald, and jowly, emptied of challenges and weary of the daily grind, he was ready to step down from the mountaintop and rest.

Or so he thought.

CHAPTER SEVEN

Finale in Philadelphia

He may have his faults, but dishonesty is not one of them.

CHARLIE COBB, 1927

☙❧

The Yankees lost the World Series to the St. Louis Cardinals in 1926, the final out of the decisive seventh game coming when Babe Ruth attempted to steal second base with two outs in the bottom of the ninth. That it was a one-run game at the time, with slugging Bob Meusel at the plate, made no difference to Ruth, whose reckless dash dominated post-Series talk. But a string of sensational developments soon shoved the Bambino's bonehead play to the back burner of the hot stove league.

On November 3, 1926, Ty Cobb told the world he was retiring from baseball. The Peach's numbers over 22 summers with Detroit were unimpeachable: 3,902 hits in 2,805 games for a .369 average, 2,087 runs scored and another 1,828 batted in, 865 stolen bases, and a dozen batting championships. All were major-league records.

His record as a manager, however, was open to criticism. Eddie Batchelor later told fellow sportswriter Fred Lieb that Ty "lacked the patience to make allowances for men who didn't think as fast as he did, nor had his mechanical ability to play ball. Like so many great performers, he was impatient with stupidity, lack of ambition, and lack of what he considered normal baseball ability. The result was that he proved to be a poor teacher and that he never could get his team imbued with real team spirit."

Cobb would always defend his mediocre bench record of 479 wins and 444 losses over six seasons, a .519 winning percentage, arguing that if he was not a managerial success, he just as surely was not a managerial failure. "What we could have done with a couple of pitchers!" he reflected in his autobiography. "If I'd had them, the Yankees would have had to wait a few years to become the terrors of baseball. In every other way but pitching, we spit in their eye and showed them the scientific way to use a bat, a glove, and a ball."

Opposite: After 22 years as a Tiger, the Peach donned the uniform of the Philadelphia Athletics in 1927.

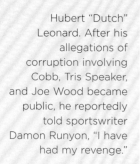

Hubert "Dutch" Leonard. After his allegations of corruption involving Cobb, Tris Speaker, and Joe Wood became public, he reportedly told sportswriter Damon Runyon, "I have had my revenge."

"I could buy myself a major-league franchise right now. Why should I bother with a few hundred dollars gained through a damned fool bet?"

—TY COBB, 1927

Frank Navin said the decision to retire as an active player was entirely Cobb's, although the Detroit owner later admitted he had made up his mind early in the season that 1926 would be Cobb's last as manager. Ty knew that if he didn't step down voluntarily he would be fired. To reporters, he insisted age was responsible for his hanging up the spikes. "I'm tired," he explained. "I can't take any chances any more. It's time to quit. I am going back to Georgia to be with my family."

One month later Tris Speaker announced he, too, was retiring. Whereas Cobb's departure had not been wholly unexpected, Speaker's was a shock. He had just managed Cleveland to a close second-place finish and played 150 games in the outfield. There seemed no plausible reason for Speaker to surrender his $35,000-a-year job.

The public soon learned that a disgruntled ex-Tiger in California was behind the resignations.

Hubert "Dutch" Leonard, often characterized as a slacker and complainer, had nonetheless been an excellent pitcher during his 11-year major-league career with Boston and Detroit. In his six seasons with the Red Sox the left-hander had been an integral member of three world championship teams, pitching two no-hitters and compiling a 1.01 ERA during the 1914 season, still the all-time low. Sold to Detroit in 1919, he became part of Hughie Jennings' rotation but gradually fell into disfavor after Cobb took over as manager. When Leonard couldn't come to terms with Frank Navin on a new contract following the 1921 season, he pitched semipro ball for two years in California. He returned to Detroit in August of 1924, becoming one of the few capable members of the Tigers' mound staff.

By the middle of the 1925 season Leonard had compiled an 11–3 record. That didn't stop Cobb from accusing Leonard, who complained of a sore arm, of being a shirker when it came to facing strong teams. "Don't you dare turn bolshevik on me," Ty yelled at him one day in front of the team. "I'm the boss here." In what turned out to be Leonard's final big-league outing, Cobb kept him on the mound despite Leonard's getting pounded for a dozen runs by Philadelphia. A few days later he put the 33-year-old pitcher on waivers. No team claimed him—a blow to Leonard's pride and pocketbook. Convinced that Cobb and Speaker had conspired to waive him out of the league, Leonard swore revenge.

In the spring of 1926 he contacted Navin and American League president Ban Johnson with allegations that he and Cobb had bet on and conspired to fix a game played between Detroit and Cleveland toward the end of the 1919 season. Also in on the alleged fix were Speaker and Joe Wood, the former Boston pitching great then playing out his career in the Cleveland outfield. According to Leonard, on September 24, 1919, he met with Cobb, Speaker, and Wood under the Navin Field grandstand and agreed that Cleveland, which had just clinched second place, should "slough off" the following afternoon's game to Detroit. The Tigers were fighting for third place and a share of the World Series money that was distributed to the top three finishers. With a Detroit victory more or less in the bag, the conspirators were said to have hired a ballpark employee named Fred West to place a bet totaling $5,500 with local bookmakers. Cobb, Leonard claimed, agreed to put up $2,000, Leonard kicked in $1,500, and Wood and Speaker said they were good for $1,000 each. Because of the size of the bet, however, West could only place $600 by game time. The Tigers, a 10–7 favorite, won the game, giving the alleged bettors a $420 payoff. Wood paid West $30 for his services, then split the balance of the winnings into three equal $130 shares.

To corroborate his story, Leonard produced letters written to him by Wood and Cobb. The correspondence seemed damning:

THE WOOD LETTER

Cleveland, O., Friday

Enclosed please find certified check for sixteen hundred and thirty dollars ($1,630).

Dear Friend "Dutch":
The only bet West could get up was $600 against $420 (10 to 7). Cobb did not get up a cent. He told us that and I believed him. Could have put some at 5 to 2 on Detroit, but did not, as that would make us put up $1,000 to win $400.

We won the $420. I gave West $30, leaving $390, or $130 for each of us. Would not have cashed your check at all, but West thought he could get it up to 10–7, and I was going to put it all up at those odds. We would have won $1,750 for the $2,500 if we could have placed it.

If we ever get another chance like this we will know enough to try to get down early.

Let me hear from you, "Dutch."

With all good wishes to yourself and Mrs. Leonard, I am, always

[signed] Joe Wood

Cobb and Judge Landis in happier days. Although the commissioner ultimately cleared Cobb and Tris Speaker of Leonard's charges, many observers joined Ty in believing Landis had used the case to enhance his own power.

THE COBB LETTER

Augusta, Ga., Oct. 23, '19

Dear Dutch:

Well, old boy, guess you are out in old California by this time and enjoying life.

I arrived home and found Mrs. Cobb only fair, but the baby girl was fine, and at this time Mrs. Cobb is very well, but I have been very busy getting acquainted with my family and have not tried to do any correspondence, hence my delay.

Wood and myself are considerably disappointed in our business proposition, as we had $2,000 to put into it and the other side quoted us $1,400, and when we finally secured that much money it was about two o'clock and they refused to deal with us, as they had men in Chicago to take the matter up with and they had no time, so we completely fell down and of course we felt badly over it.

Everything was open to Wood and he can tell you about it when we get together. It was quite a responsibility and I don't care for it again, I can assure you.

With kindest regards to Mrs. Leonard, I remain, sincerely,

[signed] Ty Cobb

After unsuccessfully shopping around the letters to some newspapers, Leonard brought them to the attention of Frank Navin and Ban Johnson. Aware of their explosive nature, they agreed to buy the letters for $20,000—hush money equal to what the pitcher estimated he had lost in salary since being waived. In September of 1926, after league owners had met in private and voted to turn over the letters to Judge Landis, Johnson presented Cobb and Speaker with the case against them. He urged them to quietly resign at the end of the season to avoid embarrassment. While protesting their innocence, the two reluctantly agreed. But when Landis continued the investigation on his own and rumors of a "scandal" involving two of baseball's greatest stars began leaking to the press, Cobb and Speaker demanded a formal inquiry during whih they and Wood—by then the baseball coach at Yale University—could clear the air and save their reputations.

Four days before Christmas, Landis made the case public. Cobb and Speaker, while acknowledging the letters were authentic, both testified they had done nothing wrong. Both men denied placing a bet or even meeting under the stands, though Cobb conceded he had innocently acted as an "intermediary" between Leonard and Wood and had recommended West as a reliable conduit to local bookies. When Wood faced the judge he swore that only he, Leonard, and a third unidentified person referred to in Wood's letter were in on the wager. Cobb and Speaker had not placed a bet, and the game had been on the square, Wood insisted.

The sensational story was front-page news for weeks, as the public waited for Landis to make a ruling. Meanwhile, Ty and his followers noisily resented the

assault on his integrity. At a rally in Augusta, citizens hung a banner that proclaimed "TY IS STILL OUR IDOL AND THE IDOL OF AMERICA." Umpire Billy Evans called Leonard "gutless," while former Tigers outfielder Del Drake insisted that "Cobb and Speaker were always on the square, working and hustling to beat the band." Ex–White Sox pitcher Dickie Kerr, commenting in Pine Bluff, Arkansas, was "not surprised" at Leonard's charges. "I met Leonard in San Francisco a year ago and he remarked that he would 'get even' with Cobb or 'die in the attempt,'" said Kerr. "He was sore because he was released by Detroit. He declared he had enough 'dope on Cobb to get him' and that he was going to use it." Leonard refused all requests to travel from his California farm to Chicago to directly confront those he accused, citing a concern for his personal safety. They "bumped off people" in Al Capone's Chicago, he explained, and Cobb himself was known to carry a pistol.

Nobody stepped forward to corroborate Leonard's charges. Circumstantially, it was clear that a bet had been placed on the game, though the exact nature of Cobb's involvement will always be debated. Ty was close friends with Speaker, a notorious gambler, so he may have initially gone along with the idea of the

While Judge Landis dawdled, the citizens of Augusta, Georgia, rallied to Ty's defense.

wager against his better judgment, then thought better of it. His subsequent dawdling seems purposeful, and as Wood wrote Leonard, "Cobb did not get up a cent." Thus, Ty presumably did not share in the winnings. The $130 payouts went to Wood, Leonard, and the unidentified third party in Wood's letter, who undoubtedly was Speaker (and whom Wood could truthfully identify under oath as "a friend of mine from Cleveland"). Ty's letter to Leonard indicates that the whole episode had made him uncomfortable.

It was one thing for players to wager on a game in which they participated—an impropriety, to say the least, but a practice that wasn't specifically banned by baseball in 1919—and quite another to have conspired to predetermine its outcome. It defies logic to think that Cobb, already a rich man, would have jeopardized his future earnings and his reputation by fixing a game for the chance to win a few hundred dollars. The Detroit-Cleveland game of September 25, 1919, appears not to have been fixed. The box score indicates that if four players were supposedly tilting its outcome, they were pretty inept. Wood and Leonard didn't even play, while Ty—who theoretically should have been thrown fat pitches to guarantee a Detroit win—had a poor day at the plate, with just one single in five at-bats. Conversely, Speaker—who should have been trying his best to lose—rapped out a single and two triples. Not that such shenanigans were unheard of during that era. It's worth remembering that just a few days after the game in question, eight members of the Chicago White Sox did the unthinkable, throwing the World Series to Cincinnati. Professional baseball was rife with incidents of gambling and game-fixing in the early years of the century, a condition

> ## "I want the world to know I stand with Ty and Tris. I've known them for 15 years. If they had been selling out all these years, I would like to have seen them play when they wasn't selling!"
>
> —HUMORIST WILL ROGERS

that led directly to Judge Landis's appointment as the game's first commissioner. During his first four years at the helm Landis threw 15 corrupt players out organized ball.

While he was deliberating on what the press had labeled "the Cobb-Speaker scandal," a second mud ball exploded in the judge's lap. Swede Risberg and Chick Gandil, two of the "Black Sox" expelled from the game for throwing the 1919 World Series, came forward with accusations that the Tigers had eased up in an important series with Chicago during the 1917 pennant race between the White Sox and Red Sox. In return, several Detroit players were given cash by the Chicago team. Although the charges did not involve Ty directly (Risberg told reporters there was "never a better or straighter baseball player than Cobb"), they added to the foul aroma surrounding his own case.

Scores of witnesses paraded in front of Landis, who left Cobb and Speaker twisting in the wind a while longer as he tackled these new allegations. The gist of the testimony, and the story accepted by the commissioner, was that the Chicago players had indeed collected a cash purse for the Tigers in 1917—but it was for defeating the Red Sox in a crucial series, not for slacking off against the White Sox. Rewarding opponents who had knocked off a team's chief rival with gifts of new suits or shoes or a small pile of bills was a common practice, one that Landis then ordered a halt to.

On January 27, 1927, Landis handed down his decision in the Cobb-Speaker case. Frustrated by Leonard's refusal to testify in person, he acquitted both men. "These players have not been, nor are they now, found guilty of fixing a game," he said. "By no decent system of justice could such a finding be made." Landis declared that Cobb and Speaker were both eligible to play for any team they wished. Within days Speaker signed with Washington.

∽

Although cleared of any wrongdoing, Ty was far from satisfied with the way Landis had handled the sordid affair. The power-hungry judge had maneuvered so as to upstage and embarrass Ban Johnson, who soon afterward resigned as American League president. Cobb later confided that powerful legal friends of his had "*dictated and forced* Landis' decision." He went duck hunting to escape the press and contemplated taking "my pound of flesh" from the game through what promised to be an ugly lawsuit. As Ty stewed in the marshes of South Carolina,

"An old friend in a new suit," as a Detroit newspaper called Cobb, enjoyed a festive homecoming when he returned to the city as a Philadelphia Athletic on May 10, 1927. A luncheon, motorcade, dinner banquet, and a new car were all part of the festivities.

Connie Mack folded his lanky frame inside a Georgia-bound train, hoping to convince one of the game's biggest drawing cards to sign a Philadelphia contract.

The two met in Augusta. Now 66 years old, the grand old man of baseball was putting together what would turn out to be his last great championship team. Ty had always respected Mack's integrity, nobility, and baseball savvy, but he initially resisted Mack's overtures. "I've had enough," he insisted. "I gave all I had and you've seen the way I was treated. If some wise guy fan should mention 'fix' to me from the stands, I'd probably go right up there after him."

"There isn't a fan who isn't for you, Ty," Mack argued. "We have a pennant contender in Philadelphia, and with you in the lineup, I just know we can win it." After mulling over several other offers, Cobb decided to return for a 23rd season, this time wearing the white elephant of the Philadelphia Athletics. Setting more records held no appeal. The chance to play for a championship, as well as the money—a $70,000 salary, a share of the spring training gate receipts, and a $20,000 bonus if the A's won the pennant—were factors. Most important, however, was the matter of vindication.

"I could not and would not leave the game with the slightest cloud over my name," Ty would explain as an old man. "Even if I appeared in only one more major league game—on my own terms—I would have proved for the all-time record and generations of youngsters to come that baseball wanted Ty Cobb to the last."

That they did. Large crowds attended the Athletics' spring training games in Florida, where Ty joined 38-year-old Zack Wheat, an 18-year veteran of the Brooklyn Dodgers, and young Al Simmons in the outfield. Rejuvenated by the prospect of playing on a contending squad, free from managerial worries for the first time in seven years, Ty smiled his way through his first day in an Athletics uniform. On March 7 he posed for countless photographs, chatted amiably with reporters, even gently tossed a ball to Thomas Edison for the benefit of newsreel cameras. That the aging inventor nearly decapitated Cobb with a line drive from a few feet away couldn't spoil the moment.

Besides Mack, Cobb, Wheat, and Simmons, the 1927 Athletics featured four other future Hall of Famers: first baseman Jimmie Foxx, 40-year-old second baseman and coach Eddie Collins, pitching ace Robert "Lefty" Grove, and catcher Mickey Cochrane. "That whole gang were tough losers," Roger "Doc" Cramer once recalled. "You have Grove pitching and Cochrane catching, and you lose 1–0, you're a little timid about going into that clubhouse."

Grove and Cochrane had broken into the majors on the same afternoon in 1925 and quickly earned a reputation as the most volatile battery in baseball. Ty took a particular liking to Cochrane, who as a cocky rookie had one day taunted the legend from behind the plate.

"What are you going to do now, Ty?" asked Cochrane, as Cobb batted with a man on first and a two-strike count on him. Ty replied that he was going to hit-and-run.

"You're crazy," said Cochrane, who called for a pitchout. Before the intentionally wide pitch could settle into his mitt, the old master reached out and slapped it to right field for a base hit. The exhibition impressed the jug-eared, dark-faced catcher, whose own drive and intelligence matched Cobb's. Now that they were teammates, it was perhaps inevitable that the two hard losers would become fast and lifelong friends.

Just as he had in Detroit, Ty freely dispensed batting advice. He taught Cochrane to aim to smack the ball back at the pitcher's head, resulting in more base hits through the middle. He also showed Al Simmons how to move up on the plate against left-handers. Both saw their batting average's jump more than 50 points in 1927. "How many guys do you know who could tell Simmons how to hit?" said Jimmie Dykes, who reached a rapprochement of sorts with Cobb.

Dykes, who came up to Philadelphia as a second baseman in 1918, had harassed Cobb through the years by standing on the middle of the bag as the teams changed positions. Ty, who superstitiously stepped on second base on his way to and from the outfield, would "come running up and have to stop and touch of the edge of the bag with his foot; then he'd give me a little blast," recalled Dykes. Cobb nicknamed the brash infielder "H. S." for "Hot Shit."

One day Hot Shit spotted Cobb instructing Simmons at the batting cage and bent an ear. The next game Dykes employed some of Cobb's batting philosophy and stroked three hits. "After the game I'm sitting in front of my locker all smiles," said Dykes. "Cobb comes by, looks at me, and says, 'Well, rockhead, you're finally learning, aren't you?' From then on I could hit left-handers real well."

Ty usually batted third and played right field for the Athletics. In his first regular-season at-bat for his new team, on April 12 at Yankee Stadium, he grounded out against Waite Hoyt. The Yankees blew past Philadelphia, 8–3, in a game that was the season in a nutshell. For 1927 turned out to be *the* year of the Yankees, with the storied "Murderers' Row" bludgeoning its way to 110 wins, followed by a sweep of Pittsburgh in the World Series. Ruth's shadow loomed larger than ever. He hit 60 home runs—a record that created little hysteria since most people assumed he would just hit more the next season—and Lou Gehrig chipped in with 47. Philadelphia finished a very distant second, 19 games out. Connie Mack caught some criticism for fielding so many graybeards. But nothing short of a natural disaster could have stopped the Yankees' juggernaut that summer.

Despite the disappointment of finishing runner-up, 1927 marked a personal triumph for Cobb. Freed from the mental shackles of riding herd over an assemblage of largely discontented players on the field and in the clubhouse, he could once again concentrate totally on playing. At times the old warhorse galloped around the field like a colt. In an early-season game at Boston, for example, he almost single-handedly engineered a come-from-behind victory. He had three hits and drove in two runs, and when pitcher Tony Welzer took his eyes off him for too long, he stole home, executing a classic hook slide around catcher Grover Hartley. It was one of three steals of home Peach would squeeze out of his worn, 40-year-old wheels that summer. Cobb iced the Athletics' 9–8 win with an unassisted double play, snagging Phil Todt's low line drive to short right field and then outracing the runner, "Baby Doll" Jacobson, to first base to end the game with a special fillip.

In early May, Ty returned to Detroit. Headlines in local papers heralded Cobb as "A Friendly Enemy" and "An Old Friend in a New Suit." He almost missed the homecoming. A few days earlier he had gotten into a rhubarb with umpire Red Ormsby, who declared his home run foul. When Ty "accidentally" bumped Ormsby, he was tossed and placed on indefinite suspension by the league.

Detroiters went ahead with plans for Ty Cobb Day. On May 10, Ty was feted with a parade and a luncheon. Midway through the event it was dramatically announced that Cobb's suspension had been lifted.

Ty traveled in a police-escorted motorcade to that afternoon's game at Navin Field. A crowd of 27,410 turned out on an overcast Tuesday and cheered as he graciously accepted a floral horseshoe, a silver service, and a new automobile from friends and fans. The ceremonies were carried live on radio station WWJ, which had just started airing games three weeks earlier. In the top of the first inning another Ty who would one day become famous in the city—announcer Edwin "Ty" Tyson—broadcast the first live description of a Cobb at-bat in Detroit, a double off of Earl Whitehill into the right field overflow. After taking the field in the bottom of the inning, Ty was besieged by autographseekers. He patiently signed programs and slips of paper for fans, some of whom might have booed him the previous summer when he was the Tigers' manager.

Although technically the enemy, Cobb was well received on subsequent road trips to Detroit. The Tigers were going nowhere under his replacement, one-time teammate George Moriarty, so Detroiters felt no guilt in boisterously pulling for an old favorite. On July 19 at Navin Field, Ty cracked a double off Sam Gibson

The Peach at bat in the 1928 season opener at Shibe Park. Playing half of the year in new surroundings posed no problems for Cobb. Displaying his usual consistency, he had a combined three home runs and 67 RBIs during his two seasons at Shibe Park— the exact same numbers he posted on the road.

> **"Good as I was, I never was close to Cobb, and neither was Babe Ruth or anybody else. The Babe was a great ballplayer, sure. But Cobb was even greater. Babe would knock your brains out, but Cobb would drive you crazy."**
>
> —TRIS SPEAKER

for the four thousandth base hit of his career. In an era far less fixated on statistics than our own, barely a mention was made of the milestone hit in the papers.

Elsewhere around the league, Cobb remained as unpopular as ever with the opposition. "Nobody liked him," insisted Willis "Ace" Hudlin, a 20-year-old sinkerball pitcher who joined the Cleveland rotation that season. "I didn't have to put up with him but a couple years. Only time he gave me trouble was at bat." Of Cobb's base-stealing, Hudlin recalled, "He'd let you know: 'I'm coming in.'" The majors' oldest everyday player had a fine season on the basepaths. He wound up swiping 22 bases in 1927, third best in the league and just four behind leader George Sisler of St. Louis.

Hudlin's teammate, fellow right-hander George Uhle, said years later that umpires, perhaps awed by the aging Cobb, gave him the benefit of the doubt on close pitches—a common complaint about great hitters in their twilight years. "His weakness was pitching inside on him. That was the one way you had the best luck with him. I hate to say it, but there weren't many umpires who'd call it a strike when it was a strike. He'd lean over home plate, and when it was on the inside corner, he would act as if the pitch was going to hit him."

Ty made several concessions to age. He took long showers after games and rested evenings in his hotel room, reading and unwinding to the soothing music of concert violinist Fritz Kreisler on his portable phonograph. "And I'd stay in that bed until almost noon the next day," he admitted. "I would breakfast in bed, entertain from my bed, and handle my outside business affairs from a bedside telephone. Only when it was time to leave for the park would I rise and dress." By pampering his tired body and conserving energy whenever possible, he would manage to appear in 134 games, including eight as a pinch hitter. He still felt strong enough to swing a 37- or 38-ounce bat.

Cobb was at his competitive best against New York, whose muscular, free-swinging lineup embodied the new age of jackrabbit ball. One afternoon he simmered in right field as Babe Ruth strode to the plate, playfully waved the Philadelphia outfielders back with his handkerchief—then struck out on three mighty swings. On his next trip to the plate, Cobb taunted the Yankees by waving a handkerchief himself. He beat out a bunt—then stole second and third.

In a year of remarkable changes, when Charles Lindbergh became the first person to fly solo across the Atlantic, Henry Ford ended production of his beloved

Model T, and the first "talkies" arrived in neighborhood theatres, some writers unabashedly enjoyed these final glimpses of baseball as it had once been played, when the game—and life itself—seemed somehow less frenzied. Joe Williams reported on one such moment during a Philadelphia–New York contest:

> Ty Cobb went around the bases in the sixth inning . . . but more enlightening was the method he used—old-fashioned stuff scorned in the Era of Ruth.
>
> He laid down a bunt, perfectly, which caught third baseman Joe Dugan totally by surprise. Cobb slid into first, beating Dugan's hasty throw. How long since you've seen a first base slide?
>
> Next, when Hale hit a short rap to center field, and when anyone else would have stopped at second, Cobb pumped his aged legs and went for third. Combs' throw to Dugan had him out cold. Locating the ball with a quick glance over his shoulder, Cobb slid left, then contorted himself to the right. There was a geyser of dust and when it cleared, he was seen to have half-smothered the throw with his body, and as Dugan scrambled for the ball, Cobb was up and dusting himself off.
>
> The whole sequence was beautiful to see, a subtle, forgotten heritage from the romantic past.

Despite such nostalgic flourishes, the Athletics rarely solved the Yankees problem that summer. With the pennant lost, Ty played his final game of the season on September 22, leaving in the fifth inning after going hitless in three at-bats against the Indians. He showered, shook hands all around, then departed for his annual postseason hunting trip.

He left behind some remarkable numbers: a .357 batting average, fourth best in the league; 104 runs scored; 93 RBIs; and a miserly 12 strikeouts in 490 at-bats. This was vindication, and then some. While Ty enjoyed a bountiful big-game hunting expedition in Wyoming and Arizona, the baseball public wondered whether it had seen the last of the Georgia Peach. Mack, who attributed his club's strong showing to Cobb's leadership, wanted him back in 1928, but he couldn't afford him at the same terms. He told Ty he could pursue offers elsewhere.

Returning to Philadelphia from out west, Ty told reporters during a stopover in Detroit, "I am sound physically, but there is no telling what might happen if I tried to drag on." But after discussing employment with a couple of clubs, Cobb announced on March 1, 1928, that he had reached an agreement with Mack. The undisclosed salary, probably about $40,000, wasn't a major factor in Cobb's decision, which contradicted his professed desire to spend more time with family and spare his battered body another season of painful slides and spills. The longing to play in one last World Series, while somewhat diminished by now, played a part. So did the chance, after a quarter century of organized ball, to finally play alongside his old friend Tris Speaker, who had been released by Washington and signed to a one-year contract by Mack.

"Baseball was in his bones—he couldn't stand to watch other guys doing something he had damn near invented," said Frank "Lefty" O'Doul. The failed 31-year-old pitcher, who was trying to make the New York Giants as an outfielder,

Despite all the mileage on his battered 41-year-old legs, Ty still displayed flashes of his old brilliance during his final season. Here he legs out a triple against Cleveland as short-stop Joe Sewell's relay throw to third baseman Johnny Hodapp arrives late and wide of the bag.

sought Cobb's advice when Ty briefly worked out that spring with the National League team in Augusta. Following the old master's instructions to loosen his grip and spray the ball to all fields, O'Doul went on to hit .349 lifetime, with a pair of batting titles and an eventual berth in the Baseball Hall of Fame.

Like most sequels, the Cobb-Speaker farewell tour was a sorry anticlimax. For the second year in a row the Athletics opened the season with an 8–3 loss to the Yankees, who went on to grab the pennant by two and a half games. Much of the blame for the near miss was attributed to Mack's insistence on starting his two slow-footed veterans in the outfield, where balls dropped in with alarming regularity. "If this keeps up," complained Al Simmons, who chased down many of the long drives that eluded Cobb and Speaker, "I'll be an old man myself by the end of the season."

Although his reflexes had noticeably slowed, Cobb still could command respect. In 95 games he hit for a .323 average, and in a June 15 contest against Cleveland he stole home for the 54th—and final—time in his career. Billy Rogell,

Benched in the middle of the 1928 season, Cobb joined Tris Speaker and Eddie Collins in watching a new generation of stars ably take their places. After Ty's retirement the young Athletics would go on to appear in three consecutive World Series.

then a young infielder with the Red Sox, remembered one game that final season. "He was in a terrible, terrible slump . . . He hit a blooper into left field and he had to slide into second base. He hit the bag and that bag flew. He tore that bastard right off. He got up, sparks in his eyes. 'Jesus Christ,' I thought to myself, 'I don't want to tangle with that old bastard.'"

Such fire was all but extinguished on July 27, when Ty was hit in the chest by a George Connally pitch. That game against the White Sox turned out to be his last major-league start. The painful injury pushed the already ailing 41-year-old to the bench, alongside Speaker and Eddie Collins. There the three dead-ball relics remained throughout August and September, as Mack used younger troops in hopes of catching the mighty Yankees, who were destined to once again sweep their opponents in the World Series.

"Say farewell to the most admired, envied and hated of ballplayers."

—*NEW YORK EVENING WORLD*, REPORTING
COBB'S RETIREMENT

The man routinely described as a "terror" ended his big-league career on a more sanguine 9/11 in New York. Late in the afternoon of September 11, 1928, with the Athletics trailing the Yankees, 5–3, at Yankee Stadium, Cobb pinch-hit for Jimmie Dykes leading off the ninth. He failed to get around on right-hander Hank Johnson, popping a pitch back of third base, where shortstop Mark Koenig made the routine catch.

The record books slammed shut when Koenig squeezed his glove. Six days later, Ty formally announced his retirement inside a Cleveland hotel room. The statement he handed reporters read:

> Never again, after the finish of the present pennant race, will I be an active player in the game to which I have devoted 24 seasons of what for me was hard labor. I make this announcement today because of the many inquiries constantly coming to me concerning my future plans.
>
> Friends have urged me to try it one more season so that I could round out a quarter century of continuous service in the American League, but I prefer to retire while there still may remain some base hits in my bat. Baseball is the greatest game in the world. I owe all that I possess in the way of worldly goods to this game. For each week, month, and year of my career, I have felt a deep sense of responsibility to the grand old national sport that has been everything to me.
>
> I will not reconsider. This is final.

That was it. The statement made no mention of his final numbers, many of which seemed beyond reach. Rows of figures told only part of the story, anyway. It was Ty's hurricane-force personality that had made him baseball's centerpiece for much of his career. He was well aware of his place in baseball's history, a place that remained secure despite a sour curtain call. Even at the end, when his cement legs had him grounding into double plays and he was being thrown out by fielders with popgun arms, the fact that he was, after all, *Ty Cobb* was enough for most fans, including a young Philadelphian named James A. Michener.

"They weren't what you'd call really good," the famous author, remembering the summer of '28 at Shibe Park, wrote many years later, "but by God they were Speaker and Cobb, and I saw them."

CHAPTER EIGHT

The Long Way Home

*I only know that summer sang in me
A little while, that in me sings no more*

EDNA ST. VINCENT MILLAY

In the spring of 1929, baseball prepared for a new season without its most storied competitor. Although few infielders or pitchers were mourning his absence, the notion of America's game being played without the Georgia Peach for the first time since Theodore Roosevelt was in the White House was newsworthy enough to warrant dispatching a film crew to Cobb country.

"Well, Ty," asked the man from Movietone News, "how's it feel to be down here hunting in Georgia instead of training in a ball camp?"

"Wel-l-l," replied Ty in his familiar high-pitched drawl, "I had about 25 years of baseball and I'll have to admit that I got pretty well fed up on it. And I'm obliged to say that I'm very happy not to have on my mind having to report for spring training. I have played ball for so long, and it was such a task, I was really happy to get out. And I've been very happy since I've been out. I've had a lot of inquiries from people who wondered about my feelings, my ability to retire from the game, and they've wondered just how I could retire. Well, I'll be honest and tell you that baseball is quite a task, and I feel that I've served a long time, and now I'm looking forward to the things that I have wanted to do for so many years. As yet, I haven't had any desire to reenter the game."

As the newsreel cameraman cranked away, Ty turned to one of his hunting dogs.

"This old friend of mine here," he continued, "he's a dog, it's true, but he's a great friend. Now, he won't boo me and he won't criticize me. But I do want to say this, that I'm not finding any fault with the fans or anyone else because I feel deeply obligated to everyone for all the kindnesses and all the nice things they've done and they've said about me and my career as a ballplayer. Of course, that's a closed incident as far as actively engaging in baseball. But I do want to have the fans realize that I still appreciate them."

Opposite: A restless 71-year-old Cobb, in the midst of another move.

That two-minute bit, part of the usual between-features newsreel fare in movie palaces across America, was how millions of fans got their first glimpse of the great Ty Cobb in retirement. His legendary ferocity was nowhere in sight. In fact, the 42-year-old Peach sounded not only gracious and contented, he seemed practically genial. But Ty could no sooner learn to enjoy a life of idle retirement than his dogs could learn to tap dance. His restless, competitive, and ornery nature wouldn't allow it. As the years passed, much of his time would be spent coming to grips with his unsavory reputation, his disintegrating family, and ultimately, his own mortality.

∞

Initially, Ty reveled in his freedom from the daily rigors of baseball. He traveled widely and indulged a variety of pastimes, including big-game hunting, fishing, golf, and even polo. In 1929 he and Charlie visited the European continent, England, and Scotland in grand style. In Scotland Ty fulfilled a lifelong dream by visiting Keith, "the big league of upland bird hunting, a pilgrimage place for the world's finest shotgun artists." There he impressed Sir Isaac Sharpe, the world-famous trainer of hunting dogs, with his superior shooting skills. The following year he participated in his first organized golf tournament, shooting an 83 over 18 holes to win a cup at the Augusta Country Club. These activities presumably salved some of the sting he felt from missing out on the two World Series championships the Athletics captured immediately following his retirement.

In 1932, as much of the rest of the country wallowed in the depths of the Great Depression, Cobb moved his family from Augusta to a magnificent estate at 48 Spencer Lane in Atherton, California, about 35 miles south of San Francisco. The estate included a seven-bedroom house, servants' quarters, a guest house, and a swimming pool, all spread over several tree-filled acres. The splendid trappings befitted his elevated station in life. Because of his diversified investments in General Motors, Coca-Cola, and other companies, he was a millionaire at a time when the unemployment rate in Detroit and other big cities approached 40 percent and a new car could be bought for less than $500. He was famous, a man of means and substance. He also was a man with whom it was impossible to live.

Charlie and the five children had never found Ty easy to get along with, but it was worse now that baseball didn't take the mercurial patriarch of the Cobb clan away from the house for seven or eight months each year. Worn out by her husband's sarcasm and afraid of his irrational rages, Charlie wanted out of the marriage. During the 1930s she filed for divorce on three separate occasions, only to change her mind each time—probably for the sake of the younger children, who were by then in their teens. Her first suit, filed in 1931, charged Ty with "cruel treatment," a broad term that could include mental, physical, or emotional abuse. Based on the stories told by old Augustans today, and considering Ty's reputation, all three probably applied.

Neither of Charlie's brothers, Alfred and Roz Lombard, could stand their famous brother-in-law. One day in the early 1920s, J. Marvin Wolfe, a print shop operator who also owned the Augusta ball club and park, was returning to his home, just a couple of houses away from the Cobbs' residence. A terrible argument between Cobb and one of the Lombard brothers attracted his attention.

The culmination of Ty's professional career was his near-unanimous election in 1936 to the Hall of Fame then being planned in Cooperstown, New York. Cartoonist Stookie Allen used the occasion to celebrate the Peach's achievements.

When Coca-Cola released a set of "All-Time Winners" cardboard posters in 1947, Ty naturally was among them.

Cobb, not wanting to pose for photographs with Judge Landis, was purposely late for the 1939 induction ceremonies at the Baseball Hall of Fame. Thus the official portrait of the charter class of inductees was missing the game's number-one immortal. On hand were (seated, from left) Eddie Collins, Babe Ruth, Connie Mack, Cy Young, (standing, from left) Honus Wagner, Grover Cleveland Alexander, Tris Speaker, Nap Lajoie, George Sisler, and Walter Johnson.

> **"I honestly believe that dogs have souls. A dog will live with you and he will die with you. How many dogs have followed their master to the grave and died there?"** —TY COBB

Asked what was going on, the enraged brother exclaimed, "This son of a bitch beat Charlie with a bat so bad she can hardly walk!" Wolfe, whose brother was married to Charlie's sister, had little use for Cobb himself. But he intervened between the two, reportedly coaxing a pistol away from the infuriated brother, who vowed, "I'm gonna kill him!" He didn't, of course, but the effect was nearly the same. The Lombard family, important people in Augusta, froze Ty out of their immediate circle.

"It was no peaceful home from what I understood," Eugene "Woody" Wolfe, Marvin's son, said of the Cobb residence in Augusta. "The kids would just scatter when he came home. Dad wouldn't let us have anything to do with him." If the social ostracism didn't directly lead to Ty's decision to move to the West Coast, thousands of miles from his wife's side of the family, it certainly made it an easier one to make.

Ty's acrimonious relationship with Charlie might help explain his falling out with Ty Jr. The Cobbs' oldest child had already witnessed his father's propensity for violence. One infamous afternoon in 1921, he watched as his father and umpire Billy Evans, both stripped to the waist, engaged in a bloody knock-down, drag-out fight under the stands in Washington. "Come on, Daddy," the then 11-year-old boy had pleaded, peeking through a forest of players' legs. One can only imagine what ugly scenes he and his siblings saw at home as their parents argued and drifted farther apart.

When it came to raising his own children, Ty was as demanding and spare in his praise as Professor Cobb had been with him. In fact, the Peach's troubled relationship with his first-born mirrored his own adolescent difficulties. Sensitive and rebellious, Ty Jr. grew up hating baseball and feeling burdened by his famous name. Such behavior shouldn't have surprised Cobb. Two of his closest friends in the game, Mickey Cochrane and Christy Mathewson, also had oldest sons who reacted in similar fashion. Both offspring ignored the diamond, looking to make their own ways. Christy Mathewson Jr. became an aviator, losing a leg and a young bride in a crash, while Gordon Stanley "Mickey" Cochrane Jr., a mild-tempered, bespectacled youngster miscast as an army infantryman, would die in the closing weeks of World War II. Ty Cobb Jr.'s rebellion consisted of driving fast cars, playing a lot of tennis, and flunking out of Princeton. By August of 1939, when Charlie Cobb finally left her abusive husband for good, moving into a house in Menlo Park, California, Ty Jr. and his father had already fallen into an estrangement that would last through the war years.

"He is a little rounded, as a man of physical powers usually is, on retirement, but only Father Time could bench him. He has still the wedge-shaped body of the born athlete. His eye is clear and fast. As he watches 'the young fellows' doing now what he used to do better than any living man, he misses nothing that takes place on the diamond."

—THE *SAN MATEO TIMES*, DESCRIBING 47-YEAR-OLD
TY COBB IN 1933

☙❧

At the same time as his family life was unraveling, Ty was reconciling with men he had battled so long and so hard against. One was Babe Ruth, who scored points when he claimed a Georgia girl, Claire Merritt Hodgson, as his second wife in 1929. The new Mrs. Ruth was the daughter of a prominent lawyer, James Merritt, who at one time handled some of Cobb's legal affairs. "In Georgia," she coyly recalled in her old age, "I had known Ty Cobb very well." The curvy brunette, a divorcee considered by some ballplayers to be a gold digger, supported herself and her young daughter in New York by working as a model, silent-film actress, and dancer in the Ziegfeld Follies.

Given the intensity of the Cobb-Ruth rivalry, Ty's dalliance with the future Mrs. Ruth years before Babe entered her life presumably gave him a certain amount of satisfaction. Because neither Ty nor Claire "kissed and told" in their memoirs, the exact nature of their relationship can only be guessed at. It's worth noting, though, that Ty confided on more than one occasion to having various extramarital affairs while on the road. In contrast to Ruth, a prolific and indiscriminate womanizer who was described by one friend as "the noisiest fucker in North America," Cobb was generally more discreet and selective in his sexual liaisons. However, at the start of his career he had sampled the standard big-league fare of groupies and paid performers, to the point that they sometimes became a distraction. In a 1906 letter Frank Navin complained of his 19-year-old outfielder's bringing prostitutes to Bennett Park. "Very immoral guy," was the judgment of Davy Jones, who joined the Detroit team that year and played alongside Cobb for seven seasons. "God, he wouldn't care who they were. He had an awful reputation with the women there." According to Jones, a law school graduate and a reliable source of information about Cobb's early years in the major leagues, the Euclid Hotel incident in Cleveland in 1909 was the result of the house detective's having foiled Ty's desire to hook up with a pair of young sisters—"hero

worshippers," said Jones—in their room. As Cobb became older and more famous and could afford to be choosier, he welcomed fewer "baseball Annies" into his bed. He preferred women of a higher quality, those who could dance or hold an intelligent conversation at dinner, though sleeping with a comely actress or chorus girl with less refined social skills would always carry its own special charm.

Ty, who had openly considered himself the better of the two feuding icons, saw that status made official in February of 1936. That was when the first class of "immortals" was selected for the newly formed National Baseball Museum and Hall of Fame in Cooperstown, New York. Of the 226 ballots cast by members of the Baseball Writers Association of America, Cobb was named on 222 of them. Honus Wagner and Ruth, who had retired just four months earlier, were next with 215 votes. Of all the honors he accrued during his lifetime, Ty was always proudest of the election that, in effect, named him the game's number-one immortal. Three years later, on June 12, 1939, the museum was dedicated before ten thousand enthusiastic people and a national radio audience. Blaming missed train connections, Cobb arrived too late to participate in the induction ceremonies or

During the war years Cobb reached a rapprochement with old rival Babe Ruth. They played a much-publicized series of golf matches in 1941, then four years later were honorary captains at a charity all-star game at New York's Polo Grounds.

Cobb with golfing legend Bobby Jones.

to sit with Ruth, Wagner, Connie Mack, Cy Young, George Sisler, Eddie Collins, Willie Keeler, Tris Speaker, Nap Lajoie, and Grover Cleveland Alexander for the official portrait of the charter class of inductees. Years later, Ty confessed that he had been purposely late to avoid posing for photographs with Judge Landis. The commissioner would always rank near the top of Ty's "son-of-a-bitch list" for his mishandling of the Cobb-Speaker case in the winter of 1926–27.

Ty, a surprisingly sentimental man at times, immensely enjoyed the annual Cooperstown get-togethers. He could swap yarns with other aging stars from his era and throw darts at the modern game. A favorite target was Ted Williams, a pure hitter considered by many to be nearly Cobbs' equal. The Peach wasn't buying that—at least not until the stubborn Boston Red Sox slugger took his unsolicited advice and started dropping bunts along the third-base line against the so-called Williams Shift, a defensive tactic that featured an overload of fielders on the right side of the diamond. "If they had tried that shift against Cobb," sniffed Nap Lajoie, defending his old adversary, "the Peach would have hit .800 every season." Another world-class hitter who took Ty's advice, this time in financial matters, also benefited nicely. In 1936, the Yankees bought the contract of a raw kid named Joe DiMaggio from the San Francisco Seals. Ed Barrow, New York's tight-fisted general manager, offered DiMaggio $4,000 for his rookie season. "I knew Ty Cobb slightly," DiMaggio recalled years later. But Joe's brother Tom, who operated the DiMaggio family's restaurant in San Francisco, "knew him even better. Cobb came into the restaurant often, and Tom either wouldn't charge him for his meal or he would let him have it at half-price. Of course, Ty was a millionaire several times over. But he still liked the idea of a free meal."

Ty was every inch the tough and crafty negotiator that Barrow was. Keeping his involvement secret, he composed a letter for DiMaggio, who copied it in his own handwriting and signed his name. In it he told Barrow $4,000 was too low. Barrow, who believed Tom DiMaggio was acting as Joe's agent, responded with a new offer, this time for $4,500. "Hold out for more," Ty advised DiMaggio. Cobb drafted another letter, DiMaggio copied and signed it, and Barrow grumpily came back with yet an-other offer, this time for $5,000.

"That seemed like a lot of money to me, and I was ready to settle for it," said DiMaggio. "Cobb said no, so we wrote another letter." Barrow upped his offer to $5,500, but Ty still wasn't satisfied that he had squeezed every last dime out of the negotiations. "You're worth more, son," he told DiMaggio. "Don't give up now. Let's go at him again."

So, recalled DiMaggio, "Cobb wrote another letter. Again I copied it, signed it and mailed it to Barrow. In 10 days, here came the answer. Barrow sent a contract for $6,000. He also enclosed a letter in which he told me that was his final offer. It was take it or leave it."

Ty, satisfied that his behind-the-scenes finagling had reached its limit, advised the rookie center fielder to take it. "You whipped Mr. Barrow," he said. "Now, go do it to the rest of the American League."

Given his wide experience and his financial acumen, as well as his demonstrated shortcomings as a manager, it would have been interesting to see how the Peach would have performed as an owner. During his first few years of retirement, Ty twice was a major investor in syndicates looking to buy a major-league franchise. The first was a bid to purchase the Cincinnati Reds (for $275,000 in 1929), followed by an attempt to acquire the Detroit club in the early 1930s. Both bids were rejected, but Ty still managed to stay on the periphery of the game through old-timers' contests, Cooperstown reunions, and golf outings, where he usually was the star attraction. He typically played in the mid-80s and low 90s, and he was embarrassed to lose matches to women's champion Babe Didrikson at Pebble Beach, California in 1930 and, nine years later, to a 12-year-old prodigy named

Bob Rosburg. That last defeat was so galling that Ty cleared out his locker at San Francisco's Olympic Club and never returned.

Cobb enjoyed a more satisfying experience on the links in June 1941 when he and Babe Ruth played a best-of-three series to benefit the USO and other charities. The media dragged out the brain vs. brawn comparisons that had been at the heart of their diamond rivalry years earlier. Ty, who had lost little of his competitive zeal, later admitted, "I went into the Ruth matches as determined to win as I ever was on the ball field."

After winning the opening match in West Newton, Massachusetts, Ty dropped the second, played a couple of days later at Fresh Meadows on Long Island, by a single stroke. The rubber game was scheduled for the Grosse Ile Golf & Country Club, outside Detroit, where Ty parlayed his passion for amateur psychology into victory. During a practice round in Cleveland, en route to the big match, Cobb missed shot after shot, moaning to everyone that he didn't stand a chance of beating the Babe.

Ruth, his confidence boosted by Ty's supposed ineptitude, partied harder than he should have on that evening's boat ride from Cleveland to Detroit. The following day arrived steamy and hot. As a gallery of 2,500 followed the two competitors around, Ty easily beat his sticky and hung-over opponent, happily claiming what he called "The Has Beens' Golf Championship of Nowhere in Particular."

After Pearl Harbor, Cobb and Ruth regularly met at exhibition baseball games benefiting war-related charities. Approaching 60, nearly bald, and some 40 pounds heavier than he had been in his prime, Ty nonetheless could still swing a bat with authority. To outwit someone—or to "slip him the oskafagus," as he liked to call it—remained a favorite pastime. During an old-timers' game played at Yankee Stadium on September 28, 1947, Cobb approached the plate and offered an apology to catcher Wally Schang. He was afraid the bat might slip out of his hands, Ty explained, so perhaps the catcher should back up a few feet to lessen the possibility of injury. Schang obligingly moved back—whereupon Ty laid down a bunt, nearly beating it out for a base hit.

That was the last time Cobb saw his old rival. Less than a year later, Ruth was dead of cancer. Eighty thousand people filed past his casket as he lay in state in the lobby of Yankee Stadium. "I can't honestly say that I appreciate the way in which he changed baseball," Cobb would write in his autobiography, "but he was the most natural and unaffected man I ever knew . . . I look forward to meeting him some day." Ruth, for his part, "didn't talk much about Cobb," said Fred Lieb, recalling a marathon bull session with Babe shortly before his death. "He said he thought Cobb was a great ball player but a no-good mean sonofabitch. Babe wasn't alone on that. Ninety percent of the players felt the same way."

About this time Charlie Cobb was finally granted a divorce from Ty, whom she charged with "extreme cruelty from the date of marriage to the present time." Although the out-of-court settlement cost him a reported $500,000, Ty remained comfortably wealthy. And he soon found a new wife. On September 24, 1949, he married Frances Fairburn, the dark-haired daughter of a Buffalo physician. Twenty-two years younger than Ty, she shared his interest in golfing, hunting, and traveling. They would remain married for nearly seven years.

Cobb married Frances Fairburn Cass, the outdoors-loving daughter of a Buffalo physician, on September 24, 1949. The bloom was off Ty's second marriage by 1955, when both partners filed for divorce, each charging the other with "mental cruelty."

Following closely on his establishment of the Cobb Memorial Hospital, Ty announced the creation of the Cobb Educational Fund to provide needy Georgia students with college scholarships. He presented these medallions to the trustees of the foundation.

During this period Ty lived the life of a country squire, playing golf, riding horses, raising show dogs, entertaining guests at his Atherton estate, and carefully watching his investments. He also corresponded regularly with old players and sportswriters. Not surprisingly, much of what he wrote was in defense of his legacy, which generally was that of a brilliant but dirty ballplayer. "It has always hurt me deep," he wrote Harry Salsinger in 1953. "It happens to be the real weak spot in whatever armor I have."

There were other weak spots the general public was unaware of. During the 1950s Cobb's tireless campaigning helped get a pair of his former teammates, Harry Heilmann and Sam Crawford, into the Hall of Fame. In the case of Heilmann, who was a popular Detroit broadcaster at the time he was stricken with cancer, Ty persuaded Hall officials to let him visit Ol' Slug's bedside to prematurely deliver the good news. Heilmann died on the eve of the 1951 All-Star Game in Detroit believing that he had been elected, although the official vote hadn't yet been taken. In the case of Crawford, the forgotten slugger who was elected six years later, "nobody, including Crawford himself, could have been more elated about it than Ty," recalled Jack McDonald of San Francisco's *News–Call Bulletin.* The sportswriter was "privy to piles of correspondence" inside Cobb's home in nearby Atherton, "answers to handwritten letters Ty had written to hundreds of influential people on Crawford's behalf." Evidently Crawford, who had feuded with Cobb for years, was not made aware of the major role Cobb played in his election until after the Peach died.

Longtime *Washington Post* sportswriter Shirley Povich remembered how the Peach also went to bat for Sam Rice, the Senators' outfielder whose accomplishments, among them a .322 lifetime batting average, had been overlooked for years by the Hall of Fame's Veterans Committee. "Sam Rice should be put in the Hall of Fame here," Cobb declared during the induction ceremonies one year in the late 1950s. "I played against Sam Rice for 14 years and he could do everything, and I'm saying his name should be here too." Ty started exerting pressure on the voters. Although the Peach wouldn't live long enough to see it, his little crusade ultimately resulted in Rice's election to the Hall in 1963. In Povich's view, "Ty Cobb was not all bad, all the time."

In early 1950, Cobb Memorial Hospital was dedicated before a crowd of 3,000. At Ty's side was Dr. Stewart Brown, who had been his teammate on the Royston Reds a half-century earlier.

Many other stories have been told about Ty's penny-pinching, which seemed to grow more pronounced the richer he became—how the old skinflint would drive miles out of his way to frequent a gas station that offered green stamps, or create a nasty scene over a three-cent discrepancy in a dinner bill. While most of the tales are true, and have been told and retold with great relish over the years, they overshadow his spurts of generosity. Cobb looked after several down-on-their-luck ex-ballplayers, including Ray Schalk and Lu Blue, sending money (often anonymously through a third party) or providing for medical care. Mickey Cochrane appears to have been another beneficiary, though his family, understandably protective of the catcher's reputation, has always insisted he never accepted any money from Cobb.

Cobb's largesse extended beyond the game and its performers. The projects that most occupied his time during the 1950s were the Cobb Educational Fund and Cobb Memorial Hospital, good works that continue to flourish to this day.

Both filled a void in Ty's life. Although he had chosen baseball over college, he understood the benefits of higher education. In 1953 he announced the creation of a fund, named after his father, that would provide scholarships for needy college students in Georgia. One stipulation was that recipients have already completed their freshman year, thus demonstrating their drive to achieve. "We want stars," claimed Cobb, "stars in medicine, in law, in teaching and in life." After a half century, Cobb's original endowment of $100,000 has grown into assets of several million dollars. From that base, administrators of the Cobb Educational Foundation annually dispense 100 or more grants ranging between $150 and $20,000 each. As of 2003, a total of 6,876 scholarships worth more than $9.7 million had been awarded—an average of about $1,400 apiece.

"Ty Cobb, the greatest of all ballplayers — and an absolute shit."

—ERNEST HEMINGWAY, 1948

Earlier, Ty had honored his parents by donating $100,000 to kick off a drive to build a modern hospital in his hometown of Royston. A federal grant and contributions added another $110,000 to the building fund. The 24-bed hospital was dedicated in early 1950 before a crowd of three thousand people, with Ty's new wife turning the ceremonial gold key. On hand was a buddy from the Royston Reds days, Stewart Brown, who had grown up to become, in Ty's words, "one of Georgia's outstanding country doctors." The nonprofit Cobb Memorial Hospital—"the hospital built with a bat"—has since expanded into one of the premier healthcare systems in northeast Georgia, its seven facilities serving the needs of four counties. For the rest of his life Cobb donated all money earned from his writings and paid public appearances to his two pet projects. When he died, one-quarter of his estate was left to his educational foundation.

Cobb Memorial Hospital helped Ty reconcile his differences with his oldest child. In his early thirties, Ty Jr. had finally decided to get serious about a career, graduating from medical school and setting up a practice in Dublin, Georgia. But soon after they patched up their differences, tragedy struck. In 1952, Ty Jr. was diagnosed with a malignant brain tumor, putting him in a "precarious & hopeless position," Cobb wrote a friend from New York, where top neurosurgeons were unable to save his son. Ty Jr. was 42 when he died.

Ty Jr.'s death came on the heels of another blow. The previous year, Herschel Cobb, whom Ty had helped set up as a Coca-Cola distributor, had died suddenly of a heart attack. Cobb's middle son was only 34. His sons' unexpected deaths undoubtedly contributed to Ty's frenzied search for meaning and a solid place in the world. Between bouts of high-stakes gambling and drinking, he brooded over missed opportunities with his children. "When you get older, you wish for companionship," he reflected. "I was just a loner; I couldn't have that with my children."

By 1956 Frances had had enough of Ty's erratic behavior. She confided to her friends that she was physically afraid of her husband. In this she joined half of America. Ty's propensity for making headlines hadn't ended just because he was approaching age 70. In California, news items described how he had punched out a heckler in a nightclub, shoved a prominent businessman into a fish pond, and been hauled off to jail for abusing a policeman. Stories circulated around Arizona about the time he had pitched a salt shaker at a waiter and the incident in which he had kicked a taxi driver in the seat of the pants. His "son-of-a-bitch list"—actually a little black memo book containing the names of Dutch Leonard, Judge Landis, Eleanor Roosevelt, utility companies, and everyone else he had a real or imagined beef with—grew almost by the day. Whenever someone threat-

Fifty years earlier, the outfield of Davy Jones, Sam Crawford, and Ty Cobb had hawked fly balls and sped around the bases like young colts. Now, at a 1957 banquet honoring Crawford's (center) induction into the Hall of Fame, the three were old warhorses, swapping stories and doing their best to keep their ties out of the gravy.

ened litigation, Ty would ball up his fists and snarl, "Get in line, bub, there's a hundred ahead of you."

All this was too much for Frances. Charging Ty with "extreme mental cruelty," she was granted a divorce on May 12, 1956 in Nevada, where they maintained a second residence in Lake Tahoe. The exact terms of the settlement weren't published, but Ty kept most of his money and both homes. Not that he found the sprawling, empty Atherton estate appealing. At times his three surviving children, all married and living in California, dreaded sharing the West Coast with their cantankerous father. "In this house," Ty sighed to a visitor in the spring of 1957, "I'm just a lonely old man." He continued to accept invitations to old-timers games, but he steadfastly refused to put on a uniform. "I wouldn't want to be remembered as a doddering old man," he said. Instead he signed autographs for fans who weren't even alive when he last played.

By 1959, Ty was a lonely, sick old man. He had relocated to Cornelia, Georgia, near Royston, where he planned to live out his days in a mountaintop home he hoped to build. He had been diagnosed with prostate cancer, as well as diabetes, high blood pressure, and a weak heart. If that wasn't enough, he suffered from impacted bowels and his kidneys were failing him. Ignoring his prescribed medicine, Ty chose to kill the pain by drinking a quart of Jack Daniels bourbon, mixed with milk, each day. "This has an effect of dulling somewhat my senses and nerves," he explained.

Over the winter of 1959–60, Ty had most of his cancerous prostate removed.

Approaching his 72nd birthday, Ty talked hitting with one of his grandchildren, Mary McLaren.

Radiation treatments followed. "I'm on the threshold of old age," he said, his skin hanging like crepe paper, "and believe me, it's quite an adventure."

Al Stump was about to come along on that adventure. In 1960 the veteran sportswriter from Santa Barbara, California, was hired by Doubleday to assist Cobb in writing his autobiography. The two men split the $6,000 advance, but for once money was a secondary consideration. Despite his oft-expressed desire to "set the record straight," Ty had for years ignored repeated requests from publishers and movie producers for his life story. He once explained to Harry Salsinger that "those Jewish boys promise but pay no attention" to the truth. The proposed book or movie would invariably portray him as "jumping down every man's throat with spikes and in general be a 'hell cat' … every boy who saw such a picture would think ill of me." For a time Salsinger, whom Ty trusted, looked to have the inside track as Cobb's collaborator. But as it developed, neither Salsinger (who died in 1958) nor Cobb would live to see what Ty liked to call "my true record" between covers.

Stump and Cobb worked on the book together in fits and starts throughout 1960 and into early 1961. During this period Stump watched in equal parts fascination and horror as Ty—half-crazed by booze, medication, and constant pain—battled terminal cancer and everyone who crossed his path as spiritedly as he had the Athletics and Red Sox a half-century earlier. Among Stump's many adventures was a hair-raising ride down a mountain during a blizzard so Ty could hit the casinos in Reno, Nevada, as well as an incident in which Cobb fired several pistol shots into a motel parking lot to hush whoever it was that had just disturbed his nap. Upon moving to Cobb's Atherton house to continue work on the book, Stump was flabbergasted to discover that Ty's electricity had been shut off in a protracted dispute over a $16 discrepancy in the bill. Stump wound up working under a single light bulb connected by extension cords to a neighboring house owned by Ty's daughter, Beverly. Even Ty's periodic cobalt treatments involved a certain amount of intrigue. He invariably quarreled with the staff, especially when they tried to take away his alcohol. "We'll have to slip them the oskafagus," he told Stump. Ty managed to fool the nurses by placing his false teeth in a glass of Scotch.

Stump worked doggedly, enduring Cobb's wild mood swings while shaping Ty's candid and insightful reminiscences into one of the finest sports autobiographies ever. The book, published in August of 1961, was followed a few months later by Stump's engrossing magazine article, "Ty Cobb's Wild Ten-Month Fight to Live," which has since become a staple of baseball anthologies. Taken together, they reveal both sides of what Stump called a "badly disturbed personality."

Cobb's most lucid moment with Stump came on Christmas Eve of 1960. That snowy evening he took his collaborator to the Royston cemetery, to a stone burial vault that he had just had built to accommodate his parents and sister. Ty's mother had died in 1936, shortly after he had been voted into the Hall of Fame. Florence had died eight years later. Ty had had all three family members disinterred.

"My father was the greatest man I ever knew," Ty said, weak with pain and emotion. "He was a scholar, state senator, editor, and philosopher. I worshipped him. So did all the people around here. He was the only man who ever made me do his bidding."

Cobb and Coke

It was perhaps inevitable that two American icons, Ty Cobb and Coca-Cola, would enjoy a long, satisfying relationship. Both were proud products of the state of Georgia, born just a few months and whistle stops apart in 1886, and both grew up to become integral parts of the national experience in the early decades of the 20th century.

Arguably the greatest commercial success in history (the company estimates that the soft drink is consumed hundreds of millions of times around the world each day), Coca-Cola was created on May 8, 1886, when an Atlanta pharmacist, John Smith Pemberton, stirred up a batch of syrup inside a three-legged brass pot in his back yard. Satisfied with the taste, he took a jug of it to the local pharmacy. There it was mixed with carbonated water and placed on sale as a soda fountain drink for a nickel a glass.

Pemberton never realized the financial potential of his "soda fizz," selling off shares of the business until his death two years later. Atlanta businessman Asa G. Candler, his brother John, and a couple of Pemberton's original investors (including bookkeeper Frank M. Robinson, who named the drink and penned the now-famous Coca-Cola script logo), made the syrup a success. Under their direction the company began its tradition of heavy promotion, with the Coca-Cola trademark showing up on everything from souvenir fans to complimentary calendars. Innovative approaches to advertising included the placement of colorful signs in trolley cars and loans of ornate leaded glass chandeliers to soda shops. After World War I, an investment group headed by Atlanta banker Ernest Woodruff bought the company for $25 million.

Ty's first commercial endorsement was a newspaper advertisement in September 1907 that had the 20-year-old star stating, "I drink Coca-Cola regularly throughout all seasons of the year." He did more than drink it; he eventually started investing in it. At the urging of Woodruff's son Robert, Ty borrowed $10,800 from Woodruff's bank, the Trust Company of Georgia, in 1918 and bought his first three hundred shares at $36 a share. The value skyrocketed after the company expanded distribution beyond the South in the 1920s, selling the beverage nationally and then overseas. A mushrooming network of regional bottlingplants, aided by massive advertising and innovative marketing (the company introduced the contoured bottle in 1916, the six-bottle carry-home carton in 1923, and the metal open-top cooler in 1929), helped account for the sales boom.

As Ty continued to prosper during the decade, drawing annual salaries in the $50,000 range and earning tens of thousands of dollars more in dividends and endorsements each year, he could afford to purchase additional shares. He gave stock tips to his teammates and urged

"On days when we are playing a double-header I always find that a drink of Coca-Cola between the games refreshes me to such an extent that I can start the second game, feeling as if I had not been exercising at all, in spite of my exertions in the first."

–TY COBB'S TESTIMONIAL IN AN EARLY ADVERTISEMENT

Ty's first commercial endorsement was this 1907 ad.

them to invest for the future, though few had the inclination or resources. "I remember when I first came along as a kid, making $4,000 a year, and he was telling me to buy General Motors and Coca-Cola stock," said second baseman Charlie Gehringer, who broke into the majors in 1924. "Which was good advice. But you had to live, too, besides buying stock."

Coca-Cola weathered the stock market crash and the Great Depression in good shape, never failing to pay a dividend. Much of the credit for that goes to Robert Woodruff, who became company president in 1923. It was Woodruff's objective to capitalize on the bottle business and place Coke "within an arm's reach of desire" of everyone. In 1928, Coca-Cola's bottle sales, including millions at ballparks, finally surpassed fountain sales. Umpires, however, were not impressed. Bottles were a nuisance. For decades, until owners finally banned bottles from their parks, more than one umpire was knocked unconscious by a glass missile thrown by an irate fan.

Woodruff, a gruff, competitive fellow with a passion for the outdoors, got along famously with Cobb. They frequently hunted together on Woodruff's thirty thousand–acre estate, Ichauway, in south Georgia, betting on who would bag the most birds. During one hunting trip Ty confided he was considering the Tigers' managerial job. Woodruff, a good judge of people, advised against it.

"Why do you say that?" asked Cobb.

"You're too damn mean," replied Woodruff.

Ty's friendship with the chairman made him privy to insider "dope," which he passed on to selected friends and family members. In a lengthy letter to sportswriter Harry Salsinger in 1953, for example, he touted "a most sensational coin control dispenser" then in development, which was expected to cause shares to rise sharply in value when it was unveiled. "I am buying more [stock] now, have advised my daughters & Ty Jr.'s widow," Cobb wrote. "My information comes from the top . . . you can guess who he is."

In 1940 Ty bought a bottling plant in Twin Falls, Idaho, and set up his son Herschel as manager. Another son, Jimmy, also became associated with the plant after World War II. Later, Herschel and his wife acquired additional bottling plants in Bend, Oregon and Santa Maria, California. During this postwar period the company introduced the Peach to a new generation of sports fans on a set of "All-Time Winners" cardboard posters, first distributed in 1947.

Cobb died a multimillionaire. Estimates of his wealth–most of it tied up in stocks, bonds, and real estate–ranged between $6 million and $12 million. According to *The Sporting News* in 1961, his Coca-Cola stock alone was worth nearly $1.8 million. Twenty years later, the *Baltimore Sun* determined that a share that had originally cost Ty $40 would then be selling for about two hundred times that amount, or roughly $8,000. The real thing, indeed!

In retirement Ty was a guest on several television programs, including his September 28, 1955 appearance on *I've Got a Secret*. The popular quiz show was aired live every Wednesday night from a CBS studio in New York. After whispering his secret ("I have the highest lifetime batting average in history") to the show's affable, chain-smoking host, Garry Moore, the Peach proceeded to stump panelists Bill Cullen, Henry Morgan, Jayne Meadows, and Kitty Carlisle. Once Ty's identity was revealed, Moore ran down a list of the guest's other notable records – to which Cullen added, "He spiked a lot of second basemen, too." "He was a mean one," Moore agreed. Ty, who was 68 and slightly deaf, was urbane and gracious that evening. He received $80 and a carton of Winston cigarettes for winning, then asked Moore's permission to individually shake hands with the panelists before making his exit.

> **"Baseball today is putrid, and you can blame it on the lively ball and the home run. There are too many lopsided scores. What's happened to those grand old one-run, last-inning finishes?"**
>
> —TY COBB'S VIEW OF BASEBALL IN THE 1950S

Ty, his eyes welling with tears, continued slowly, "My father had his head blown off with a shotgun when I was 18 years old—*by a member of my own family*. I didn't get over that. I've never gotten over it."

The past weighed heavily on Cobb. When an old friend, comedian Joe E. Brown, visited him in Atherton the following spring, Ty was full of self-recrimination. Maybe he'd been too aggressive, he told Brown, had gone a little too far. "I always had to be right in any argument I was in," he confessed, "and wanted to be first in everything." Later Ty added, "Joe, I do indeed think I would have done things different. And if I had, I would have had more friends."

In April of 1961, tests showed that Ty's cancer had spread into his brain. He flew back to Cornelia, where on May 22 he drew up his will. An inventory of his estate, the bulk of which was left to his three children and a trust fund for his 15 grandchildren, was never filed. But contemporary estimates of his wealth ranged between $6 million and $11.8 million. Whatever the amount, it was of no use where he was headed. When Ty entered Atlanta's Emory Hospital on June 5, he knew he would only leave it feet first. From his hospital bed he mailed a photograph of his mausoleum to Stump. "Any day now" was written across it. No longer able to endure the pain of the cancer coursing through his back and skull, he finally surrendered to a variety of drugs. He slipped in and out of consciousness, regularly praying with a local Baptist minister when he was sentient. "He loved to talk about how much Christ meant to him during his suffering and as he faced the future," said Reverend John Richardson of Atlanta. But Ty remained in character up to the end. On the table next to his bed was a paper bag containing $1 million in negotiable securities, weighed down by his favorite Luger pistol.

Who can say what thoughts danced through his drug-addled mind at this stage? Did the faces of those he abused throughout his long life emerge Marley-like from the shadows, goading him with scenes of what might have been? Or did a greater fear—that of being forgotten—creep over him? As Robert Wilkins has observed, "Fear of being forgotten after death is one of man's most deep-rooted anxieties. It is uncomfortable to think that we will not be alive 100 years from now; it is even more disturbing to think that hardly anyone then alive will

Ty standing outside his Atherton home in 1957, prior to moving back to Georgia for good.

The adventure that had been Ty Cobb's life ended on July 17, 1961, in Atlanta's Emory Hospital. Two days later, sandlot players stood at attention, caps in hand, as his body was carried from a Cornelia funeral home to a waiting hearse.

remember that we existed at all." Forced to face his own mortality, Ty had in his final years embraced those old standbys—religion, good works, and autobiography—in an attempt to validate his existence. Whether it was all enough to save his soul or his reputation remains open to conjecture.

"More than anything else, Ty Cobb wanted to be remembered," said his hospital nurse, Betty Jo Parsons. The planned Cobb memorial in Royston—a building eventually turned into a city hall because of a lack of funds, artifacts, and visitors—would have pleased him, even if he never would have admitted it, she added. "He acted as if he didn't care whether the world remembered Ty Cobb for a minute. But he cared. He cared so much."

The hearse bearing Cobb rode silently past the sign the local chamber of commerce had erected a year earlier to honor Royston's most famous son.

Baseball's greatest performer, his body wracked by cancer, diabetes, and cardiac problems, finally passed away at 1:18 on the afternoon of Monday, July 17, 1961. He was 74 years old.

"For the last dozen years he had been trying to go home again," Ralph McGill wrote in his eulogy in the following day's *Atlanta Constitution*. "He could never quite make it, and it angered him that here was something with which he could not come to grips and have it out. Try as he would, Ty Cobb could not find the old dream in the hills of north Georgia where he was born. But he made it at last. He went to sleep for the last time on the sunny afternoon of July 17 just about the time the players of his day would have been taking the field for batting practice. He died in a coma-like sleep. He went home as quietly as if his father had come and taken him in his arms and carried him away."

A light rain fell as Ty was placed in the Cobb family vault two days later. "Ty—old Ty—is at rest for the first time in his life," cried one female mourner. The melodrama was lost on the uniformed Little Leaguers in attendance, a few of whom offended the prevailing solemnity with whispers and self-conscious grins. Stern looks from adults stopped the fidgeting. Some in the crowd of four hundred or so watched the disciplinary tug-of-war in silent amusement. Fathers and sons, they knew, can sometimes be that way.

"He forced a lot of his trouble," Tris Speaker said of Cobb, "but a hell of a lot of it was dumped on him."

CHAPTER NINE

Bat Out of Hell

*How much of the Cobb story is myth and how much is fact?
It's hard to separate one from the other. Did he sharpen his spikes?
Many say yes, but add that in great measure it was an advertising
program, telling the opposition to "keep out of my way." Was he
overly belligerent? Not necessarily, but because he was Ty Cobb each
incident became front-page news all over the nation. In terms of
individual performance, his record is awesome. A number
of his records have been broken, each time by a different individual.
When you consider maybe six of his marks took as many men
to erase them, you can see how truly great he was. Was he better
than Babe Ruth? An excellent case can be made for either
player. Cobb has figures to back his claim, but in contests like
these the New York exposure means a lot. Ruth cemented his claim
as the best by having a large personal following among
newspapermen. Cobb had no such support.*

*Here's what I think. If, in the Celestial League, the St. Peter's
Angels were to play Lucifer's Legions, it would be good sense
to wager on whichever team offered Cobb in its lineup.*

RETIRED SPORTSWRITER EDGAR HAYES, 1985

❦

For Tyrus Raymond Cobb, it's been a long road, dead or alive.

One hundred years after he first broke into the major leagues, nearly everyone intimate with his singular playing style is long gone, leaving the shepherding
of his complicated fame largely in the hands of a variety of pop-culture custodians. Taken collectively, what has emerged from the commingling of the factual
and fictional treatments of his life is the pervasive image of a brutal, bigoted,
friendless, haunted creature, a free-swinging, bourbon-guzzling ogre who presumably tortured small animals when he wasn't gleefully using his sharpened spikes

> **"Life's too short to have enemies. I read that about Cobb, that he had a lot of enemies. If you got enemies, they try to hurt you. Run into you. I don't want people throwing at my head."**
>
> —PETE ROSE, 1985

to saw milk-drinking infielders in half. "Baseball is war!" a thoroughly repulsive Tommy Lee Jones shouts in Ron Shelton's 1994 biopic, *Cobb*. "I love it!"

Mainstream news media, also not known for nuance or analysis when it comes to Cobb, has done its part in reducing a confounding and self-contradictory character to a comfortably predictable stereotype. In early 2004, when *NBC Nightly News* reported on Pete Rose's admission that he had bet on baseball, producers trotted out the usual bad-boy suspects in an attempt to put the story in historical context. As grainy film clips of Babe Ruth and Cobb played across millions of television screens, the voice-over described the playful Bambino as "a womanizer," while his grim rival was described as "violent and neurotic." A few months earlier, when the press took Baseball Hall of Fame president Dale Petroskey to the woodshed for revoking invitations to activist-actors Susan Sarandon and Tim Robbins to Cooperstown's planned *Bull Durham* film festival, at least one defender of the First Amendment used the controversy as an opportunity to take a swipe at the Hall's first inductee. "Somebody should ask Petroskey about that great American racist, Ty Cobb, being in the Hall," wrote Nick Canepa in the *San Diego Union-Tribune*. The lauded ESPN "SportsCentury" documentary series, which has been regularly re-telecast since its debut in 1999, could not resist concentrating on Cobb's many personal shortcomings during its profile of the player, though the cable network emphasized its rankings of the 20th century's greatest athletes were based strictly on athletic ability. (For the record, the panel of judges determined Cobb to be number 20. Babe Ruth was named the second-greatest athlete, behind hoops legend Michael Jordan.)

In today's culture, personality has overpowered performance to the point that someone unfamiliar with Cobb's accomplishments is left wondering exactly what it was that caused his contemporaries to name him the first person to the Hall of Fame. "Ty Cobb's image is pretty well set now in the minds of most fans and baseball writers alike," essayist Ted Hathaway decided more than four decades after the Peach's passing. "If Cobb's greatness is acknowledged, it is often done so grudgingly."

For better or for worse, much of what the public today knows about Cobb— or thinks it knows—can be traced back to the article "Ty Cobb's Wild 10-Month Fight to Live," which Al Stump wrote for the December 1961 issue of *True*. It came

Robert Wuhl (right) and the real Al Stump on the set of *Cobb* in 1994.

out at the same time as the insightful but sanitized autobiography Stump had collaborated on with Cobb, *My Life in Baseball*, was in bookstores. Stump's article, which was a lurid first-person account of his experiences as the Peach's ghost-writer, got much broader play than Cobb's posthumously published memoirs because of its sensational storyline and the magazine's extremely large circulation. More than 40 years after it first appeared, the widely anthologized article still makes for riveting reading, and all subsequent biographical treatments of Cobb (including this one) are required to draw upon it for a glimpse of the man in the terminal stage of his life. But there are some nagging questions about Stump's dark and devastating portrait, even as its impact on Cobb's public legacy remains clear.

Al Stump, circa 1955.

Stump was born in 1916 in Colorado Springs, Colorado, and was raised in the Pacific Northwest. After graduating from the University of Washington, he went to work at the *Portland Oregonian*, getting married and starting a family on a reporter's modest salary. Toward the end of World War II, he entered the navy as a correspondent and was assigned to the aircraft carrier U.S.S. *Hancock*. The most profitable part of his tour of duty was the six months he spent at a hospital in Santa Barbara, California, recovering from a severe skin malady. He fell in love with the area and, after making his first-ever magazine sale to the *Saturday Evening Post*, used the eye-popping $5,000 paycheck to quit the low-paying grind of daily newspaper work. He moved his family from Washington, and for the next two decades, until he took a staff job in 1968 at the Hearst-owned *Los Angeles Herald-Examiner* during a contentious strike, supported himself as a freelance writer. His byline appeared in *Argosy, Saga, Esquire, Sport,* and other popular men's periodicals. Once, during the 1950s, he had stories in five different national magazines on the newsstand at the same time.

"When you go to the Baseball Hall of Fame, it has what it calls the 'immortals.' Ty Cobb is one. Baseball can call you an immortal. I thought only God could do that."

—DIRECTOR RON SHELTON

"Stumpy" affected a certain style, consistent with what some thought were his Alan Ladd looks. He dressed dapperly and was generous to friends, some of whom knew him as a soft touch for loans that often went unpaid. To Stump, whose literary hero was Ernest Hemingway, home life was never quite as alluring as the testosterone-soaked environment of sports, politics, crime, and entertainment he inhabited as a writer. He pursued interesting stories, enjoyed his flirtations, and at the end of the day could usually be found inside any number of favorite watering holes. There he could unwind and exchange gossip, tall tales, and mild boasts with his cronies or a captive bartender. Among his claims was that he was the co-inventor of the "greyhound," a drink comprised of grapefruit juice, vodka, and lime. "Al was a workaholic," said his second wife, Jo Mosher. "His only hobby was drinking."

Stump's collaboration with Cobb on his autobiography was the first book the writer, then in his middle 40s, had ever worked on. (He would go on to write five more, including a collaboration with golfer Sam Snead.) Stump was fond of stating that Grantland Rice, the dean of American sportswriters, had highly recommended him to Cobb, a bit of self-puffery that ignored the fact that Rice had died several years before Ty finally decided to publish his memoirs. Actually, Stump was approved by Ty and his publisher, Doubleday, after several other writers were dropped for various reasons—the most common being an inability or unwillingness to deal with Cobb's irascibility, especially after cancer had handed Ty a death sentence.

Stump's relationship with the dying ballplayer was anything but chummy. Afterward he liked to say he "quit once and was fired twice" as he and Cobb argued over what should remain in the book and what should be left out. For example, Ty chose not to go into any detail about his father's death, and his marital woes and other family problems were not mentioned. Conversely, he was very forthcoming in describing his ruinous relationships with early teammates and the 1926 Cobb-Speaker scandal. Stump later explained he was moved to tell "the true story" about Cobb in his follow-up piece in *True* because, as Ty's ghostwriter, he was upset by the book's omissions and "sugar coated" nature. This seems specious, for Stump, who attended editorial meetings in New York with Ty and the publisher, understood his role as collaborator going into the project. Ty described the arrangement in a letter written to a Nevada friend on June 8, 1960, the day before Stump was scheduled to arrive in Royston to begin work. His ghostwriter "will do by tape, forming questions & answers a conversational procedure my part reciting from my early youth on to my retirement. select from all this what they think might be usable, then final composition continuity, polishing up which I insist Doubleday and myself will decide whats to be [sic]."

In writing what he considered his corrective and cathartic piece for *True*, Stump clearly was less motivated by the chance to iron out history or cleanse his guilty conscience than by the sizable check that an account of the ballplayer's "wild" final months promised—not to mention the payoff on any movie rights he might be able to sell. Freelancing has always been a precarious existence, even for established writers like Stump. During the time Stump was working on Cobb's memoirs he was going through a divorce. In addition to alimony and support payments for his four children, he also had his own living and office expenses to meet. The exact amount *True* paid Stump for his 10,000-word story could not be found. But based on the article's length, its subject, and the very generous rates large-circulation magazines paid its top contributors during this era, an estimate in the range of $3,500 to $6,000 seems right. Much higher payouts were not unheard of for the right story. (A few years earlier, Cobb himself had received $25,000 from *Life* for a two-part series.) Even a figure at the low end of the range was roughly equal to the annual wage of teachers and factory workers in 1961.

Whatever Stump was paid, for years he made no attempt to turn the article into a book-length biography, presumably because he was contractually prohibited from publishing a title that would directly compete with *My Life in Baseball* as long as Doubleday kept it in print. However, he was free to shop around the movie rights to his magazine piece, eventually selling them to filmmaker Ron Shelton. A tie-in book deal also was negotiated, with the publisher stipulating that the *True* article comprise the opening chapter to what became *Cobb: The Life and Times of the Meanest Man Who Ever Played Baseball*. Shelton's movie and Stump's book came out in 1994, each ratcheting up the level of malevolence originally contained in "Ty Cobb's Wild 10-Month Fight to Live."

Stump's article was tailor-made for *True*'s audience of armchair adventurers. *True*, which promoted itself as "the world's largest selling men's magazine," was a staple of barbershops, barracks, firehouses, and other masculine enclaves. Issues regularly served up stories about safaris, treasure hunts, flying saucers, lost mines, the Abominable Snowman, and the Loch Ness monster. Stump's penchant for consistently delivering wildly colorful anecdotes in his profiles of sports figures, politicians, criminals, and show-biz personalities is troubling to anyone who knows how writers of the day regularly twined fact with fiction in putting together their stories. Stump once profiled Jon Lindbergh, a record-setting deep-sea diver and the son of famed aviator Charles Lindbergh, for *True*. "I was rather upset about the article he did on me," recalled Lindbergh, a low-key fellow who declined to go into a blow-by-blow account. "He really stretched the facts and embellished it." Because of Stump's sensationalizing, Lindbergh added, he refused the magazine's request for a follow-up article.

Every writer has his own method of crafting a story. According to Jo Mosher, who became Stump's second wife while working as a travel columnist at the *Herald-Examiner*, Stump liked to sit back, have a few drinks, and "egg someone on." Said Mosher: "Al was not a character himself. He was quiet. But he loved oddballs. He'd encourage them to act up, to really be bad. He'd get good stories

like that." One has to wonder if that methodology was in play during any of Stump's private moments with the ailing, unstable, and frequently disoriented Cobb. If so, then how much of what this old-school writer related, from the hair-raising car ride down a snowy mountain pass and the tearful scene in the Royston cemetery on Christmas Eve, to the conversations with unnamed "informants" and Cobb's revelatory confessions, can be trusted not to have been embroidered or contrived? The only people present during the article's most powerful scenes and the sharing of its most dramatic dialogue were Cobb and Stump—and Cobb was not alive to pass judgment on the story's veracity when it was published. Ted Williams, a straight shooter if there ever was one, insisted Stump was "full of it" when the writer claimed Williams and Cobb had had a permanent falling-out over a silly argument while picking an all-time all-star team. Stump described the anecdote in detail in "Ty Cobb's Wild 10-Month Fight to Live." Williams claimed Stump had simply invented the story for effect—hardly the first offense of its kind in journalism, but at the same time no ringing endorsement of the writer, either.

Stump disingenuously told readers in his *True* piece, "During the final 10 months of his life I was his [Cobb's] constant companion." Actually, the events he breathlessly seamed together occurred over the course of a few intermittent working sessions with Cobb from early June 1960 to the following May. At best the two collectively spent only a few weeks together over the course of about a year, with Stump saying his goodbyes to Ty a full two months before he passed away. The rest of the time Stump steadily worked on the book manuscript of *My Life in Baseball* at his California beach house, using material from earlier biographies by John McCallum and Harry Salsinger and Cobb's *Life* pieces. He made little effort to check the reliability of these sources or of the stories the addled and pain-wracked Cobb told him. As a result *My Life in Baseball*, for all of its wonderful re-creation of the game's early days and Ty's stories of "inside baseball," was marred by numerous factual errors. To be fair to Stump, he never considered himself a historian. He was first and foremost a storyteller, though he bristled at the term "barbershop writer," as those who specialized in men's magazine fare were called.

However one chooses to describe or judge Stump's style, there is no denying its influence on how Cobb has come to be remembered since his death. For example, in the *True* article he dramatized Ty's drunken boast that he had killed a man in 1912, though a sober and more reflective Cobb was dodgier about that claim in his autobiography—passages that Stump had ghostwritten. This purposeful shading of the facts was significant. Prior to 1961, Cobb had been characterized in many unflattering ways, but never as a murderer. However, with Stump ignoring any ambiguities about the alleged murder in his article, the image of Ty Cobb as a bona fide "killer" quickly became an unquestioned and endlessly recycled part of baseball lore. "Killer Cobb" is now a staple of pop culture. In the 2000 movie *Nurse Betty*, to cite just one example, Morgan Freeman chastises fellow hit man Chris Rock for the unorthodox manner in which he has just carried out a murder: "If I'd told you a Ty Cobb story, would you have taken a bat and beaten him to death?" Some of Cobb's cultural custodians have felt the need to embellish the body count. When Ron Shelton's film *Cobb*, which was based on Stump's article, was released as a "director's cut" DVD, it included Shelton's commentary: "We know Cobb killed at least one man. He probably had killed others during his lifetime, too." There was absolutely no proof Cobb killed one man, much less others. If anything, that story—like many others involving Cobb—has been satisfactorily debunked by baseball historians. Nonetheless, uncontested comments like this not only kept alive, but also enhanced, the Peach's reputation for actually committing homicide—a reputation first given wide circulation in "Ty Cobb's Wild 10-Month Fight to Live."

Near the end of his *True* piece Stump summarized Cobb's funeral in a single misleading sentence: "From all of major-league baseball, three men, and three men only, attended his funeral." Some variation of the game's implied dissing of the Georgia Peach has worked its way into almost every creative treatment since. Whether it's an article, book, or film, it provides a neat wrap to any Cobb story— baseball's bad-ass abandoned and unmourned in death. In the opinion of Ty's still-agitated daughter-in-law, Shirley Cobb (who had married Jimmy in 1951), Stump "meant to deceive people with that. The *Los Angeles Times* later used the line and had just three people *total* coming to the funeral. Throughout the entire article he didn't care if what he wrote was derogatory or exaggerated or untrue. It was just a money maker for him."

Stump, who did not attend the funeral, almost certainly got his information from *The Sporting News*, which reported three baseball people were among the estimated 150 mourners who gathered inside Christian Church in Cornelia to hear a pair of preachers praise the deceased. What Stump chose to omit, although "baseball's bible" included it in its coverage, was that the low-key funeral service was the result of a family decision to keep it a private affair. Ty's old friend Coca-Cola chairman Bob Woodruff had argued unsuccessfully with the Peach's three surviving children and his first wife, Charlie Lombard Cobb, for a more substantial funeral. Members of the Spink family, longtime publishers of *The Sporting News*, also thought the Peach deserved a funeral consistent with his stature.

Instead, the deceased was buried within 48 hours of his passing. This presumably was in keeping with Ty's wishes, though some have suggested a couple of contributing factors. Family members, stuck in muggy Georgia on a prolonged deathwatch, were anxious to return to their normal routines. Ty's youngest offspring, Beverly and Jimmy, both lived in California and between them had eight children waiting for them at home. The family also didn't want to give the national media time to marshal their resources and descend en masse on Royston, where probing microphones and cameras would predictably concentrate on the darker aspects of the Cobb family history. (There were, to be sure, several skeletons rattling around in the Cobb closet, starting with the shooting death of

Ty Cobb — THE Name
of the Game

If it's true that imitation is the sincerest form of flattery, then the Peach certainly would have to be pleased by the large number of namesakes he inspired. Over the years hundreds–perhaps even thousands–of admirers have named their offspring after him. An Internet search conducted in 2005, a century after he broke into the majors, revealed 60 American males named Ty Cobb. (For comparison's sake, the same search yielded six Babe Ruths, two Mickey Mantles, and only a single Honus Wagner.) As might be expected, the majority were located in southern states, though there also were Ty Cobbs in such disparate places as Sugarcreek, Ohio; Dillon, Montana; Providence, Rhode Island; and Vail, Colorado.

The search, of course, did not include any Ty Cobbs with unlisted phone numbers, or any Tys carrying different surnames. The latter category includes Ty Grisham, the son of best-selling novelist John Grisham (whose literary success has allowed the baseball-loving writer to build six Little League diamonds on his property); Ty Gretzky, whose father, hockey legend Wayne Gretzky, once paid $451,000 for the famous T206 Honus Wagner tobacco card; and Ty Rose, born during his father Pete's pursuit of Cobb's all-time hit record. "Many people consider it an honor to be named after the greatest ballplayer of them all," said Julie Ridgway, curator at the Ty Cobb Museum in Royston. Her son, Ty Ridgway, presumably agrees. "He hasn't asked to change his name," she said.

Naming a child after the Georgia Peach can be something of a burden, especially on the sandlot. "I was ribbed about it so much, I didn't pick up a baseball," confessed Ty Cobb of Burlington, North Carolina, a 58-year-old maintenance director. Mrs. Cobb verified her husband's ineptitude. "He was named after the ballplayer," she said, "but he can't play a lick." One who can play a lick—okay, a musical lick—is Ty Cobb of Gresham, Oregon, whose band, Ty Cobb and the Jukes, is a staple on the Portland blues scene.

Most Ty Cobbs of the world have learned to take their famous name in stride, enduring a lifetime of teasing while carving out their own niche. Occasionally a Ty Cobb makes a pretty big splash in another field. For several years the Reno Media Press Club has presented the Ty Cobb Award at its annual banquet. It's not in memory of the ballplayer, as most non-media types think, but to honor Tyrus Richard Cobb (1915–1997), an accomplished Nevada sportswriter for nearly 60 years. That particular Ty Cobb named his son Ty, and so to this day Tyrus William Cobb of Reno has to patiently explain to curious strangers that he was named after his father, who was named after the ballplayer, who—to add to the confusion—happened to have a lodge in nearby Lake Tahoe for many years.

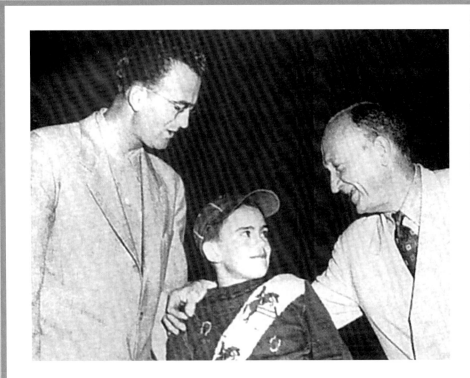

In fact, the three Ty Cobbs of Nevada often mingled over the years, said Tyrus William Cobb, who was born in 1940 and went on to a career in national security, at one time serving as a special assistant to President Ronald Reagan. "It was pretty well known that Cobb was always arguing with the utility companies," he recalled with a laugh. "Every time our lights would go out for some reason, Dad would say, 'The ballplayer didn't pay his bills.'" When the ballplayer was in the midst of his first divorce, the confusion over names caused the sportswriter's wife to be served with papers meant for Charlie Cobb.

In 1975, Tyrus William Cobb and his wife debated long and hard whether to name their newborn baby after Ty. "I thought, 'No way is my son going through all that I went through in Little League.' Finally, after six days, we settled on Tyrus Obren Cobb." The boy was known as Bren Cobb as he grew up, then switched over to Ty Jr. in college. Like his father, this Ty Cobb also works as a national security agent; his activities have included recent duty in Iraq.

Given the original Ty Cobb's controversial reputation, it's somewhat surprising to find that even African Americans have occasionally paid this special form of homage to the baseball legend. One was Alex Rivers, the Peach's longtime handyman and chauffeur, who named his first-born son Ty Cobb Rivers.

"Even if it had been a gal," Rivers often told his disbelieving friends, "ah woulda named her the same."

The Cobb vault in Royston.

Cobb's father in 1905. In 1928, the wife of Ty's brother, Paul—a former minor leaguer who had made a tidy fortune in insurance and Florida real estate—committed suicide by sticking her head inside a gas stove. And Ty's hard-luck middle son, Herschel, had been responsible for the horrible accidental deaths of two men during his abbreviated life. The first tragedy involved a stranded motorist who had run out of gas outside the Cobb home in Augusta. Herschel, then a teenager, played the Good Samaritan, providing the young man with a can of fuel. However, as the gasoline was being poured into the tank, Herschel carelessly lit a cigarette, igniting the fumes. The motorist died of his burns. The second gruesome death occurred several years later, when a water skier fell and was run over by the boat Hershel was operating. This time the victim was decapitated by the propeller.) Whatever the reason, "There wasn't much time to put it together," Shirley Cobb said of her famous father-in-law's funeral.

Ty, aware of the melodramatic send-offs Babe Ruth and Lou Gehrig had enjoyed in New York, had fretted over how his own departure would suffer in comparison. For one thing, he had outlived many of his closest friends from baseball days, as well as his sister and even two of his own children. He also was mindful of all the animosity he had stirred up during his lifetime. Yet, for all the people he had alienated, Cobb still had many admirers—more than the self-pitying ballplayer himself realized. His funeral clearly could have been an impressive large-scale affair had he (and his family) desired it. Condolence cards and telegrams from people inside and outside of baseball poured in, while the many published obituaries included glowing reminiscences from old rivals. Hillerich & Bradsby, among others, bought expensive full-page ads in several large newspapers mourning the Peach's passing. "We have lost a true friend," the bat maker declared. A number of baseball people, including household names like Ted Williams and Casey Stengel and the last surviving members of the charter class of Hall of Fame inductees, Rogers Hornsby and George Sisler, were among those planning to serve as pallbearers when they were informed of the family's wish for a private funeral. Dignitaries from outside the game, such as aging military legend Douglas MacArthur, also were planning to travel to Georgia. Some of Cobb's closest friends from baseball disregarded messages to stay home. Mickey Cochrane and Ray Schalk flew in from Chicago, while Nap Rucker traveled from his residence north of Atlanta. Hall of Fame official Sid Keener came from New York. "Cornelia, Georgia was not exactly easy to get to back then," recalled Shirley Cobb. "Traveling wasn't what it is today."

It was a long way from New York to Georgia in a cultural sense, too. Photographers were kept at a distance; there were to be no shots of the ballplayer in his casket, as had happened with Ruth and Gehrig. A cortege of 26 cars crept its way from Cornelia to the Royston cemetery 28 miles away. "Everybody was so respectful," remembered Shirley Cobb. "This is a very Southern thing, I know, but as the cortege passed by, motorists stopped their cars at the side of the road and got out." All told, upward of 400 people attended Cobb's "private" funeral, including the squads of Little Leaguers lining the path from the cemetery gate to the Cobb family mausoleum. Afterward there was a reception at the home of Harrison Gailey, a distant cousin who had befriended Ty in his final years. "I loved him, that's how I felt," Gailey later told an inquisitive biographer. All in all, the Peach's farewell was understated and dignified, as befitted his small-town Georgia roots, but it was not pathetic, as Stump implied. Ty Cobb, for all his many faults and all his quiet fears, did not leave this world unloved or unmourned. Nonetheless, it is Stump's pithy description that endures.

The reaction to Stump's story by Cobb's relatives and friends and the medical professionals who had treated him was overwhelmingly negative. While not denying Cobb's irascibility, they protested that Stump's account was biased and overdrawn and as mean-spirited as he had made the terminally ill man out to be. At one point in the article Stump made a fleeting reference to praying with Ty, who in the twilight of his sinner's life had found a measure of solace in reading and discussing passages in the Bible. Where, some might have wondered, was any extensive depiction of a more contrite Cobb, his Luger lowered and his expletives in check before the man on the cross? Surely this was as much a part of the exasperatingly complex Cobb in his final "wild 10 months" as the drunken ravings Stump attributed to him.

"I think Stump was very one-sided in his presentation of Cobb in the article," Betty Jo Parsons, one of Cobb's nurses, told a reporter in 1962. "Like so many people he seemed to shut his eyes to anything that reflected good on Ty." Georgia radiologist Rex Teeslink, then a young medical student, was Cobb's constant, around-the-clock companion for the last two months of his life. The doctor kept quiet about his experiences for 30 years before he decided to "set the record straight before it's too late." "The things that have been written, the way he has been portrayed...it's like those ten-cent novels about the heroes of the old West," Teeslink told *Sport Illustrated*'s Leigh Montville. "None of them are true. Wyatt Earp and all the rest aren't any more heroes than you or I, but because these things have been written and have lasted so long, the stories have been taken as the truth. That's how it has been with Ty Cobb, only the other way. All I want people to realize is that he was a fair and meaningful guy." Beyond the slanted nature of Stump's article, many thought the magazine sale smacked of bald opportunism and was a betrayal of trust. Moreover, because the story appeared during the holiday season and so soon after Ty's death, it was criticized as being in just plain bad taste. For years afterward Cobb's immediate family refused to cooperate with other creative projects, including a well-received 1985 biography written in just-the-facts-ma'am style by history professor Charles C. Alexander.

For uninvolved readers, however, Stump's article was a jarring, engrossing character study that brought back to life a troubled American icon who had badly faded from public memory. Bob Considine, the syndicated columnist who had ghosted Babe Ruth's autobiography, called Stump's article "possibly the best sports story I have ever read." The piece went on to win the annual Best American Sport Story award and was almost immediately anthologized, thus assuring it a far longer life and greater readership than the typical magazine story. Meanwhile, sales of *My Life in Baseball* were lukewarm, with only about 16,000 copies sold by the time the book went out of print at the end of the decade.

Stump, who for the rest of his life delighted in smoking one of Ty's pipes, died of congestive heart failure in late 1995. He was 79. Ironically, the writer had grown estranged from his children in his latter years; none of them attended the memorial service at a local marina when his ashes were taken out to sea and spread over the Pacific. Five years after his death, the Al Stump Collection of sports memorabilia went to auction. Among the personal possessions of Cobb's that had found their way into Stump's hands were Ty's dentures, which ultimately fetched $8,021 from a Pennsylvania woman anxious to take her own bite out of the Peach's past.

◎◎

"Was Ty Cobb psychotic throughout his baseball career?" Al Stump rhetorically asked in "Ty Cobb's Wild 10-Month Fight to Live." The answer, the writer concluded, was an unequivocal "yes."

Cobb was considered by many to be, in the parlance of the day, a "nutter." Fred Haney once said of Cobb the manager: "We thought that Cobb would crack up any day. One day he would be riding high and working well with his lineup, next day he'd go around with the whites of his eyes flared and be the meanest guy you ever saw. He had spells, fits. Unimportant things made him blow. Some of the

Tommy Lee Jones, a Luger on his lap and bottles of bourbon and medicine at hand, was an especially malevolent Ty Cobb in Ron Shelton's biopic.

> **"A lot of people have gloves and bats of famous players, but we are the only ones who have Ty Cobb's teeth."**
>
> —KAREN SHEMONSKY, WHO PAID $8,021
> FOR A SET OF COBB'S DENTURES

boys thought it was a case of brain fever." Furman Bisher recalled the ordeal of working with the elderly Peach on a magazine article. "You had to treat him like a stick of dynamite. You'd be getting along fine and then you'd say something that would trigger a response....You'd make just one mistake, say something wrong, and he'd be gone." Cobb's odd and often antipodal behavior caused reporters, umpires, ballplayers, and others to freely throw around such terms as "psychotic" when describing the Peach.

As any behavioral scientist today would be quick to warn, simply saying it doesn't make it so. But in a layman's effort to better understand the engine of Cobb's behavior, especially in the light of a growing interest in the relatively new subspecialty of sports psychiatry, one has to seriously consider the possibility—some would say *probability*—that he suffered from an unspecified mental illness. There's reason to suspect it may have been bipolar disorder, a manic-depressive condition caused by a chemical imbalance in the brain. Little was known about it in Cobb's lifetime. The severity of the condition, which is found in an estimated 1 to 2 percent of the population, can vary greatly. Many people walk through life not even knowing they have it. Although anyone can suffer from bipolar disorder, it seems to be disproportionately found in more creative and intelligent people. These include comedians Jonathan Winters and Robin Williams, singers Rosemary Clooney and Connie Francis, directors Tim Burton and Francis Ford Coppola, actresses Patty Duke, Margot Kidder, and Kristy McNichol, astronaut Buzz Aldrin, and musicians Brian Wilson and Axl Rose. Those suspected of being bipolar who have since died include writers Ernest Hemingway and Virginia Woolf, musicians Del Shannon and Kurt Cobain, poet Hart Crane, and actress Marilyn Monroe. All of the departed had something in common: unable to exorcise their demons, they committed suicide. According to Stump, in his final year Cobb also spoke of taking his own life, though by that point he was in constant pain and already knew he was terminally ill. A comprehensive psychiatric examination of the Peach obviously falls beyond the scope of this book; besides, his death makes moot any exhaustive and definitive clinical study. Still, such a diagnosis, were it possible, might account for his pronounced mood swings, his manic periods of rage, irritability, and thrill-seeking, the "brain fever" that so many people commented on during his lifetime.

According to Dr. Antonio L. Baum, a sports psychiatrist at George Washington University Medical Center in Washington, D.C., bipolar mania "can cause the same behavioral disturbances in athletes as anyone else. Stressors in pro fessional athletes' lives can trigger a manic episode...and the public may not wit ness the episode's manifestation. When this occurs, the athlete's mental illness is generally misunderstood by the public and misrepresented in the media." For baseball fans, the most famous example is Jimmy Piersall, whose bizarre behavior and emotional outbursts while playing for five different teams in the 1950s and '60s were uneasy reminders of some of Cobb's uglier moments. Piersall had a nervous breakdown during the 1952 season and entered a sanatorium, where he underwent shock treatment. His comeback with the Boston Red Sox included a book, *Fear Strikes Out*, that described his battle with what was subsequently iden tified as bipolar disorder. Darryl Strawberry, another self-destructive major lea guer, also was diagnosed as being bipolar. Other afflicted athletes from the recent past include golfer John Daly, tennis player Ilie Nastase, and football players Barret Robbins, Alonzo Spellman, and Dimitrius Underwood.

One doesn't ask to come into the world with a broken brain any more than one asks to be born with a deformed limb or defective eyesight. Along with genet ics, environmental factors play a key role in determining who must grapple with the handicap. Studies have shown that extreme stress brought on by the sudden death of a loved one or a similarly shocking incident can trigger or aggravate the condition. During a 10-month period in 1905–06—arguably Cobb's *real* "wild 10- month fight to live"—the teenager experienced a series of psychological shocks capable of unhinging any young mind. His father was shot to death and his mother was put on trial for his murder; at the same time he underwent a major change of cultural environment in going to the North and the big leagues, where he had to deal with the animus of his much older teammates. All of this culmi nated in a nervous breakdown so severe he had to be rushed back to Detroit in the middle of a road trip and confined for nearly two months in a sanatorium.

The ability to understand, much less correct, mental illness was much more limited a century ago. Today patients are treated with a combination of mood-sta bilizing drugs, intensive psychotherapy, behavior modification, and group coun seling. At the time of Ty's confinement, however, America's "mental hygiene" movement had just started and, in Vienna, Sigmund Freud was still developing his breakthrough theories of psychoanalysis. The distressed 19-year-old was encouraged to sleep, fish, and tramp the woods, but there really was little else to be done in 1906 beyond simply resting one's mind and body for a spell before going back into the world. Reflecting the sad state of mental-health care then, many of Cobb's contemporaries surrendered to emotional distress and opted *out* of this world. In the first two decades of the 20th century, nearly a score of active or recently retired ballplayers took their lives. The list of suicides included Detroit player-manager Win Mercer, who inhaled gas inside a hotel room three years before Ty's breakdown. Given the fact that many mental illnesses run in families, it may be worth noting that Cobb's grandson, Ty Cobb III, put a bullet through his own brain in Florida in 1986. According to Peggy Schug, her tortured 42-year- old brother had spent a lifetime drifting through a succession of colleges and menial jobs, all the while trying to cope with the unrealistic expectations his famous name created. "He was an introverted person," she said. "He never should have been named after granddaddy. It just put too much pressure on him."

Was the Peach mentally ill? Or was he simply a moody social misfit—a supremely proud, intelligent, and hypersensitive competitor who, for all his abnormal behavior, doesn't deserve one moment on the analyst's couch?

Whatever the true state of Ty's mental condition, the "psychotic" Cobb is regularly found in creative treatments of his life. Such a flawed personality generally has received greater empathy in novels, such as Harry Stein's *Hoopla* (1983) and Patrick Creevy's *Tyrus* (2002), where there is more room for the artist to ruminate and complex characters to develop, than in films, a medium that typically relies on a series of revelatory "big moments" to carry a story.

Ron Shelton was one of those fascinated with Stump's take on the troubled ballplayer. Shelton was a diamond star at Santa Barbara High School when the *True* article made Stump a local celebrity. Shelton, the product of a strict Baptist upbringing who wasn't allowed to even see motion pictures as a child, rebelled with a vengeance. During his years as a second baseman in the Baltimore Orioles' farm system, he spent much of his free time in small-town bijous, soaking in all that he could about the art of filmmaking from what he saw on the big screen. Shelton's unconventional career path to Hollywood included a graduate degree in sculpture and 10 years of odd jobs, including stints as a cab driver and teacher. Meanwhile he was writing screenplays, finally selling his first produced script when he was 37 years old. Soon Shelton was directing as well as writing films. After achieving success with sports-oriented movies like *Bull Durham, White Men Can't Jump,* and *Tin Cup,* the late-blooming Oscar nominee had the credentials to convince Warner Bros. to bankroll his version of "Ty Cobb's Wild 10-Month Fight to Live."

Shelton's *Cobb* was Stump's hyperbolic horror story writ large, with Tommy Lee Jones, a craggy-faced Texan known for his prickly behavior, playing the title character. A former Yale football player, Jones had to learn to bat left-handed to portray Cobb as a player, then shaved his head and endured hours of latex applications to resemble Cobb as a dying old man. Midway through production, the 47-year-old actor accepted an Academy Award for his supporting role as a lawman in *The Fugitive,* bald pate and all. His Oscar win helped boost expectations for *Cobb.*

"Some people won't think he's worth two hours," Shelton said of his and Jones' Cobb. "In that case, go hang out in South Carolina with Forrest Gump—he won't threaten you. That's not a statement about *Forrest Gump.* It's just that I'd rather get in your face with a movie, ask some tough questions, disturb you a bit."

Shelton's movie was disturbing to the point of its own detriment. Jones fleshed out Shelton's screenplay with consummate gusto, his nonstop transgressions including shooting off his pistol and filthy mouth at every opportunity and sexually assaulting a cigarette girl in a hotel room. The latter sequence, which has a drunken Cobb kicking the woman before dragging her into his room, where he pays her to brag about his sexual prowess after he can't perform, had many moviegoers turning their eyes away from the screen. The attempted rape was pure fabrication on the part of Shelton, who favored pyrotechnics throughout what was meant to be a meditation on the public deification and deconstruction of celebrities like the Peach. At the same time, those hoping to catch an insight into Cobb's genius as a player were disappointed. Cobb's altercations may have regularly put him in the news, but it was his on-field brilliance that made him so fascinating. The audacious base running, the unparalleled bat control, the offensive cunning—all were missing. Instead of seeing Cobb gracefully perform one of his patented fadeaway or hook slides, grabbing a corner of the bag as the infielder swiped at air, Shelton had Jones clumsily bowling over opponents. If Cobb had motored around the base paths as portrayed in the movie, he would have broken an ankle or been shipped back to Augusta.

Cobb received positive reviews in the *New Yorker*, the *Boston Globe*, and the *Chicago Tribune*. "Shelton's strong, stinging film," opined *Rolling Stone*, was "one of the year's best." Other critics were not kind to Shelton's vision. "*Cobb* feels as if it ought to have some great meaning…but it succeeds in illuminating surprisingly little about the man, other than his vicious ways," Peter Stack wrote in the *San Francisco Chronicle*. "The viewer winds up with the depressing, uneasy feeling that *Cobb* really is a celebration of a monster, with but a little glimpse of its beating heart." Susan Stark of the *Detroit News* found Jones' character "so absolutely loathsome—irascible at his best, plain vicious at his worst—that the logical defense is to regard him, dismissively, as sub-human." *Entertainment Weekly*'s Owen Gleiberman, initially excited over the teaming of Shelton and Jones, called *Cobb* "a jaw-dropping botch, a bilious and reductive attack on its own hero." Ordinary sports fans willing to accept the caricatured Cobb were let down by a baseball movie with precious little baseball action in it. Pressed for their opinion, even members of the Stump family admitted Tommy Lee Jones was guilty of chewing the scenery and that comedic actor Robert Wuhl made a poor Al Stump. (Shelton and the Stump family all preferred Richard Dreyfuss for the part, but there was no room in the budget once Jones was signed. Stump himself was given a cameo role as a barfly in an early scene.)

In the wake of Jones' performance, the dwindling number of people still alive who personally knew the Peach rushed to his defense. Generally displaying a selective and worshipful memory, they glossed over the shortcomings of "Mr. Cobb" while arguing his good side was rarely exposed. Jimmy Lanier had grown up in Augusta as a close friend of Ty's son, Hershel. "Ty was outside the movie theater, waiting for me and Hershel," said Lanier, recalling an incident from his youth. "A young man in tattered clothes, a World War One vet, came over and asked somebody for directions to somewhere and Ty stepped in and said, 'I'm going that way, I'll take you.' The man didn't know this was Ty Cobb. Later, I saw Cobb slip him a twenty-dollar bill. I saw him do so many generous things that nobody else ever saw. Those things never got in the press." In Detroit, reporters managed to track down a handful of old-timers who had once crossed paths with the Peach. "We were kids of another time, I guess," said Louis Lemieux, who recalled getting 50 cents for carrying Cobb's bats to his car one afternoon when he was seven years old. "I don't know how it is today, but we didn't compare goodness with badness back then. All you knew is how you were treated, and I can say that Ty Cobb was always gracious."

PEANUTS by Charles M. Schulz

Cartoonist Charles Schulz was an avid baseball fan and friends with Cobb's daughter, Beverly, who owned a bookshop in Palo Alto, California, that Schulz frequented. As a form of homage to the Peach, the "Peanuts" creator occasionally worked Ty Cobb's name into one of his comic strips, typically around the anniversary date of his death. This particular strip appeared on July 17, 1998, the day the Ty Cobb Museum opened in Royston.

The Peach was decidedly *not* always gracious and generous. But reminiscences like these underscored the fundamental issues of fairness and balance that have always irritated Cobb's admirers. Although Shelton and Jones had nobly proclaimed their intention to attack America's propensity for hero worship, in the eyes of Cobb's supporters Hollywood had made its case by presenting a litany of myths, half-truths, falsehoods, and exaggerations. Once again, in the rush to present a portrait of what is generally considered to be an unbalanced personality, the view itself became unbalanced.

The premiere in Royston was a disaster. Many locals had worked in the movie as extras, and they were just as eager to see Hollywood's take on Royston's favorite son as they were to spot themselves and their neighbors on the big screen. They entered the theater bubbling over with anticipation and left it silent and shell-shocked. "Everybody walked out too embarrassed to look at each other," recalled Greg Hall, a florist who had taken time off to don a straw boater and bowtie during the filming of baseball scenes at Rickwood Field in Birmingham, Alabama. Residents were so upset they finally created the hometown museum that had been talked about ever since Cobb's death. The Ty Cobb Museum opened in the headquarters building of the Ty Cobb Healthcare System in 1998. One of its proudest exhibits is Ty's Bible. Meanwhile, Hall quietly built his own humble shrine of movie artifacts in his basement, away from disapproving eyes.

Cobb was a commercial flop. It grossed less than $850,000 in its limited domestic run over the winter of 1994–95, though video rentals and overseas releases (in Germany it was re-titled *Home Run*) helped Warner Bros. recoup some of its money. The schizophrenic reviews hurt ticket sales, of course. Another part of the problem, sources close to the film confided, was Tommy Lee Jones, who proved as petulant as the Peach himself. The actor's recent divorce settlement called for his ex-wife to receive half of his income on *Cobb* and his next two movies, so he had little incentive to promote the film. Jones' peevishness upset Shelton and gave Warner Bros. another reason to yank the film after it had been released in only a dozen U.S. cities. To top it off, Jones' performance failed to produce his expected Oscar nomination for best actor, which would have caused the studio to invest much more money in its marketing.

Despite poor box office numbers, widespread publicity over the film, assisted by healthy sales of Stump's companion book (90,000 copies were sold during its first decade in print), helped drive the popular image of Cobb as a drunken, raving lunatic straight into a new century. Musical artists, fascinated by the character's repellence, took their cultural cues from the Stump-Shelton Cobb. The Seattle heavy metal band Soundgarden released "Ty Cobb," a song whose lyrics and pounding beat suggested helter-skelter violence: "Sucking on a ball and chain / Another motherfucker goes down the drain / Hard headed fuck you all / Just add it up to the hot rod death toll." A couple of brothers in Philadelphia, Paul and Ryan Cobb, decided to call their alternative guitar band Ty Cobb. "We were in a bar and we were playing one of those trivia touch-screen games," Paul told *Under the Radar* magazine. "And the question came up that asked, 'Who was the only player to beat up a fan with their own crutch?' It was Ty Cobb. And we just laughed. We thought that it sounded like a good, strong American name. But don't worry; we don't beat people with crutches." Curtis Management International, the Indianapolis-based agency that protects the commercial rights of dead celebrities like Babe Ruth and Elvis Presley, wasn't amused. The band changed its name to avoid potential copyright problems. The Cobb brothers didn't really care, said one, because the Peach "was an asshole anyway."

Today Cobb remains as much a captive to his bigotry as he does to his violence. Little was made of Ty's prejudice during his lifetime; reporters in the pre–civil rights era considered Cobb's racial attitudes to be so in line with the rest of white America as to be hardly newsworthy. However, in the years of heightened racial consciousness that followed Cobb's death, bigotry went from being an ugly, but tangential, part of the man's mosaic to its predominant and defining feature—so much so that one can argue it has disproportionately affected the public memory of his accomplishments.

In 1994, just prior to the release of Ron Shelton's biopic, Ken Burns dissected the Peach with a vengeance in the PBS series *Baseball*. The much-honored filmmaker, who has made "America's defining issue of race" the leitmotif of his historical documentaries, used Cobb as a one-dimensional foil for his centerpiece hero Jackie Robinson, who many knowledgeable baseball fans complained was as excessively deified in the series as Cobb was unduly demonized. Millions of viewers saw the stock Cobb: a beastly, murderous, emotionally bankrupt bigot with no real qualities beyond that of bedeviling pitchers and solving the stock market. Old canards were dusted off, including one that had Ty in retirement charging five dollars apiece for autographs. (A quick digression is in order here. Cobb, like any celebrity flooded with mail, was not unhappy to occasionally discover a check accompanying an autograph request, but that was never a condition for signing. On these occasions everybody benefited. The small amount of money was donated to his educational fund and the fan got a valuable autograph on the back of the endorsed check. Ted Williams actively encouraged this practice to benefit his Jimmy Fund for young cancer patients.) One "talking head" even opined that, all things considered, it might have been better if the game had never had Ty Cobb at all. While many cultural critics and ordinary baseball fans praised Burns' 18-hour-long series for its scope and ambition, *Commentary* magazine spoke for a sizable number of disappointed viewers when it described the film as "politically correct baseball" that was, at its core, "a tedious lecture on race."

Lee Blessing's *Cobb*, a multilayered production that has been performed on stages in New York and elsewhere to solid reviews since 1989, was more effective than Shelton and Burns in using the Peach as a prism through which to explore the issues of race and celebrity. The Minnesota playwright, whose script unavoidably drew upon Stump's article, employed the device of having three quarrelsome Cobbs of varying ages onstage at the same time. "He seemed so fractured as a personality," Blessing explained. "He was so successful on the ball field, so successful financially, so unsuccessful in his family life, that I just automatically started thinking of him as more than one person. Besides, Cobb was such a contentious human being, that I thought nothing made more sense than to watch him argue with himself for ninety minutes." Throughout Blessing's play, Ty is taunted by Negro Leagues great Oscar Charleston, who some called "the black Ty Cobb" during baseball's apartheid era. The fleet, powerful center fielder personified the experiences of the typical black player of the period. Despite two decades of excellence in the Negro Leagues, Charleston's name and achievements were unknown to mainstream America; relegated to anonymity, he died as a broken-down baggage handler in Philadelphia. "I am the greatest ballplayer that ever lived," brags Blessing's Cobb, who, according to legend, diminished that claim in 1926 by refusing to accept Charleston's challenge to a batting contest. As Blessing observed, some who watched both players in their prime thought it was more appropriate to refer to Cobb as "the white Oscar Charleston."

By the late 1990s, the creative works of Shelton, Burns, and Blessing, among others, had helped establish Cobb as the great metaphor for baseball's historic racism, though his actual influence on the issue of allowing blacks into organized ball was virtually nil. Cobb's mulish refusal to play against "darkies," which was shared by the majority of his contemporaries in organized ball, was nothing to the machinations of such world-class bigots as Adrian "Cap" Anson and Judge Landis in keeping the major leagues an all-alabaster affair until 1947. Nonetheless, the volatile nature of Cobb's bigotry sets him apart and continues to haunt him and his supporters to this day.

Time brings change, as any journey through today's South clearly illustrates. Had the Georgia Peach come along a generation or two later than he did, it's not unreasonable to assume that, like millions of Southern whites, he would have adopted a more enlightened view about race—or, at a minimum, kept his prejudices to himself, as many unreconstructed Southerners have learned to do. As it was, there are signs that Ty began to soften his views somewhat in the 1950s,

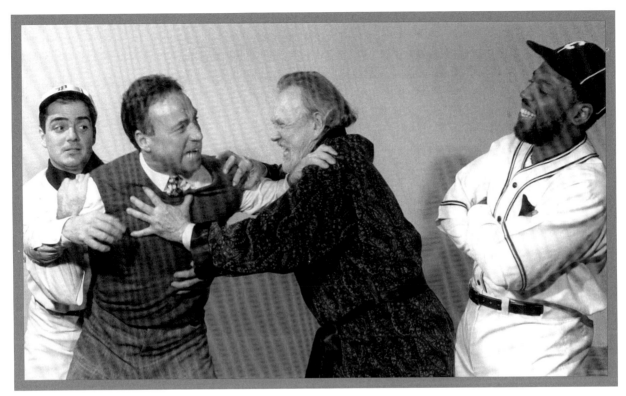

Lee Blessing's play, which has been staged across the country since 1989, features three Cobbs, all taunted by Negro Leagues great Oscar Charleston.

as he increasingly chewed over the many mistakes he had made during his life. One friend from that period recalled him regularly bragging on the black nurses that worked at Cobb Memorial Hospital, "though, of course, he could never bring himself to associate socially with blacks." That would have been out of the question for a true son of the segregated South in the 1950s, a time and a place percolating with racial rancor. Still, when there was little being done to address the medical concerns of blacks in north Georgia, Cobb Hospital employed one of the best African-American physicians in the region, Dr. J. B. Gilbert, to provide them with affordable quality health care. Dr. Gilbert, who had started practicing medicine in 1928, also treated white patients at Cobb Hospital and eventually became its chief of staff. As always, a whiff of old-fashioned plantation paternalism can be detected in Cobb's dealings with blacks. But outside of Ted Williams, how many other sports figures of the day were engaged in philanthropic work on any meaningful scale?

Ty came to accept the desegregation of baseball long before his old employer did. He told a California reporter in 1952—six full years before the Detroit Tigers fielded their first black—that he approved of the decision by the Dallas club in the Texas League to sign Negro players. "Certainly it is okay for them to play,"

> **"There is small doubt that Cobb was the greatest of all players, though some of his contemporaries held out for either Ruth or Honus Wagner. Their opinions may have been formed by hate."**
>
> —NEW YORK COLUMNIST JIMMY CANNON, 1961

he said. Not only was the growing influx of blacks in the majors and the Deep South inevitable, it also didn't bother him. "I see no reason in the world why we shouldn't compete with colored athletes as long as they conduct themselves with politeness and gentility," Cobb said, unaware of the irony of his comments about comportment. "Let me also say that no white man has the right to be less of a gentleman than a colored man; in my book that goes not only for baseball but in all walks of life."

A half-century after those surprising comments, many refuse to believe the old Tiger was truly capable of changing his stripes. Just prior to the start of the 2004 season, pressure from civil rights activists caused Augusta commissioners to withdraw a proposal to change the name of the local minor-league ballpark from Lake Olmstead Stadium to Ty Cobb Field. The proposed honor, timed to coincide with the centennial of the Georgia Peach's minor-league debut, would have been an "insult to many African-Americans and some white citizens," argued John R. Maben, former president of the Augusta chapter of the NAACP. Many Augustans, eager to maintain harmony in their community, agreed. "It's setting a bad precedent as far as the racism goes," one fan told a reporter from WJBF-TV. Said another: "I don't think we should name the baseball stadium after him—definitely not somebody as mean as he was." Cobb's latently evolving views on race, the success of his nonprofit health-care system, and the fact that his educational fund had helped hundreds of black Georgians attain college degrees—none of these was enough to save the Peach from the censure of the community with which he had long been associated. The name Ty Cobb simply was too vivid a reminder of Georgia's discriminatory past.

At the same time, a plan to recognize Cobb's brief career in Anniston, Alabama, also came under attack. Calhoun County commission chairman James "Eli" Henderson had headed a drive to have the state place a historical marker at a SouthTrust bank built on the site of a rooming house Cobb boarded at while playing with the Noblemen. Permission and funding were in place, and SouthTrust had already agreed to erect a temporary display case exhibiting memorabilia associated with Cobb's stay in Anniston. As commemorations go, this one promised to be small and innocuous. However, support evaporated once Cobb's toxic encounters with race, most dating back three-quarters of century and more, became part of the discussion. Nobody wanted to antagonize Anniston's populace, evenly divided between blacks and whites. Once again, activists were intolerant of the Peach's intolerance.

"We are so judgmental today," said Henderson. "Let's face it, 1904 was a long time ago. Everybody today knows racism was wrong. It's just like everybody used to smoke cigarettes and eat all kinds of food that was bad for you and other things we knew nothing about back then. We have to look past all that." With the Cobb project scrapped, Henderson has concentrated on that other Lost Cause—a memorial honoring the county's 5,000 Confederate volunteers. Supporters have been able to move forward on that "without any real problems," he said.

And so it goes. To his eternal detriment, Tyrus Raymond Cobb—a uniquely gifted performer and a fascinatingly complex human being—will always be his own worst enemy. To aficionados of inside baseball, the Peach's charm will continue to rest in the head, and for collectors who have written six-figure checks for one of his uniforms or bats, his name will always carry an almost mystical cachet. But modern storytellers, the gatekeepers of his image, will continue to find it more convenient and entertaining to concentrate on—and frequently embellish—the more tantalizing aspects of an imperfect life lived at full throttle. For all he accomplished on the diamond and off, Cobb's deeply flawed character will always be the cornerstone of his legend.

This was already evident 20 years ago, when Pete Rose was in the process of overtaking Cobb as baseball's all-time base-hit champ. A reporter mawkishly asked Rose if he thought the Peach was watching the proceedings from heaven.

"From what I've heard," said Rose, "that's not where he's at."

TYRUS RAYMOND COBB

DETROIT-PHILADELPHIA, A.L.-1905-1928
LED AMERICAN LEAGUE IN BATTING
TWELVE TIMES AND CREATED OR
EQUALLED MORE MAJOR LEAGUE
RECORDS THAN ANY OTHER PLAYER.
RETIRED WITH 4191 MAJOR LEAGUE HITS.

Ty Cobb's Batting Record

Minor Leagues

Year	Club	G	AB	R	H	BA	2B	3B	HR	RBI	BB	SO	TB	SA	SB
1904	Augusta	37	135	14	32	.237	6	0	1	—	—	—	41	.304	—
1904	Anniston	32	128	22	40	.313	4	**8**	0	—	—	—	60	.469	10
1905	Augusta	103	411	60	134	**.326**	13	4	1	—	—	—	158	.384	41
	Totals	172	674	96	206	.306	23	12	2	—	—	—	259	.384	51

Major Leagues

Year	Club	G	AB	R	H	BA	2B	3B	HR	RBI	BB	SO	TB	SA	SB
1905	Detroit	41	150	19	36	.240	6	0	1	15	10	—	45	.300	2
1906	Detroit	98	350	45	112	.320	13	7	1	41	19	—	143	.406	23
1907	Detroit	150	605	97	**212**	**.350**	29	15	5	**116**	24	—	**286**	**.473**	**49**
1908	Detroit	150	581	88	**188**	.324	**36**	20	4	**108**	34	—	**276**	**.475**	39
1909	Detroit	156	573	**116**	**216**	**.377**	33	10	**9**	**107**	48	—	**296**	**.517**	**76**
1910	Detroit	140	509	**106**	196	**.385**	36	13	8	91	64	—	279	**.554**	**65**
1911	Detroit	146	591	**147**	**248**	**.420**	**47**	**24**	8	**127**	44	—	**367**	**.621**	**83**
1912	Detroit	140	553	119	**227**	**.410**	30	23	7	90	43	—	324	**.586**	61
1913	Detroit	122	428	70	167	**.390**	18	16	4	67	58	31	229	**.535**	52
1914	Detroit	97	345	69	127	**.368**	22	11	2	57	57	22	177	**.513**	35
1915	Detroit	156	563	**144**	208	**.369**	31	13	3	99	118	43	274	.487	**96**
1916	Detroit	145	542	**113**	201	.371	31	10	5	68	78	39	267	.493	**68**
1917	Detroit	152	**588**	107	**225**	**.383**	**44**	**23**	7	102	61	34	**336**	**.571**	55
1918	Detroit	111	421	83	161	**.382**	19	**14**	3	64	41	21	217	.515	34
1919	Detroit	124	497	92	**191**	**.384**	36	13	1	70	38	22	256	.515	2
1920	Detroit	112	428	86	143	.334	28	8	2	63	58	28	193	.451	14
1921	Detroit	128	507	124	197	.389	37	16	12	101	56	19	302	.596	22
1922	Detroit	137	526	99	211	.401	42	16	4	99	55	24	297	.565	9
1923	Detroit	145	556	103	189	.340	40	7	6	88	66	14	261	.469	9
1924	Detroit	155	625	115	211	.338	38	10	4	74	85	18	281	.450	23
1925	Detroit	121	415	97	157	.378	31	12	12	102	65	12	248	.598	13
1926	Detroit	79	233	48	79	.339	18	5	4	62	26	2	119	.511	9
1927	Philadelphia	134	490	104	175	.357	32	7	5	93	67	12	236	.482	22
1928	Philadelphia	95	353	54	114	.323	27	4	1	40	34	16	152	.431	5
	Totals	3034	11429	2245	4191	.367	724	297	118	1961	1249	357	5861	.513	892

World Series

Year	Club	G	AB	R	H	BA	2B	3B	HR	RBI	BB	SO	TB	SA	SB
1907	Detroit	5	20	1	4	.200	0	**1**	0	0	0	3	6	.300	0
1908	Detroit	5	19	3	7	.368	1	0	0	4	1	2	8	.421	2
1909	Detroit	7	26	3	6	.231	3	0	0	5	2	2	9	.346	2
	Totals	17	65	7	17	.262	4	1	0	9	3	7	23	.354	4

Bold indicates led league or Series

Bibliography

Alexander, Charles C. *Ty Cobb*. New York: Oxford University Press, 1984.

Bak, Richard. *Cobb Would Have Caught It: The Golden Age of Baseball in Detroit*. Detroit: Wayne State University Press, 1991.

Bingay, Malcolm W. *Detroit Is My Own Home Town*. Indianapolis: Bobbs-Merrill, 1946.

Blessing, Lee. *Cobb*. New York: Dramatists Play Service, 1991.

Cobb, Ty. *Busting 'Em and Other Stories*. Reprinted edition (orig. 1914). Jefferson, N.C.: McFarland, 2003.

Cobb, Ty (with Al Stump). *My Life in Baseball: The True Record*. Reprinted edition (orig. 1961). Lincoln: University of Nebraska Press, 1993.

Cobb, Ty (ed. William R. Cobb). *Memoirs of Twenty Years in Baseball*. Marietta, Ga.: Wm. R. Cobb, 2002. A compilation of Cobb's syndicated newspaper memoirs, which ran serially during the 1925–26 off-season.

Creamer, Robert W. *Babe: The Legend Comes to Life*. New York: Simon & Schuster, 1974.

Curran, William. *Big Sticks: The Phenomenal Decade of Ruth, Gehrig, Cobb and Hornsby*. New York: William Morrow & Co., 1990.

Donovan, Frank. *Wheels For a Nation*. New York: Thomas Y. Crowell, 1965.

Falls, Joe. *Detroit Tigers*. New York: Collier Books, 1975.

Farrell, James T. *My Baseball Diary*. Reprinted edition (orig. 1957). Carbondale: Southern Illinois University Press, 1998.

Fiffer, Steve. *Speed*. Alexandria, Va.: Redefinition, 1990.

Fountain, Charles. *Sportswriter: The Life and Times of Grantland Rice*. New York: Oxford University Press, 1993.

Freel, Margaret Walker. *Our Heritage: The People of Cherokee County, North Carolina, 1540–1955*. Asheville, N.C.: Miller Printing Co., 1956.

Gropman, Donald. *Say It Ain't So, Joe! The True Story of Shoeless Joe Jackson*. New York: Citadel Press, 1992.

Holtzman, Jerome. *No Cheering in the Press Box*. New York: Holt Rinehart Winston, 1973.

Holway, John B. *Blackball Stars: Negro League Pioneers*. Westport, Conn.: Meckler Books, 1988.

——————. *The Sluggers*. Alexandria, Va.: Redefinition, 1989.

Honig, Donald. *Baseball When the Grass Was Real*. New York: Coward, McCann & Geoghegan, 1975.

——————. *The Men in the Dugout*. Chicago: Follett, 1977.

James, Bill. *The Bill James Historical Baseball Abstract*. New York: Villard, 1986.

Lieb, Fred. *Baseball As I Have Known It*. New York: Coward, McCann & Geoghegan, 1977.

——————. *The Detroit Tigers*. New York: G. P. Putnam's Sons, 1946.

Lochbiler, Don. *Detroit's Coming of Age, 1873–1973*. Detroit: Wayne State University Press, 1973.

Lodge, John C. *I Remember Detroit*. Detroit: Wayne State University Press, 1949.

Lutz, William W. *The News of Detroit*. Boston: Little, Brown, 1973.

MacFarlane, Paul (ed.). *Hall of Fame Fact Book*. St. Louis: Sporting News Publishing Co., 1983.

Mack, Connie. *My 66 Years in the Big Leagues*. New York: Winston, 1950.

McCallum, John D. *Ty Cobb*. New York: Praeger, 1975.

Michener, James A. *Sports in America*. New York: Random House, 1976.

Mize, Jessie Julia. *The History of Banks County, Georgia, 1858–1976*. Homer, Ga.: Banks County Chamber of Commerce, 1977.

Okkonen, Mark. *The Ty Cobb Scrapbook*. New York: Sterling Press, 2001.

Rice, Grantland. *The Tumult and the Shouting*. New York: A. S. Barnes, 1954.

Riess, Steven. *Touching Base: Professional Baseball and American Culture in the Progressive Era*. Westport, Conn.: Greenwood Press, 1980.

Ritter, Lawrence. *The Glory of Their Times*. New York: Macmillan, 1966.

Russell, Francis. *The American Heritage History of the Confident Years, 1865–1916*. New York: American Heritage/Bonanza Books, 1987.

Seymour, Harold. Baseball: *The Golden Age*. New York: Oxford University Press, 1971.

Smith, Ken. *Baseball's Hall of Fame*. New York: Tempo Books, 1980.

Sobol, Ken. *Babe Ruth and the American Dream*. New York: Ballantine, 1974.

Spink, J. G. Taylor. *Judge Landis and 25 Years of Baseball*. St. Louis: Sporting News Publishing Co., 1974.

Stump, Al. *Cobb: A Biography*. Chapel Hill, N.C.: Algonquin Books, 1994.

Articles:

Alvarez, Mark. "An Interview with Smokey Joe Wood." *Baseball Research Journal* (1987).

"Baseball in the Dead Ball Era." *The National Pastime*, Spring 1986.

Batchelor, E. A. "Cobb, Great Player and Great Showman, a Tiger for 20 Years." *Detroit Saturday Night*, August 29, 1925.

Bisher, Furman. "A Visit with Ty Cobb." *Saturday Evening Post*, June 14, 1958.

Cobb, Ty. "They Don't Play Baseball Anymore." *Life*, March 17, 1952.

———. "Tricks That Won Me Ball Games." *Life*, March 24, 1952.

Creamer, Robert W. "The Firebrand That Was Cobb." *Sports Illustrated*, August 19, 1985.

Cremer, Jack Francis. "Detroit's Baseball Players as They Really Are." *Detroit Saturday Night*, October 16, 1909.

"The D.A.C. Heritage." *D.A.C. News*, April 1965.

Gipe, George. "Ty Cobb's Anger Led to Baseball's First Strike, a Comedy of Errors." *Sports Illustrated*, August 29, 1977.

Gleiberman, Owen. "Dropping the Ball." *Entertainment Weekly*, December 2, 1994.

Granahan, Tom. "The Day the Tigers Walked Out, But the Game Went On." *Detroit Free Press Magazine*, April 15, 1984.

Grayson, Harry. "Ty Cobb Wanted to Pitch." *Baseball Digest*, May 1943.

Haney, Fred. "My Most Unforgettable Character." *Reader's Digest*, June 1964.

Hathaway, Ted. "Cobb as Role Model: Ty Cobb in Juvenile Periodical Literature: 1907–1929." *Nine*, Spring 2003.

Holland, David. "The One and Only Cobb." *American Mercury*, September 1956.

Lardner, Ring W. "Tyrus, the Greatest of 'Em All." *American Magazine*, June 1915.

"Last Inning of an Angry Man." *Sports Illustrated*, August 21, 1961.

Montville, Leigh. "Last Remains of a Legend." *Sports Illustrated Classic*, Fall 1992.

Papalas, Anthony. "Lil' Rastus Cobb's Good Luck Charm." *Baseball Research Journal* (1984).

Roberts, Doug. "Ty Cobb Did Not Commit Murder." *The National Pastime* (1996).

Ross, Lillian. "Keeping Up with Mr. Jones." *The New Yorker*, April 4, 1994.

Stump, Al. "Ty Cobb's Wild Ten-Month Fight to Live." *True*, December 1961.

Tomlinson, Vic. "Vic Tomlinson Anylizes [sic] Ty Cobb." *D.A.C. News*, September 1916.

"Why Ty Cobb Is Tired–and Retired." *Literary Digest*, November 20, 1926.

Woolf, S. J. "Tyrus Cobb, Then and Now." *New York Times Magazine,* September 19, 1946.

Illustration Credits

Page 1: Burton Historical Collection. 3: Author's collection. 4: Burton Historical Collection. 6: Burton Historical Collection. 9: Burton Historical Collection. 11: Ernie Harwell. 12: Burton Historical Collection. 14: Burton Historical Collection. 17: Burton Historical Collection. 18: Georgia Department of Archives and History. 20: Burton Historical Collection. 24: Burton Historical Collection. 26: Georgia Department of Archives and History. 29: George Brace. 30: Burton Historical Collection. 32: Detroit Free Press. 34: George Brace. 37: Burton Historical Collection. 38: George Brace. 40: Burton Historical Collection. 42: Author's collection. 44: Burton Historical Collection. 46: National Baseball Library. 49: Author's collection. 50: Burton Historical Collection. 52: Author's collection. 56: Burton Historical Collection. 59: Burton Historical Collection. 61: Hillerich & Bradsby Archives. 62: Detroit Saturday Night. 65: Library of Congress. 66: Detroit News. 69: Burton Historical Collection. 70: National Baseball Library. 72: Burton Historical Collection. 74: Burton Historical Collection. 75: National Baseball Library. 76: Augusta History Center. 78: Burton Historical Collection. 81: National Baseball Library. 82: Burton Historical Collection. 85: Royston News-Leader. 86: Burton Historical Collection. 88: Author's collection. 91: Detroit News. 92: Burton Historical Collection. 95: Detroit News. 97: Burton Historical Collection. 98: National Baseball Library. 101: Author's collection. 103: National Baseball Library. 104: Hillerich & Bradsby Archives. 107: Burton Historical Collection. 108: Burton Historical Collection. 111: Burton Historical Collection. 113: Author's collection. 114: Burton Historical Collection. 115: Burton Historical Collection. 118: Burton Historical Collection. 120: Burton Historical Collection. 123: Author's collection. 124: National Baseball Library. 127: Private collection. 128: Detroit News. 131: Burton Historical Collection. 134: Jack Miner Sanctuary. 135: Burton Historical Collection. 136: Private collection. 139: Private collection. 140: Burton Historical Collection. 142: Detroit News. 144: National Baseball Library. 146: National Baseball Library. 149: Library of Congress. 151: Burton Historical Collection. 152: Burton Historical Collection. 154: Detroit News. 157: Burton Historical Collection. 158: Hillerich & Bradsby Archives. 161: National Baseball Library. 162: Burton Historical Collection. 164: Burton Historical Collection. 167: Burton Historical Collection (top) Coca-Cola Archives (bottom). 168: National Baseball Library. 171: Hillerich & Bradsby Archives. 172: Author's collection. 175: Burton Historical Collection. 176: Burton Historical Collection. 177: Cobb Memorial Hospital. 179: Burton Historical Collection. 180: Detroit Free Press. 183: Coca-Cola Archives. 185: Private collection (both). 187: Burton Historical Collection. 188: Burton Historical Collection. 189: Private collection. 190: Burton Historical Collection. 193: Jennifer Smalley. 194: Jo Mosher. 197: National Baseball Library. 201: T.W. Cobb. 202: Royston News-Leader. 205: Jennifer Smalley. 210: United Features Syndicate. 213: Burton Historical Collection. 215: Burton Historical Collection. 216: Author's collection.

Acknowledgments

This book is the result of many contributions, large and small, from a number of people and institutions. I would like to acknowledge the help of the staffs of the Ty Cobb Museum in Royston, Georgia, particularly Julie Ridgway; the National Baseball Library in Cooperstown, New York; the Burton Historical Collection of the Detroit Public Library, especially Dave Poremba; the Vincent Voice Library at Michigan State University; and the George B. Catlin Library of the Detroit News, especially Jeannette Bartz and Pat Zacharias. I am indebted to Lucy Copas of Royston, who hunted down several rare photographs of the Cobb family and arranged for their reproduction. Mike Opipari in Detroit, Jason Machem in Royston, and John Evans in Murphy, North Carolina, also provided photographic assistance.

Few of Cobb's contemporaries are still alive. However, those that I spoke to over the course of doing this book and its predecessor added significantly to the final product, contributing anecdotes, insights, and background information. My thanks to Eddie Batchelor Jr., Eugene "Woody" Wolfe, Archie Yelle, T. W. Cobb, John Bogart, Herman "Flea" Clifton, Edgar Hayes, Shirley Povich, Willis Hudlin, Bill Kennedy, Jasper Miner, Kirk Miner, Bobby Reeves, Stanley Roginski, Milt Gaston, Eddie Forester, Charlie Gehringer, Eddie Wells, George Uhle, George Sanders, Ray Hayworth, Harry Heilmann Jr., Bill Moore, and Ray Fisher. I'd especially like to thank the members of Ty Cobb's family who agreed to interviews: daughter-in-law Shirley Cobb, nephew Paul Cobb, and grandchildren Peggy Schug and Charlie Cobb.

Thanks also to Ernie Harwell, who wrote the foreword; Kathy Johnson, who researched the Hillerich & Bradsby archives at the University of Louisville; Wesley Fricks and Greg Hall, a pair of Royston natives and authorities on "Mr. Cobb"; John Goodman of Philadelphia, who researched the 1912 strike game between the Tigers and Athletics; Jo Mosher and Jennifer Smalley, who filled me in on the life of Al Stump; Ernie DuMouchelle, who provided copies of correspondence between Cobb and Harry Salsinger in the 1950s; Bill Dow, who interviewed Jon Lindbergh for me; Phil Mooney, head archivist at Coca-Cola headquarters in Atlanta; and the pseudonymous "K" on the West Coast, who lent me a tape of Cobb's 1955 appearance on *I've Got a Secret*. Also lending assistance at various times were Larry Amman, Charles Alexander, Bill Plott, Eli Henderson, James Riley, and Donald Honig.

Finally, a tip of the cap to Ron Shelton and everybody else involved in the filming of *Cobb* at Rickwood Field in Birmingham, Alabama, in the spring of 1994. Wearing a bowtie, plus-fours, and a newsboy cap inside an authentic wooden ballpark, alternately cheering and booing Tommy Lee Jones, was an "extra" I had never foreseen when I first started writing about the Peach.

Index